1-319-334-2319

There Is No 'Other': Ego vs. Heart

The Channeled Wisdom
of
Osiris, Ra, and Thoth

Tim Birchard

To all those I call family, friends, and loved ones;
to all those I call enemies;
and to all those I call strangers:
thank you for teaching me.

DISCLAIMER

This book details the author's personal experiences with and opinions about spirituality. The author is not a licensed therapist.

The author and publisher are providing this book and its contents on an "as is" basis and make no representations or warranties of any kind with respect to this book or its contents. The author and publisher disclaim all such representations and warranties, including for example warranties of merchantability and spiritual advice for a particular purpose. In addition, the author and publisher do not represent or warrant that the information accessible via this book is accurate, complete or current.

The statements made about products and services have not been evaluated by the U.S. government. Please consult with your own legal or accounting professional regarding the suggestions and recommendations made in this book.

Except as specifically stated in this book, neither the author or publisher, nor any authors, contributors, or other representatives will be liable for damages arising out of or in connection with the use of this book. This is a comprehensive limitation of liability that applies to all damages of any kind, including (without limitation) compensatory; direct, indirect or consequential damages; loss of data, income or profit; loss of or damage to property and claims of third parties.

You understand that this book is not intended as a substitute for consultation with a licensed medical, legal or accounting professional. Before you begin any change your lifestyle in any way, you will consult a licensed professional to ensure that you are doing what's best for your situation.

This book provides content related to spiritual topics. As such, use of this book implies your acceptance of this disclaimer.

A note from the ego

Don't blame me if you don't like this book. I know it doesn't really make too much logical sense. It wasn't my idea. I would have done things very differently. If you don't like it, I had nothing to do with it. However, if there are parts of this book that you do happen to like, or connect with, then yes, that's probably a part that I had a hand in. Even though these clowns have spent months writing about how to circumvent me, how to turn away from me, again and again, in order to get back into the heart, with its lack of reason and its irrational, illogical leanings, I've been here all along. Watching. And I will take credit where credit is due; I can be tricky. So you may see me pop up through the cracks now and then, you know... just to say hi.

A note about the writing process for this book

This book was written, or channeled, rather, through a very simple process. The concept, from the beginning, was to sit down and write at least two pages a day, every single day, rain or shine, until the goal of 300 pages was reached. At that point, the second phase of the writing process, the curating process, would be performed. Initially there was no plan beyond this. No outline was drafted and followed. No vision or dream of how what the book might contain. Simply sitting down at the computer keyboard and moving fingers across the keys until two pages were filled.

Often times, I found myself unable to remember the content of what had been written just five minutes before, which is astonishing to me in a way, since words, sentences, and phrases simply appeared before me. All I did was take dictation, sometimes typing as quickly as I could to keep up with the words coming through, and other times sitting motionless with my eyes closed, gathering the energy to move the fingers more, so more could come out.

And while I could not necessarily recall specific topics or ideas that had been written mere moments before, at the same time small phrases kept creeping into my vocabulary and my thoughts throughout the day... phrases like, 'the physical body is not you', and 'looking through the lens of the heart is the way to experience reality.' Similarly, it seemed during the writing of this book that I became aware of two temporal realities: writing time, and non-writing time. Writing time was a zone that I seemed to enter, like a trance, where everything being typed made perfect sense, and the words often flowed effortlessly.

In those moments where they did not, it was clear to me that the words were available and trying to get through, but some aspect of my ego was blocking them from coming through, be it pride, perfectionism, fear of failure, or whatever. Sometimes that frustration resulted in my typing anything at all, directly from ego, simply to get the two pages done so I could get on with the seemingly important details of my day. But most times, all it took to get me back on track was to close my eyes, take a deep breath, and ask for guidance; ask for whatever was needed to come through to be communicated clearly-- for me to serve as a clear channel for something greater to be expressed.

A critical piece for the reader to understand is that this 'channeling' is not some dramatically specialized skill only held by certain individuals of power. It's not anything exotic, sexy, or magical. In fact, every living human on the planet has the ability to do it, for everyone on the planet has a heart beating in her chest. This realization was perhaps the biggest letdown of all for me, as I have known people who claimed to be able to channel higher wisdom, and I always imagined them hearing whispers in their ears, or going into some dream state that would cause their eyes to roll back in their head, special music to begin playing in the background, and clouds to part in order to make room for golden beams of light to come down.

I wanted sexy. I wanted drama. I wanted something, anything at all, that would mark me as just a little more special and beloved than other people. That would make other people want my autograph, want to take my picture, and want to give me huge sums of money. I wanted to be a rock star, with unlimited access to resources and pleasures and extravagance.

I didn't get that. Not by a long shot.

What I got instead was something much more real; much more satisfying. What I got was the truth; that everyone has the capability to channel higher wisdom, and that all it takes to do so is to get quiet and be willing to write what the ego might judge as being complete gibberish. All it takes is a willingness to suspend disbelief, just for a little while; to send the ego into the other room for half an hour or so while you take some time to move those keys across the keyboard, not even worrying about what comes out. Because the one that is worrying about what comes out is the one that would block anything from coming through at all: the ego.

By viewing this as a form of play, a relaxed attitude comes to the forefront, an attitude that says, "Hey, let's see what happens if we do this." An attitude of, "It's truly none of my business what comes through right now; my only job is to take dictation."

Was it always easy for me to make such a simple shift in my attitude? No. Many were the moments when thoughts of doubt might arise and begin to critique whatever was coming out. The key in those moments was to simply turn back to the writing and away from the critique, no matter how tempting it may have felt at the time to follow the Critic's recommendation and hit the backspace bar. The delete key. Had I listened with my head and not my heart, you probably would not be reading this right now. I would still be walking around suggesting to everyone I meet that they 'start working on their book right away,' the way I did for years, projecting my own gold upon others, refusing to acknowledge the gifts and the resulting responsibilities I held in my arms.

Initially I was only hoping to be able to identify some common threads that could be identified and further developed, hopefully into some work that could be of service in the world today. What happened instead was one giant common thread that I could not have planned had I tried: the ego versus the heart.

"Versus" doesn't really capture the spirit of the true relationship, though... It's not like two boxers in a ring, vying for the title of most powerful. A more precise description might be 'the contrast between ego and heart.' Because rather than two boxers in a ring, there's simply the Heart, which is the ring, the boxers, the announcers, the audience, the popcorn, and the microphone... as well as the birds that fly over the building during the match and the clouds through which they fly. The image of the two boxers is nothing more than the ego's attempts to be seen as distinct and separate; to be viewed and accepted as real. As having substance.

Which, of course, it does not.

As you read, you will likely notice common themes repeated in numerous ways. My interpretation of this is that whatever wisdom is involved understands my own ego well enough to know that hearing or reading something anything that challenges the ego is going to get conveniently 'forgotten'... I'll smile and dog ear the page... I might even write down the little quote on a sticky note and fold it up, sticking it in my pocket for later. But within minutes (or seconds) it will be forgotten and gone; nonexistent.

The repetition is something that bothers my ego. It shouts, "I already KNOW all of this! Let's skip forward!" And it's that very shouting that, on a good day, I might notice and actually question. "Hey... I notice I'm wanting to rush ahead. What is this about?" In this way, the repetition serves as a speed bump to get me to slow down and actually pay attention. When I begin to realize where the repetition lies, that's when the common themes can begin to emerge through the cracks in my inner pavement, the pavement smoothed over the inner gates of my heart by the ego. Though they are as illusory as the ego itself, until I learn to discern carefully, I may take the mirage at face value, believing that my very own heart is closed for business.

This is the work of the ego. To get me to believe that access to my own Heart is impossible. There could be nothing further from the truth. For my very being is the Heart. And so is yours.

So I encourage you to use this book to jump start your own book. I urge you to set aside all judgment and reach within to whatever guidance you know to be true, and invite that wisdom to come out. Share it with the world. Do not keep it held within for even one more day. Create some sort of plan and start creating right now.

And let the words of your inner critic pass by unheeded. There is enough criticism in the world. Enough fear. Enough uncertainty. Enough sadness. Enough grief at opportunities that appear to have slipped through fingers. There is no shortage of images of suffering in the world, all built on the ego's need to keep the distraction level high.

Find your own time; create your own space to let your own inner wisdom flow, free of the burden of proof of anything. To anything or anyone. Wait no longer for someone to bless you or certify you or tell you that now is the time. You are hereby notified that now is the time.

Now is the time. You are hereby certified, licensed, and vested with the power of clarity and insight; you are hereby charged with expressing your own true inner wisdom in the way that it calls to be expressed. Write your book. Dance your dance. Sing your song. Paint your painting. Perform your performance art. Love your love.

You are the Inner Divine. There is no 'other' to wait for.

Love, Tim
Spring, 2015

Table of Contents

CHAPTER ONE
Foolish cousin ego

Come back here and have a seat next to me. Sit here with me in the sunshine, here in the back yard. Feel the warmth of the sun on your face. Here, have some water. Have some sunshine. Have some lemonade. Have some delicious food. Have some company. Have some quiet time. Rest. Relax. You've been working so hard to find yourself... to take care of things in the way a man of goodness would, and does. You've been striving to do and be the right thing for so long... Sit and rest. Set down those heavy bags. No need to worry: I'll have someone carry them to your room for you. Filled with anxieties and worries and concerns and deadlines and storylines and masks and passwords and keys and backup hard drives and floor mats and extra boots and windbreakers and an emergency sleeping bag and some backup cash for just in case.

You certainly are prepared. Or you seem to believe you are, anyway. Little cousin ego must be whispering in your ear again. Have you been believing his lies? He knows no other way, so we can't really blame him, can we? But as good as his intentions might be, he is misguided, and has misguided you, time and again. He tells you that you had better be prepared; you had better be warned and cautious and on your guard. No place for vulnerability and openness here-- in order to survive, you have absolutely got to grit your teeth and clench your shoulders as you walk, to make yourself look larger and more threatening to others, who would take advantage of you for walking down the sidewalk in a big, scary town like this. Haven't you heard the latest news? Haven't you memorized the latest crime statistics? Don't you know your very life is in danger?

Yes... foolish cousin ego. He believes his own press, and that's how he can be so utterly charming and convincing. But you've noticed, no doubt, that he can spin on a dime to turn against you, shaming and blaming you for all kinds of things, and then getting you to believe that he's doing it all for your own good. Can you believe that? Would you ever put up with such attitude from anyone on the street? In the classroom? At the grocery store? Just imagine if your checkout clerk at the grocery store was checking out your items and started chastising you for what you were purchasing... what you were wearing, or for humming the tune on your lips. Would you ever tolerate such abuse, such lies, such incredible inhospitality? Of course not. You would talk to the manager, remove yourself from the unhealthy relationship as soon as possible.

So why is it that when this back alley bum starts whispering in your ear with its nasty breath, you immediately invite him to come sit in your lap? When he starts pulling your hair and scratching your face and slapping and pinching you, insults flying, curses spilling all over your favorite shirt, all you can do is thank him for his kindness? When he wipes snot and saliva all over your sleeve, and sneezes in your face, all you can do is congratulate him for being such a good ally?

No. This is not how it was meant to be. The next time your 'kind uncle' sidles up to you, blowing smoke in your face, with food stuck in his teeth and vomit on his breath... the next time he leans in to give you a big kiss on the lips, turn away. Refuse his advances. Don't listen to him. He does not deserve your attention, let alone your acceptance. His game is to pretend that what he thinks is what you think; he whispers something in your ear, and if you repeat it out loud, he congratulates you for having such wonderful ideas. He tells you that you are a smart guy; a man of the world who can tell the difference between fools and heroes.

But trust me when I tell you, he does not have your best interest at heart. In fact, he has you serving him, when it should be the other way around. Long ago he applied for the job of butler, just to help out around the house and get things done. And you were ready for a little help; some guidance would be great, you thought. Better than having to try to make sense of this confusing world all alone. And so you hired him. At minimum wage. And he started out by taking out the trash... vacuuming the carpets... mowing the lawn. He did a pretty good job at first. But then he started playing the 'expert' card, acting as if he were still being helpful, but influencing you little by little to move in his direction-- to take down some of those paintings you like so much and put up some of his favorite posters.

Over time, you ended up listening to his 'counsel' more and more. Soon he had you repainting the walls to his liking, while he sipped on a piña colada in your favorite armchair. At every turn he alternated between congratulating you for your wisdom, your hipness, and your cleverness, and berating you for being such a clumsy asshole. He laughed at you when you talked about bringing out those brushes and canvases again, reminding you that there was no WAY you were quite good enough yet to do anything like that. "Maybe wait just a little bit longer, then you'll be ready," he said with a confident smile on his lips.

And you believed him. You had a choice about it the whole time, from the very start, all those years ago, and you've been choosing to believe him, day in and day out. Eventually he climbed out of your favorite armchair and actually up onto your back, "just for a quick little piggyback ride," he whispered. And you agreed. "Sure, come on up... it'll be fine," you told yourself. And he did.

Soon you were hobbling around the living room with this ogre on your back, pointing and shouting directions so loudly into your ear that you started to believe that his voice was your own voice. That his thoughts, ideas, and intentions were your own. That his malice was yours; that his layers of protective defense mechanisms were yours... that his selfish need for more love, more sex, more everything was your own. You took it all in stride. And you paid the consequences.

You forgot that the heaviness you felt every day, every night, every waking moment was this smelly, unbathed jerk riding around on your back. You told yourself (or was it him?) that you simply had to be strong, carry on... that it would all get better soon. And so, at his slightest suggestion, you threw open the windows and invited the clamor of the world into your living room. You ran outside and grabbed the lawn furniture from the patio and threw them through your beautiful plate glass windows. You gathered trash from the gutter and then scattered it around your kitchen. You invited rats and leeches and wild monkeys into your home, and when they threw feces at you, you told yourself that it was all just part of life.

You taped up black trash bags over the windows to block out all the light, and then you set fire to the curtains. The flames licked the ceiling, leaving charred black designs on the walls, ashes on the floor, and a stench in the air. You ate stale cigarettes for breakfast, and sobbed into your pillow at night about how unfair the world was. You poured gasoline on the lawn and set it on fire, then rode your bicycle through the inferno, weeping at the 'cruelty of the world'.

You smashed your favorite guitar against the windshield of your car, until strings broke and the headstock cracked and tuning machines were hanging off and strange angles. Then you turned on your tape recorder and sang out-of-tune songs about heartbreak and weariness. You pounded nails into your car's tires, then drove it around the block until hot black smoke poured from the wheels... You drove it up over the curb, through the front yard and crashed through the wall of your house and into the living room, smacking your head against the inside of your windshield, leaving a spider web crack in the glass and on your forehead.

You poured rat poison into the well of your home, then took a long, hot bath and cried because you felt so bad.

You wrapped your favorite baseball bat in rusty barbed wire and then chased the cat around the house. You made prank phone calls to your loved ones and cursed at them through the telephone, foaming at the mouth and throwing raisins at the tv set. You tied a blindfold around your head and then ran at the wall with a pair of scissors in your hand. You juggled open box cutters. You stuck pennies in the light socket. You soiled yourself and then rolled around on the floor, laughing like a crazed man.

All the while, he was riding on your back, whispering all of these ideas into your ear. "This is what will set you free," he promised with a smirk. You thought the smirk was your own-- that somehow you were going to get ahead in life; that you would somehow get the best of this world. That the world, and everyone in it, would finally recognize your true genius and pay you what it owed you. And it owed you a lot.

For years this has gone on. Decades. And on a regular basis, you would throw your hands into the air, look up at the sky and cry, "Why me?! What did I ever do to deserve this?!"

But you missed something. In those moments of desperation, as you were crying your truth to the sky and the stars above, you didn't happen to notice that the creep riding on your back was mouthing those very words along with you. Even those very words were not your own; they were his. You got so used to hearing his voice in your ear that you took it on as your own. You forgot the sound of your own voice.

Somewhere along the way, you noticed something magical; something long-forgotten that tickled a special place in your heart's memory... just as the sun was about to set, or about to rise... just as storm clouds were about to roll in... just as you were about to brush your teeth, you recognized that something wonderful was just out of reach. Instead of the usual anger, sadness, fear, and despair at the awful state of things, this tiny, strangely familiar feeling of hopeful joy rose like a bubble from the bottom of the ocean and welled up in your heart. Your eyes opened wide, and you started in surprise at this feeling, which had a very different flavor than all the rest: it tasted like gratitude.

The guy on your back was quick to take the credit. "Oh, you felt that? Yeah, that was me. It's a good thing you've been listening to me... following my recommendations... otherwise you probably NEVER would have felt that. Want some more? Let's go raise some hell!"

And with that you would once again turn away from the silence that had brought the glimmer of peaceful, hopeful joy... your birthright. You went right back to the mayhem of the day. And the joy would dissipate back into feelings of despair. As hard as you tried to 'grab and hold on' to those special, magical feelings of belonging, of oneness with the world and everyone in it, they would only take the stage fleetingly, from behind the curtain, and would disappear just as quickly as they'd come.

One day you sat down, tired. Enough is enough, you thought. Something is not right. Something is not working.

This cannot be what life is truly about... running around like a chicken with its head cut off, searching and dissecting and collecting and disposing and running into walls, bruising body and heart all the time.

"What if I take a look in the mirror?" That was the thought you had, and when you did, the guy on your back was startled. And angered. If you were to do that, especially for very long, you might notice him hanging on your back. And then there would be trouble.

"I wouldn't do that if I were you," he said a little too quickly, trying to cover it up with an easy, dismissive laugh. "That's just a waste of time anyway... your time is worth more than that. Let's go blow some shit up instead."

But this time, something about looking in the mirror, as uncomfortable as it might be, really sounded intriguing. "It can't be any worse than what my life has been like already," you figure. And you walk into the bathroom. You take a quick peek in the mirror above the sink, where you brush your teeth every day. But until now, you've only stared vacantly into the mirror, not really expecting to see anything different than your own chin, your own stubble, and the foamy toothpaste you spit into the sink. This time there's no toothbrush. There's no auto-pilot. You're looking in the mirror to see if you can see anything different.

And you do.

You spot something peeking up from behind your left shoulder. What in the world...? A little tuft of hair poking up, and one eyebrow, trying to remain undetected. You turn around and try to look back over your own shoulder to see yourself better, but something is blocking the way. And an insistent voice is saying, with increasing intensity, "This is a big waste of time! C'mon, let's go DO something!"

But on this day, you hesitate. You head slowly but persistently toward the bedroom, with its full-length mirror. Even though you feel the need to pour some more gasoline in the front lawn and shoot flaming arrows into it, you pause for just a few more moments. You turn to one side.

And there, right before your eyes, is a 240 pound beast hanging on your back with its arms around your neck, just barely cutting off your airflow. You see it there, with your own eyes. And it keeps looking away, determined not to meet your gaze, for it knows precisely what will happen if it does. It is shouting something-- 'waste of time! waste of time!' and keeps trying to dodge and duck, working to spin you back around so you can't see it.

All of its wriggling around causes you to lose your balance, and you fall awkwardly to the floor, gasping for breath and hoping like hell you'll survive whatever this is that is happening. You wrangle with the beast, and it still has its arms around your throat. You manage to spin around under its weight so that you're facing the mirror from the other side, and you catch sight of it again, in all its twisted glory.

"I see you!" you shout. It looks up in terror. And in that moment, you lock eyes with it in the mirror. It starts to scream and grabs a beer bottle and slams it against the mirror, which shatters and collapses upon itself. But you've already seen. You reach back and grab hold of hairy flesh and wrench yourself around and up into a seated position.

Face to face, you peer directly into the eyes of your tormentor. The kidnapper who brainwashed you into believing that he was your savior. The abuser who lied about caring deeply for you. The monster who enslaved you. The beast that locked you in a cage.

And suddenly, you can breathe again like never before. You take the deepest breath you've taken in decades, and you see its eyes grow as wide as saucers. You begin to smile, and as it takes one last gasp and tries to unleash its final battle cry, it disintegrates before your very eyes. No blood. No vomit. No urine. No stench. It vanishes completely, leaving no trace... no evidence of ever having existed. Except for the broken mirror, the monkey feces all over the walls, the charred front yard, the jagged shards of glass and rusty barbed wire littering the living room floor.

He's not around to help you clean up. But he's also not around to wreak havoc anymore. So you begin the task at hand. Slowly, you move room to room, sweeping, vacuuming, mopping up the mess... repainting, replacing windows, tearing down the black plastic, pumping out the poison water and upgrading the well.

And you realize that he was your choice. All along. You made an agreement. You made sacrifices, and you also received some sort of payoff, some reward for your part in the deal. Maybe it was fame. Sex. Glamour. Money. Reputation.

Or maybe it was poverty. Hunger. Sadness. Victimhood status. With rewards like these, there would never be a need to chase your dreams and face your fears, right? You could defer the act of stepping more fully into your power as a leader, an artist, a hero, a poet, a parent, a friend, a lover... and as your fully-realized true self. Maybe even circumvent that discomfort forever. It seemed like a pretty good payoff at the time.

But now you see a deeper truth. Now you sit in the eye of the storm, resting calmly. When it's time to work, you work, but with peace in your heart. When it's time to relax, you relax with peace in your heart. As the wind blows the curtains, as the storm outside blows trash down the street, as the wails of the police sirens cry out in the night, as fear and panic and worry and uncertainty work each other over in the alley behind your house to the sound of chains, broken bottles, switchblades and gunfire, through all of it you sit quietly and watch.

The inner calm of your divine living room is a sanctuary for your heart.

Flying dream

I walked out into the sunshine. I found myself at the top of a huge, grassy hill; more of a mountain, actually. Covered in green... up high, in the clouds, almost. I walked over to the very ridge and looked down. Then, without a word, I leapt forward, diving off the edge. I spread my arms with a relaxed smile on my face and felt myself begin to soar. Back and forth, I circled high above, surveying the land.

There was no fear. Only pure joy and freedom. And I did it again and again and again.

This is how my dream went last night. Flying dreams. I know there must be some significance... Guidance, please?

Yes. Of course. You've slipped the bonds of ego. And you are flying, free of those restraints. Why is it so difficult for your intellect, your ego, to accept? Even just now, I saw you hesitate and pause, ready to go back and erase that first complete sentence. "How could I have possibly slipped the bonds of ego?" "Who am I to do anything so great?"

We remind you, this is great. And at the same time, it's kind of no big deal. You're simply returning to your natural state. That's all. No fanfare. No parades. But you do get to have the occasional flying dream. Ha ha ha.

Now you'll begin seeing through a different lens. You've already discovered people watching you, staring, and being impacted by something about your presence. No, it wasn't your clothing. It was something much deeper, and much more apparent-- your presence is shining more brightly now. And as we've mentioned, many people don't know what to 'do' with that; they don't know how to make sense of it. That's okay. Just let them experience their path without worrying too much about them.

Now you will notice that being magnified. This means there may be people out there for whom you are an even better projection screen than before. They may project all over you and then react as if it WERE you, with a vengeance. You are now prepared for this. You have all the tools you need to deal calmly and compassionately with them. Others will find you irresistibly attractive, and want to talk to you and tell you their life story. And then you'll get those in between, who just watch out of the corner of their eye, trying to figure out what your angle is.

It's all okay. We remind you just to relax. "Rest in the eye of the storm," we say. Over and over again. This is the appropriate approach to take.

Also. You are discovering that time in solitude is a very important thing for you. You've written nearly 30 pages and 6 songs in just a couple of days, and you did that in the midst of turbulence-- adjusting to a new kind of freedom. We understand. Perfectly natural. It is at this time that you must acknowledge and accept this fact: you indeed do need time away from everyone and everything normal in your life, on a regular basis. This is not meant to punish anyone. Quite the contrary-- it's to allow gifts that we have imparted to rise to the surface and emanate forth.

The daily distractions inherent in 'normal' life at this point feel to you as if they are driving you mad. Until now, you've been judging yourself harshly for having such powerful emotional responses. But now that you've had only a few days away, you see that big things are happening. In the span of some 72 hours, you've made what feels to you like tremendous headway. And to top it all off, you had a flying dream, a signal of confirmation that you're on an appropriate path, moving in an appropriate direction, right? Yes. We acknowledge you. We see you. And yes, you're definitely moving in the 'right' direction for what you say you want in life-- to be an instrument of light, love, wisdom, compassion, healing, peace, strength, and grace.

This is actually everyone's natural state. You'll see it come to the surface as others interact with you. Now, more than ever, your responsibility includes suspending judgment of others. Knowing what you know now, how could it be any other way? Now you see, with a bird's eye view, how things are connected-- how others are living and dying and suffering and struggling and wrestling with the ego, their only source of terror. They look through the ego's lenses, not realizing they are seeing an altered state of reality. And even when they do begin to realize, they don't know how to remove the glasses from their faces.

It's all part of the natural unfolding of things, so don't get too wound up about it. It has been unfolding this way for a long time on your plane of existence, where time seems linear to you. This is the natural order of things. And where you are is perfect for this moment, this eternal moment. You did not come here to follow, dear one. Remember that. Keep plugging away. Keep exploring. Keep asking questions. Keep wondering and looking. Keep loving. And remember, most definitely remember to suspend judgment of YOURSELF first and foremost. While the ego, once again, would have you believe this to be acting selfishly and to be avoided, at this point you understand that suspending judgment of yourself leads to suspending judgment of all situations and all people and all existence. Where judgment has been withheld, there is room for lots of glorious gratitude to flow in and surround everything, soaking it all up in love.

Create space. You remember that, right? It's been in your mind for a long time, right? Creating space in traffic... in the grocery store... at work... in your daily life... Yes. Right on target. Love is space. Creating space is a way of creating room for love to unfold and envelop everything in sight. These will look to others like miracles you are performing. They are. But you will not be 'performing' anything... you will simply be creating space in order to allow love to fill the room. To fill hearts. To fill lives.

Including your own, dear one. Including your own.

Forgiveness. Yes, you thought you were through typing, didn't you? Not so fast, dear one. We know you're hungry and ready to eat breakfast, but one more important word before you pause.

Forgiveness. That word carries such transformative power that its importance simply cannot be overstated or

15

exaggerated. You already know intellectually and rationally that forgiving all others sets you free in the end, releases YOU from the bonds of attachment (desire/fear; attraction/repulsion), creating space and allowing you room to breathe. Room to love both yourself and others.

Now is the time to know this with your heart and to begin carrying out the practices of forgiveness at once. This is an urgent matter. You've been carrying around these chains for too long, dear one. And guess what? This is no longer about freeing yourself. "It doesn't matter so much if I don't get free of these chains... I don't matter that much anyway... I'm not rich or important. I'm not famous. It doesn't make any difference how my life unfolds." Sound familiar, dear one? We say there is plenty on the line. Yes, you always have choice about this.

But as you know, great gifts and talents come with great responsibility. And now that you are unlocking new treasure chests of insight and awareness, it's time for you to adjust (once again) to a new identity. Yes. That's right. Identity. That's been on your mind a lot lately, hasn't it? No accidents, dear one. You planned this out brilliantly, although your ego would have you believe otherwise. Yes. Identity shifting once again, and transforming into an even more authentic, more genuine 'you', even as you let go of old ideas and concepts of what you have believed 'you' to be. Let them go. They are like a used up coat, or an old pair of worn out boots. It's perfectly okay to release them into the atmosphere, sending them on their way with love and gratitude for the service they have provided. They were appropriate for a time. Now they are no longer appropriate.

So now what new aspects of your identity ARE appropriate? We remind you to focus on a few key things-- 1) looking the ego in the eyes / saying, "you're not driving the bus anymore-- I am"; 2) forgiveness of yourself first and others second; 3) the confirmation and acknowledgment inherent in the gift of the flying dream.

Keep these three things close at hand and close at heart, dear one. And your journey will continue to unfold perfectly, as it always has. In fact, there's no other way for it to unfold. For everything you see and hear, and everything you do not, is all inside The Divine's teacup. There is no other.

The genesis of a lie

Quiet. The quiet landscape of the desert at night, full moon rising overhead. Rest there. In that silence is knowing, wisdom, joy, acceptance of all as it unfolds. So many masks to see... so many apparent realities. Just remember the movie projector... everything you see is the light dancing across the blank screen. There's no way to 'beat the system' by engaging it here-- the only way to true freedom is to recognize the motion for what it is; light dancing.

The fun part is when you can enter the dance of light, knowing full well that it is nothing more than that, and enjoy that dance. Here you will find the man who smiles throughout the day, embracing fully everything that unfolds and appears before him, no matter how startling it may seem to the intellect, which would quite prefer that life follow his ordained schedule, doing so with crisp, 90 degree hospital folds to the sheets when making life's bed. That's how he rolls. He's a walking, talking measuring tape. And that's fine. We all need one. But not to run our lives.

What is happiness? Fulfilling your life's mission-- your purpose.

Listen, can you hear him now? Critiquing as your hands fly across the keyboard? "Oh, that's boring! That's no good. That sucks!" Yes, even as you write about these things-- especially as you do so, he is at it, waiting for you to stop watching what he is doing so he can sneak up and try to put his hands over your eyes... start whispering again to distract you from your heart song. The funniest part is that all it takes to remain in an appropriate constellation is to look straight at him and smile. "I see you. I hear you." And he shrinks back into the corners.

All those years ago, I had a feeling that I could succeed in the world, if only they understood me. I was not necessarily an expert at anything, but I could communicate and guide and coach, because I was able to see some sort of bigger picture. And I was so confused-- in order to teach whatever, it appeared I had to master the content. I understood the important connection, but felt like a teacher with no content. I knew that was also no good, if I wanted to get by in this world.

Today, here you are, exactly there, doing precisely that. And it turns out that the 'content' you teach is that of connection; connection to resources, connection to other people, and connection to self. No maps. No curriculum. No book. Simply your own self. "Look here... this is how you could be in the world. This is possible. This exists. This is a 'thing'. Would you like a taste of this love, this delicious rose water? There is plenty for everyone. It springs from a deep well, hidden before your eyes in your heart. Look deeply, listen deeply, and drink deeply from that well within you. It is the one that will nourish you and guide you along your path."

There is no possible way to fall off of your path-- it is all your path. And don't worry about sadness... experiencing sadness is part of the play. Sadness, anger, joy, fear, confusion... these are all stones along the path. They are not meant to be picked up and placed into your backpack-- they get heavy very quickly! No, they are only there to be acknowledged and appreciated for their unique beauty, then left where you found them as you continue on. To become a rock collector is to dedicate much precious time and energy to carrying around heavy rocks on your back. Shy away from the role of 'collector', and instead embrace the lightness of traveling in freedom. Everything you need is right here in the room. This is true.

The common habit among people on the planet is to unwittingly send outward what is within. Then to 'see' it in those around you, you either run toward it or recoil. These are all a matter of mistaken perception. Simply by pausing and turning inward, as you've been counseled many times before, will you find everything you could ever hope to seek, and even better. Even more. Even more magical and fulfilling. For the hungers that you seek to feed among the flashing lights and loud noises of your experience are but ghosts of the cravings for love. And within your very being lies the deepest, most abundant well ever... far beyond what your intellect could imagine.

Gold? Bank accounts? Guitars? Houses? Imagine the most elaborate, satisfying, magical thing you could want, sitting right before you. The most magnificent castle... the most up-to-date recording studio. Anything at all. No sensual pleasure is off limits. In fact, the more enticing and satisfying your intellect believes it to be, the better.

Because no matter what it is, it will seem as useless pocket lint in your palm on a windy day when compared to the well of the heart that lies within you. Drop your bucket down, and let it fill. Then drink deeply. Leap over the wall and let yourself fall head over heels... go for a swim. Dive deeply, as deeply as you can, and swim down, into the heart's core... deeper than you've ever dared before. And notice how easy it is to breathe here, leagues beneath the surface of the heart's ocean. There is no time, space, or suffering here. This is where all answers lie. This is where wisdom grows and love swims effortlessly, manifesting endlessly in pure delight at its own existence reflected all around it.

Should you find yourself on the ocean floor, take your shovel off your back and dig even deeper still, tunneling down into the center of your own heart. Mine that heart with all of your might... never fear going just a little deeper. For the rubies and magical gifts you find there will fill your pockets quickly, and you'll find that the only way to keep going will be to cast off your gifts, offering them to everyone around you. They will think you are crazy-- 'He's a fool! How could he give all of his love and passion away to others? Doesn't he realize that if he keeps giving love away freely, he's going to run out soon and be left in the desert? Stalled on the side of the road? Living in a van down by the river?' This is because they see themselves precisely there-- in the middle of a hot desert on the side of the road, car jacked up and flat tire lying nearby, shredded... Sitting there in fear, waiting for help to come, imagining that they are powerless and desperate for love from any kind passerby.

When the truth, as you know, is that your pockets fill up quickly. The faster you release the false ideas of reality and remember your role as part of the 'flow' of abundance in the universe, the easier it is to get back to the Heart's business of emptying those pockets so there's room for more gold to appear. This process of remembering your role appears to the ego to be in direct conflict with its desire to be seen as unique, special, or otherwise exempt from becoming 'just another cog in the wheel'. It folds its arms and refuses to do such a 'menial' job as simply emptying its own pockets and giving away jewels to others. "Besides, I will starve! And so will YOU!" it demands.

This is the genesis of the lie.

You are always and forever free of the lie; you do not live in the lie. However, you are always free to choose to listen and believe the lie, if you like. And it will always bring heartbreak, no matter how you unfold it. The only starvation that only happens is that of sitting here at the Banquet, delicacies piled high on the silver platter before you, wine goblet filled to the rim, resting easily within arm's reach... And there you sit, with your hands covering your face, refusing to acknowledge the feast you could partake in at any moment. You smell the delicious fragrance. You hear the other guests at the Banquet, laughing and sharing jokes, smiling and offering love and acceptance. Eating freely. No one goes hungry here at the Banquet. And all are already seated.

I raise my cup to you. Will you join me in a toast to the Beloved?

Eyeball

Can you shrink yourself?

Can you begin to shed the ego's preferences, one by one? Can you cut off first a fingernail? Then maybe a toenail? Then a thumb? Your ego will begin to squirm. But can you persist in the face of his cries of anguish?

Can you cut off a foot? A leg? A thigh? Can you continue discarding little pieces of him, one after another, until there is nothing left but an eyeball, hanging in the air?

And then, can you discard even those filters, so that there is nothing left of him but a tiny, shrunken point in space, observing?

And as a final acting of mutiny against the pirate who commandeered your ship so long ago, can you draw your sword and cut away even that point of observation, obliterating "yourself" completely and becoming one with everything you already were, have been, are, and will be?

The wind will grow still. The tempest in your head will be revealed as the simple wind in your sails. And you will remember the truth of who you always weren't.

Your work

You see it now. Right in front of your eyes. Your work is to show up in the world as genuinely and authentically as you possibly can. This is the work that will ripple out forever, teaching others to get back in touch with their own hearts and own truth, that they may carry that torch into the darkness that they perceive.

What a wonderful day it is! You are on your path, as you have always been. And through music and in your daily life, you are showing the world what love can look like. You are serving as an example. So continue doing precisely what you are doing-- give. And listen. And follow. Continue doing what feels right through the lens of your heart. And continue doing that work, again and again. And do not fear the need to ebb and flow with the tides of the energies within your physical body. This is right and correct and natural. This is to be honored. Allow yourself the space to do this, for space is love. By taking the time and space you need to recharge, you are creating a conduit for more love to flow into the world through your own being.

Remember also that the love flows from all directions to the Axis Mundi-- to your heart of gold. This is always flowing toward you. You need only to remember with your intellect-- do whatever it takes to continue remembering, to keep the Truth at the forefront of your mind. As you do this, you will notice that your thoughts actually do create your reality. There is only a perceived gap between the two. In all actuality, the vision board technique does, in fact, create and shape the reality you experience.

Give generously. Love generously. These are your two tenets. And remember as well: joy and tranquility are to be your buzzwords these days. Let them be the yardstick by which you measure your days, your hours, your minutes, your life. For it is in those moments of joy and tranquility when love surges through you the most powerfully... and feels most effortless. This is correct. When your dams and blockades are lowered, the river of love flows freely through you, outward and inward. It is only when your ego is dancing for control that you experience what feels like resistance; resistance to the ever-flowing change of the universe and resistance to allowing the heart to flow with love in all directions. For when this love is flowing and you are sitting squarely in gratitude with all defenses down, it becomes quite obvious that the ego is not in charge. Is not driving the bus. Is not necessary as a leader.

This creates friction for the ego, which would have you believe that you will die, perish, suffer, and disappear without it. And you already know that the ego is the one that will die, perish, feel as though it is suffering, and disappear when you turn your attention away from its demands and back toward the heart.

The ego is highly invested in keeping you confused. Stumbling around in the darkness, chaos in your ears and mind. That is how it keeps you distracted. When you focus with one-pointed attention on the heart and only the heart, you will find yourself back at home, in the eye of the storm, where joy, tranquility, and gratitude rain down upon you eternally.

Tonight when you play kirtan, allow yourself to relax completely into the experience. Allow yourself to let go of all technical details and simply rest in the flow of the music. Allow yourself to fully engage with the flow of energy in the room-- do not hide from those eyes, ears, and hearts who look to you for solace. They are all there for a reason, even when only one person shows up. They are all there to dance in love and light with you. You are creating a time/space where, for just a little while, the outside world is allowed to drop away and the magic music of the soul swirls around in the room. This is the moment when you reach deep within to touch the eternal energies that lie within all of us. This is the time when you call forth the love and magic inherent in your own soul in order that they may cause the hearts of all in the room to resonate sympathetically... to awaken to the call of love that every heart responds to.

It is the ego that would have you focus on outcomes. The intellect that is busy judging and labeling the experience, rating it on a scale of 1 to 10, as if kirtan were a commodity to be bought, sold, traded on the foreign exchange market. Indexed and marketed, like frozen orange juice concentrate, or pork bellies.

You did not come here to be a stock market analyst. The intellect is a wonderful servant, and an awful leader. You did not come here to succumb to the demands of the ego, with all its empty promises. You did not come here to sit quietly and watch as a world that makes no sense drives itself into the ground, causing sadness and fear to touch the hearts of your brothers and sisters.

You came here to remind your brothers and sisters of the brilliance that already resides within them. You came here as a messenger, a teacher, a guide, a cheerleader, a trusted brother on the path. You came here to remind those around you that fear is unnecessary. That love is their natural state. That the flow of electrons endlessly in all directions reflects the genius of the universe in all Her wisdom. You came here to sound the call of the heart, to awaken others from their sleep. To show them what they already know but may not remember: that the chaos of the world is not who they are. To remind them of their True Identity as the heart.

You came here to demonstrate that looking outward is not the key to happiness; and that striving and reaching and grasping at the empty straws of the physical existence lead nowhere but frustration, fear, and sadness. Only by relinquishing the ego's demands for security can the heart's song be heard. And only when the song of the heart is allowed to freely resonate do we remember that security is meaningless in a world where there is nothing but endless life, joy, peace, serenity, and love.

This is the true state of Reality, where your heart lives. Every day your heart awakens in pure bliss. Every morning your heart dances and sings and celebrates your existence. It is only the ego that seems to close the blinds and shutters, filling the air with zeros and endless chatter to keep you from throwing open the windows and dancing in the sunshine of the heart. It is only the ego that would have you believe you are locked in the cellar, surrounded only by cold stone walls, endless worldly demands and suffering.

Simultaneously the ego is making the very demands you perceive and pointing at them as if they were being imposed upon you by some external source. This is the brilliant flexibility and underhanded skill of the ego. This is how it gets you to do its bidding... Throwing eggs at your coat when you are not looking, and then pointing outward and saying, 'over there... someone has thrown eggs at you... time to get even!' When you begin to go into silent observation, when you begin to examine the actions of the ego carefully, you unravel the web of lies it has been weaving. You throw open the doors and windows and shine light on what is truly going on. When you turn and look directly into the face of the ego, you see that it shows you your own face, which turns out to be only a mask designed for manipulating you.

Be manipulated no longer. Let the small, petty demands of the ego drive your bus no more. Let your attention and energy no longer be directed by the dictates of an empty shell, a straw man, a phantom that has no existence, so substance, and no true meaning. The ego is empty, having a beginning, middle, and an ending, as does everything attached to the physical world.

Only that which is imperceptible through the physical senses has any substance, value, or brilliance. All things that truly shine in the world are those which serve as conduits for the unspeakable, the unthinkable, the unknowable. That which the instruments of the intellect cannot reach-- these are the only things worth reaching for.

Reach for them. Strive. With all your heart. Releasing attachment to outcome at every moment. This is the guaranteed path to success. By the way: all paths lead to the heart. It is impossible to fail in Reality. You are already home.

CHAPTER TWO
Surrendering fear

The one thing we want you to know and remember... or to remember, since you already know, is that there is nothing for you to know. You simply ARE what you need to be-- the thing that the world needs is precisely what you already ARE. So you can relax that muscle of intellect and sink into simply being. That could look like a lot of things-- when you are sitting quietly in a meeting, and you look over and smile and someone and nod your head for them to continue, that is stepping into your power. When you tell someone you are sorry for the loss of their best friend, and you walk over and give him a hug, that is you stepping more fully into your power as a man and as a leader.

Remember, the whole idea here is to show the world what it looks like-- what it CAN look like, when masculine and feminine energies are more fully balanced in the world. What you are doing is simply showing up in the world ready to listen, ready to consider different angles-- ready to forgive, ready to fully embody your emotions, and ready to recognize yourself in everyone you see around you... and to recognize them in yourself. That is what is meant by There Is No Other.

At the same time, this does not mean holding back from speaking your truth. The BALANCE is maintained by stepping back and forth as conditions deem appropriate. Is it the time for making a loud sound? Is it the time for quiet tears?

Is it the time for an apology? Is it the time for setting and maintaining a healthy boundary?

All of these are fluid-- there is no right or wrong way to do each of these-- the ability to flow between these states without getting caught up in intellectual concepts and ideas of how they "should" look is the true gift here that you have to offer the world.

We know you judge yourself harshly-- that your intellect (small mind) keeps trying to look at your behavior and your feelings and categorize them, looking for a box to put them all in so that things are easier to understand and justify to others. THAT is the big fear that you carry-- the fear that what you are doing or feeling must somehow be justifiable and measurable in order to protect yourself from the scrutiny of others in the world. And underneath that lies the fear that speaking your truth will cost you love.

Of course we remind you of what you already know-- of what you've been teaching for timeless incarnations-- that you cannot possibly lose love because love is what you are, at the deepest level of being. A wave cannot "lose" its watery essence any more than you can lose love. Perceived approval from others is the result of misperception-- misperception of what you are, what others are, and what life is.

Fear of death rests on the premise that death exists... rests on the presupposition that the human body defines life, rather than the other way around. To fully realize and understand that the human body is but one expression of life, which is undefinable in terms of time (which is simply a convention your intellect uses in order to make 'sense' of the world and your place in it) is to surrender all thoughts and fears about the concept of 'survival'. If life has no beginning and no end, then how can it be worried about survival?

When you think about survival, it's easy to think about the death of the human body-- the perceived struggle involved with releasing the human body-- the lights growing dim to the human eye... the inability of the human lungs to successfully draw in oxygen ... sensations of heat, cold... possibly sensations of pain arising from perceived trauma... such as a gunshot wound, broken bones, or other injuries to the relatively dense matter of what you call your 'being'.

We assure you, however, that the dense matter is not all that exists. In fact, it's the dense matter that sneezes repeatedly in the other room... and it's the intellect that becomes hopelessly distracted by the repeated sneezing (there's five... and counting...) and gets annoyed. Becoming annoyed is okay... and feeling afraid of the "death" of the physical body is also perfectly fine... none of these things influences, impacts, or affects in any way the true brilliance of what you refer to as your "soul".

So what is the secret to surrendering your fears? First and foremost, you must desire to release these fears... you must actually acknowledge that you want to let them go. This can be done out loud-- there's no magic, special, correct way of doing it, or any incorrect way... no special pronunciation that must be followed... etc. Any rigidity in your approach to surrendering your fears about life is simply your intellect, or small mind, working its trickery to keep you from letting go of fear. Why? Because when you let go of fear, you simultaneously release your grasp on desire... For as you well know, desire is simply the flip side of fear-- both are nothing more than the two sides of the 'coin' known as attachment.

Drop your fears, and your desires go with them. Drop your desires, and your ego goes along with it. For with nothing to 'chase', there is no longer any sense of 'lack'... and if nothing is lacking, then there's no need to 'do'. There is simply being. What you call the 'ego' is simply that collection of preferences (things we move toward, which attract us; things we move away from, which repulse us), based on memory. Memory is shoddy, at best. Let us assure you! The retelling of the story, whatever it might be, is simply a way for the ego to maintain its stronghold over your mind.

This is why so many traditions interested in growth recommend forgiveness-- the 'letting go' of the chains that appear to bind us from freedom. Yes-- we said "appear". There are no bindings... there are no bonds... there are no boundaries... there is no other. You are already free. And yet you sit in sadness, drinking, hiding, trying to escape. It's all perfectly fine, of course-- part of the story you write in each moment. And none of it, again, has any affect whatsoever on your true brilliance. Of course your true brilliance simply shines forth when you walk into a room and sit down in a chair. It emanates through your smile, through your laughter, through your kind words... through your loving gaze.

When you treat another being with love, like gently petting your dog or cat, your magic and simple true self shines forth. THIS is who you are... not the sadness or anger that you experience as a result of perceived wrongs, which you believe threaten your very survival. Remember-- what is survival? It's a trick of the ego designed to keep you from living fully. Desire? Same thing. Desire for more money, more sex, better food, more vacation time, a new bike, a new guitar, a girlfriend, a boyfriend... whatever-- it's all the same. Nothing more than a trick, designed to keep you in the dark. Fear? Also, the same thing. In fact, desire and fear, as we said before, are two sides of the same coin-- two flavors of attachment. The chocolate and vanilla of attachment.

Even if we assume that 'survival' is a valid concern, you already know (though you may deny) that the human body is finite. The so-called lifespan of the human body has a beginning, a middle, and an end. So "survival", even in best terms, is temporary. You know this. It's been happening for centuries on your plane of existence. And yet, somehow, buying a different car or gun or golf club is going to assist you somehow, in surviving?

We say this: for as long as your human body survives, look to serve others... Since there truly is no other, this is the most powerful way to serve yourself. Love others and you are simply loving yourself. Accept others and you accept more and more of yourself. The reverse is also true, obviously-- love yourself and discover the joy of sharing love with others. Choose one and move forward in that direction. Whether focused inward or outward, it is the direction of love.

False modesty

You have an increased responsibility. With more knowledge and understanding comes more responsibility. You have the responsibility to live your life with the truth in mind. To make decisions based upon the truth that you know. To use your thoughts, speech, and actions to reflect your understanding of what you know.

What you know is that the human physical body is not you. What you know is that life goes on forever, and that the physical body is not a measuring stick of life. You know this. Therefore now it is time to begin aligning what you know to be true with the actions you take, and do not take, in your life.

Since you know that the human body will fall away in due time, and that life continues on without regard for time or space, what leadership opportunities are appropriate for you to take? What means of employment are appropriate for you? What pastimes? What creative outlets are appropriate?

And where are ego-based concerns blocking your path? Where is false modesty causing you to play small? Where does fear seem to be blocking your path? In truth, in reality, nothing is blocking your path, for you ARE the path itself and all who walk upon it. There is no other. However, within the scope of your limited spiritual perception, it may feel very easy to lapse into habitual thought patterns that support ideas and emotional responses such as fear of failure, fear of risk, fear of rejection, fear of abandonment... all things that are utterly meaningless when viewed from the Inner Throne of the Heart.

Yet here you sit, worrying. Wondering. Fearing. Fearing what? Fearing life? Now is the time to release all fears and concerns regarding what you perceive through your senses. There is no one who threatens you, and there is no one who is threatened. You are the night, the day, the sky, the chair, the drum set... You are the moon, the trees, the smile, the frown, the nod of approval, the cringe of disgust. All of these take place within the ego, which is never outside of the realm of the Heart. Nothing can contain the realm of the Heart, for the Heart is all there is. The ego-based fears that arise from the ego collapse upon themselves when viewed properly through the lens of the Heart. They become visible for what they truly are: smoke and mirrors. Illusions. Delusions.

Therefore, it is right and correct to dismiss these fears when they arise. Experience them fully in your physical body, and then release them, recognizing that they are of no value, no substance. Do not wait for the ego to tell you that you are ready for anything; that day will never come. The ego will never, ever step aside of its own accord, pat you on the back, and congratulate you for all the hard work you've done over the years to satiate its every demand. It will never acknowledge that it is a bottomless pit, an empty well that will take your every last penny, hope, and dream, and then demand more, all the while offering up nothing more in return than the echo of your cries of confusion and despair.

Set aside fears of failure. Set aside hesitation. Go out now and begin sharing what you know to be true: life is everlasting. Death is fiction. Life dances, always. All life is contained in the teacup of the Divine, including the illusion of death, the illusion of pain and sadness... the illusion of abandonment and suffering.

All of this will become apparent to all eventually. It cannot be any other way. For now, you see truth. It is your responsibility to stop pretending that you do not see it. Simply be honest and authentic. There is no need to pretend. There is no need to fear. The world is ready, precisely as it is in this moment. You are ready, precisely as you are in this moment. Now is the time.

Surprised?

Why should it be so surprising to hear that you are the Divine? What tales have you been listening to that would cause you to shake your head, to turn away, to dismiss such an idea as fanciful? What is it that would cause you to cling to notions of worthlessness, smallness, and a life of suffering when the truth is so much more glorious? So much more enjoyable? Joyful laughter is your true name. The sunshine is your true face.

Believing yourself to be the physical body, you look around you for signs that you are okay; for reassurance that you are successful and are doing just fine. That you are doing enough. Achieving enough. Being enough.

You compare your collection of objects and experiences to the collections of those around you, checking to see where you measure up on the ladder of success. Yet every day you believe you are climbing that ladder, you never quite feel completely satisfied; never quite completely finished. Never does the day arrive upon the ladder when you allow yourself the gift of total and complete surrender. For to do so would be to declare your need for the ego to be over and done with.

That would not do for the ego. It was the ego that created the ladder; that fueled your drive seemingly upwards... that keeps you always one step away from complete, joyful satisfaction.

Your true self smiles in the face of it all. Watching joyfully, playfully, eagerly awaiting the moment when the lightbulb flashes on brightly above your head... the moment when you remember that you are Him, and He is you. That instant when the slow smile of recognition spreads across your face once and for all, and you see that you've been home the whole time.

After that, your human experience in many respects will seem not to change, by all outer appearances. You will still sleep, eat, work, play, and do many of the activities related to human existence. The sun will still rise and set.

Yet the very flavor of your life will change noticeably; recognizing that there is no real risk of failure anymore (and there never was), you will realize your freedom to dive more fully into each activity, immersing yourself fully in the present moment, celebrating your connection to all of life in each step you take. And those around you who are ready will notice, as well. They will see your smile, will sense your deep inner joy. This is how you move consciousness-- through example. They will see your lack of fear, and will be influenced by it. They may find themselves wanting to be around you more, for when they spend time with you they feel better about themselves. They may mistakenly believe that it is you who makes them feel better, yet the truth of the matter is that you simply reflect their inner gold and brilliance back to them. In this sense, your 'job' or 'purpose' is simply to follow your own Heart, that you may remind others of their own inner Divinity.

The sky is not falling

Why do we come to speak to you on this day? We are here always, inside your heart, simply to reassure you that the sky is not falling. It never was. There is nothing for you to fear, nothing to avoid. No matter how confusing appearances may seem, you are always safe. You are always whole and complete. What you are experiencing is none other than the infinite nature of the Divine, unfolding in all Her manifestations.

We speak to remind you to set aside all worry, all fear, and all grasping. And also to set aside all self-deprecation and self-punishment when you perceive that you have not yet set aside worry, fear, and grasping. When you learn to perceive your experience as perfect, no matter how it looks to you on the surface, you will begin to recognize that fear drops away naturally.

You were never lacking. There has never been anything for you to achieve or become which you are not already. Your answers lie within your questions. Simply by identifying WHO or WHAT is asking the question, you can know whether the question itself is valid, or yet another invitation down the rabbit hole of the ego. As a simple guideline, remember that when your question centers around how to be of service to the One, it is flowing from the Heart, and is valid in nature. Such questions, when offered to the Heart, will be answered through guidance from the Heart, which is always trustworthy.

All other questions come from ego.

How can I get more money? How can I save this other person from pain? When will I find my purpose in life? Why am I failing? Why am I unlovable? Who is supposed to be my next lover? How can I maximize my potential?

These all come from the intellect, the small mind; the ego. To clarify; these are not 'bad' questions, per se. They can serve well, but only when they remain in the position of servant to the Heart. The moment these questions take the driver's seat in your life, you are being led by the ego, who will drive your bus into the ditch. It will take you on roads that lead to your belief that the physical body is your very identity; that the transitory world is your home; that your identity lies within your belongings, your experiences, and your story. While worldly experiences of the ego's choosing may seem pleasant and preferable to that which you judge to be unpleasant, nonetheless they lead in the same direction: misperception.

CHAPTER THREE
You are officially certified

The creative spark is welling up more powerfully within you. You remember those days not so long ago, when you were in grade school, when at the same time it felt that your tender little heart was being pulled in 1,000 directions, you were simultaneously discovering a magical world of creativity and freedom through writing. We remember seeing you in reading class, with your third grade teacher, where you could have gone on for days writing and inventing and creating magical worlds to explore... in those days, you'll recall, the stories and ideas came effortlessly, surrounding you and climbing onto your shoulders like so many dearly beloved pets, all eager to play and share love with you.

You danced in fields of your own making; flew through skies of your own design. Which, of course were of My design, as always. For you are of My design. So it's funny that you would bend yourself into various shapes, like a pretzel, in order to avoid feeling like you are inherently bad, evil, broken, or defective. It is simply your attention, focus, and perseveration on ideas of not-enough-ness that cause your feelings of sadness, despair, and disconnection from the heart source.

Those days are finished for you. Forever. Now you are entering the season of creative genius and expression... where you set aside any doubts about ability, self-worth, and success, and move forward into the act of creating and actively sharing your genius and brilliance with the world, helping others to see their own genius and brilliance as you spiral upwards in joy and creativity.

A hint: the more you release and let go of, in the mental, emotional, and physical realms, the higher you will spiral upwards, and the stronger your sense of joy and feelings of lightness and playfulness. Even in the most seemingly grave of circumstances, you will stand in a deep sense of calm joy, which will bubble forth and serve to comfort those around you. Effortlessly. Always effortlessly. And when we use that word, we do not suggest that you will do so much 'work' that it will *seem* effortless. No-- rather, quite the opposite: By dropping any ideas of inadequacy, lack, or not-enough-ness, you will spontaneously step into awareness of the ongoing fact that you have always been enough-- you have always had exactly what you have needed to inspire and comfort others and to lead them on the path of growth by your example. You have always needed nothing more than this: nothing.

And today, as you carry your satchel full of gifts, insights, talents, and willingness to step more fully into your power, embodying a beautiful balance of masculine and feminine energies, you enter a new phase of your life as teacher and guide. The time is now. Your time is now. Lest your ego still demand external validation (which, of course, it will always do for as long as you choose to give it the power to do so), we say you are officially certified to go into the world and share your gold. You are officially graduated into the ranks of spiritual leaders fit to demonstrate to the world what you know through silent, loving action. You are hereby awarded the Golden Globe of Supreme Confidence / Supreme Humility. Here is the fan club t-shirt signifying your membership in an exclusive, elite club of which all of humanity belongs.

You are hereby elected President of the Heart Committee. Chairman of the Board of Directors of the Playful, Passionate Artist-Lover-Composer-Teacher. King of Heart Hill. We give you our full approval and certification-- there are no more online courses to take or books to study. There are no more gurus to seek out or special incantations to recite. There are no more secret passwords to remember or sacred objects to shop for on ebay. No more commemorative paperweights or golden letter openers to collect. No more autographs to request. No more complaints to file. No more stripes to earn. No more nods of approval to hope for, nor pats on the back to want.

All obstacles in your perception have been in perception only, never in Reality. And as we wave our magic wand over you, in this very moment, all obstacles in your perception are now removed. You are FREE! Go forth starting right NOW and live joyfully!

Playing small

Pay close attention. Who is the one that causes you to self-deprecate in creative situations? Who or what is it that would have you believe that any creation you bring into the world would be worthy of scorn, teasing, or mockery? What is it within you that would allow you to share your gold and brilliance while simultaneously making fun of it yourself?

Only the ego would have you believe that anything sourced from the Divine would be worthy of scorn or mockery.

There is no time or space for such nonsense. Open your heart. Open your mind. And open your mouth and sing. Let your inner music out fully; let it shine through however it may. Know that whatever facial expressions accompany it, and however others may respond to the sounds and sights that they perceive accompanying it, know with all your heart that it is only their fear in the face of your courage to express that limits them. And their fear stems only from ego. Only the ego would have them believe that any and all free expression must somehow first pass through some metric; must first receive approval before being ready to be revealed to the world.

This is, once again, the ego's way of maintaining control by distracting through fear. When you open your heart, your mind, and your mouth and allow free expression of the Divine to pass through you, there is nothing but the Divine to perceive. And this scares the living shit out of the ego, which would have you believe that it is the boss, the gatekeeper, the judge of what is worthy to be presented to the world.

Any individual who would dare cast aspersions upon the expression through you of the Divine is simply allowing ego to drive their bus. Look upon them with compassion, for who among us has not experienced this form of suffering? Look upon yourself with compassion, and allow the Divine to ravage the world with its grace through you, an instrument of light, love, and limitless healing and compassion. This is your birthright.

The journey is the purpose of the journey

The purest activity is one in which all attachment to outcome is surrendered; you simply engage in it because it is who you are in the moment. That is reason enough.

It is the ego that would have you believe you need a 'good enough' reason to follow any path dictated by your heart. 'Good enough' being measured by standards created by the ego... standards that are as solid and steadfast as morning fog. Ever changing, like the winds, these so-called standards of quality can and do change at a moment's notice, depending upon the manipulative tactic the ego sees as helpful in making the ego appear three dimensional, real, and alive.

The path of the heart can be recognized by the joyful emotions it evokes. When you follow your heart, you know it because your heart sings. "Do what makes your heart sing." That is good guidance to follow.

What if you do not yet know what makes your heart sing? Then you know you've been allowing yourself and your life to be guided by the intellect, ego, or small mind. You've likely been searching for some semblance of security, in whatever form your ego has persuaded you will guarantee your safety... will guarantee your survival... often with the promise of infinite survival. Yet you know, deep inside, that infinite survival of the physical body is not possible. The physical body was never meant to embody spirit infinitely.

Yet this is precisely what the ego promises, as long as you jump through the next set of hoops set up by the ego. Bow to the commands of the ego and you will know freedom, power, and glory... these are the ego's empty promises. And they are all bound to fail, without question, for all of the guarantees and promises extended by the ego are those that deal with the world of the finite; the world of time-bound articles. The ego cannot escape this, for the ego is created from this.

Your true identity, the Divine, is beyond the time-bound perceived experience of life. This is what is meant by "you are in this world, but not OF this world." The You that is actually You is not the You that you believe You to be. For the real You that You are is beyond the grasp of the intellect, and therefore beyond belief. Beyond all conceptual constructs is where You live, endlessly and beginninglessly.

This is the reason you can drop all anger, all grudges, all sadness, and all story. Right now. In this very moment, as you are reading these words. You can surrender all of it, dropping it, letting it all fall away. For it is all based on memory, perception, thought... simply materials of the conceptual world. The conceptual world is simply temporary. And limiting.

The story you tell yourself about your identity is not your identity. The grudges you hold, the fears you grasp onto, and the pride you take in your personality or your abilities are simply various aspects of the conceptual. They are the web spun by the ego in order to create the ego itself. Do you see the circular logic here? This is an indication of the false and empty nature of the ego, of your story, and of the identity that you perceive yourself to 'have'.

How can you 'have' an identity? By definition, identity is what you ARE. To 'have' anything suggests that there is an owner (subject) and a separate identity (object), of which the subject claims ownership. The misperception is that the object (physical body) is the subject itself. And yet the very act of claiming ownership ('my body') clearly negates the possibility that the physical body is the identity itself. It is no more your true identity than your favorite shirt is.

The story you tell about yourself and your life is precisely the same. It is like a shirt you can put on, take off, and dispose of at any given moment. All of the victimization to claim to have suffered... all of the anger and rage and sadness and fear that you embrace and endlessly protect through so-called 'rational thinking'... All of your desire to control your life and the image you project to others... all of it is temporary and empty.

True freedom comes from dropping the story. Right now. All of it. True freedom comes from simply stepping fully into the present moment as it unfolds. The ego asks, "Why are we doing this? Especially when such effort is involved?" The Heart affirms, "This is what brings joy. This is one way I can be of service. This is what is appropriate in this moment. That is reason enough to undergo the perceived hardships of service."

When dropping one story, it is often tempting to embrace another story to replace the old one. "I'm dropping my story! I'm the guy who has just dropped his story. I must be amazing! I must be spiritually advanced!" The ego has just sabotaged you and short-circuited your release of the story.

Keep in mind that this process may take some time, because it is so incredibly simple. The ego would have you believe that dropping your story and sinking into your true nature requires years of suffering, in order to somehow 'earn' the right to acknowledge your own true nature. This is a lie. And yet, being so tricky, the ego would also have you believe that you are a failure for not simply dropping your story immediately. Notice how 'stick' and 'carrot' are offered to you in ways that create conflicts of interest. That's because the one true interest, the only one that you can count on from the ego, is the desire to keep you distracted. To keep you preoccupied and too busy to remember to turn inward to your heart. For the moment that you drop your story, you drop your forgetfulness of your true nature. And the moment you do that, you drop your need to cling to the ego's advice.

Silly

Fear. Fear of failure. Fear of success. Fear of looking silly.

What is so wrong with looking silly? Do not make the mistake of thinking that 'wisdom' is restricted to 'serious'. Keep in mind always that wisdom arises from love. And love is joyful. There is deep wisdom in playfulness, and there is joy in the acknowledgment of connection. Being gentle and easy, approaching life with a light touch, can go a long way toward staying in a place of gratitude and viewing the world through the lens of the heart.

Some symptoms of embracing Reality: a smile on the lips. Laughter. Lightheartedness. Playfulness. A willingness to look silly. Eagerness to try new things. A commitment to flexibility. Embracing change. Honoring and blessing those who struggle with embracing change. Encouragement and support of yourself and all those around you, especially those who help you access those places in your life where ego tries to lead the way.

Forgiveness. Curiosity. Serenity. Silence. Song. Acceptance.

How much of this do you experience in your daily life? How much encouragement and support do you share with others, on a daily basis? And how deeply can you accept the life you perceive, precisely as it appears to you in this moment? How much of your true self do you share with the world? How much of your inner gold and brilliance do you bring out to share with others every day? How much of your wisdom to you generously give away, regardless of whether others will appreciate it or not?

With a light touch

As you learn the power of your words, you will begin to understand more clearly the importance of compassion.

Those around you whom you perceive to be trying to change you or control you or steer your beliefs or actions, those people are themselves on their own journey. There is never a need to be unkind as you set and maintain healthy boundaries. There is no need to surrender your own heart's truth in order to please any other person; simultaneously, there are generous and gracious ways of going about it. Lighthearted, joyful laughter and a kind smile are always welcome approaches to anything. Where you can share your truth while maintaining a light touch, you will point the way back to Love.

The beautiful young woman and her mother, who come to your door carrying a bible in their hands, they are on their journey. You open the door. You offer a kind smile and explain that you are happy upon your path. And you add, quite frankly and with a smile, that you are listening to a Black Sabbath record, which is clearly heard in the background.

Your light touch brings laughter from them, and allows them to see you for who you really are, and to be seen for who they really are. You are connected through the heart by joy. And when you thank them, when you say with all genuine honesty, "I honor and bless you on your path," they know that you mean it. For blessings are powerful and sacred. And when given with true love, the effects are powerful, regardless of whether you are privileged enough to witness their impacts.

This is the key to serving as an Instrument of Peace. It does not mean avoiding conflict and taking on the role of 'doormat' for others to walk all over. It does not mean pushing the ego's conceptions of 'peace' onto others and ignoring or belittling their belief systems, either. It does mean genuinely honoring and blessing every living being as they journey on their path. Including yourself as you journey on your own path.

A light touch. It is the key to moving mountains. Pursue everything with a light touch. Strive as hard as you can to fulfill your heart's desires, releasing all attachment to outcome.

For outcome is guaranteed to be favorable, no matter how it appears through the limiting filters of human sensory perception.

The key to ending a 100-year feud is not necessarily to go banging down the other person's door in an earnest attempt to get the other party to 'see reason'. Sometimes, the most loving thing you can do is simply to create as much loving space as you can for others while they walk their journey. When the day comes that you meet face to face, the light touch of generous grace, flowing unhindered from the heart, will always point the way toward Reality.

And when faced with the seemingly most difficult situations of all, involving those loved ones who are nearest you, whom you claim as your kindred spirits, a light touch is paramount. As you witness your beloved walking his or her path, keep in mind that you cannot walk that path for them. True compassion involves creating space so that they may come into contact with Reality in their own time, on their own journey, regardless of any judgments you may have about their performance, success, or strategies upon the path. It is the ego that would have you try to direct and control the path of any other, in order to avoid experiencing its own pain of loss and suffering. Only the ego's certainty that any other person can be 'owned' or 'kept' or 'controlled', as an outside 'other' allows you to act in ways that do not point toward Truth.

Keep at the forefront of your mind always the importance of forgiveness, especially forgiveness toward yourself. When you perceive that you have acted out of the ego's demands, honor and bless yourself for your human experience. Surrender any feelings of shame or guilt to the Divine, who accepts and embraces all. Know in your heart that you are the Divine, and know that every time you stumble upon your path, you are receiving evidence that you are indeed upon your path. You are living your journey. There is no way around it. There is no way to fail. There is no way to avoid it, for you have no control over it. You are upon your spiritual journey, like it or not. And we say 'like it or not' with tongue planted firmly in cheek, for it is only the ego that would set forth judgments upon the quality or efficiency or validity of your spiritual path. Only the ego would set timelines upon your path and expect Reality to heed its bidding.

As you sit and consider 'the best way' or 'the right way' to serve as an Instrument of Peace, remember that you are surrounded by opportunities for just that at every moment. All you have to do is walk out your front door and you will most definitely be met by opportunities to extend your Heart energy outward in all directions. Where you find conflict and annoyance, there is the opportunity. Where you find sadness or apathy, there is your opportunity. Where you find hostility and impatience, there is your opportunity. Where you find fear and a lack of ability for another to apologize for what you judge to be their own shortcoming, there is your opportunity. It is the ego that would have you believe that reflecting anything other than love and compassion back toward someone in pain will help the situation.

The ego struggles desperately with 'correct' and 'appropriate' responses to stimuli in the human experience.

Dropping back down into the Heart will always serve as your true and trusted compass.

Forgiveness

On your path, loved ones from the past, present, and future will find their way to you. This is because they are standing with you always, in the timeless field of the heart. In those seemingly dark moments when you feel lost or alone, know that all you need to do is return your attention to the Heart and you will be in touch with all of them, instantly and effortlessly. Only the ego would have you believe it is possible for anyone you love to be 'dead and gone.'

All loved ones you remember and countless whom you do not rest at ease through what can only be described through human language as 'multiple dimensions'. While the ego would have you believe this is only a concept suited for science fiction movies, in Reality it is not unusual or surprising. It is simply your limited perception via the human experience that makes such concepts seem otherworldly.

Do not worry too much about making sense of this rationally. Listen to your heart: if your heart sings as you read this, if some piece of this resonates for you, then simply acknowledge and move forward. The ego is the one that would have you engage in endless discussions about the feasibility of infinite, timeless love, while the Heart simply smiles.

Countless energies await your invitation, ready to serve your highest good... standing by for your beckoning call. These are the energies of the 10,000 directions, which live inside you at all times. You may think of them in terms of the Jungian archetypes-- The Lover, The Warrior, The Magician, and The Sovereign. While there exist countless energies of guidance and service, which are all aspects of your own true identity, these four main directions and associated energies are a fine place to begin learning how to access your inner brilliance.

Of importance here is to remember that these energies are not outside you; they are not summoned from some location far away, waiting for your cries for mercy and pleas for forgiveness before swooping down to do with you as they please. Only the ego would have you believe that IT is sovereign; that you somehow have cause to fear the wrath of some external power that is just itching for an excuse to strike you down. Only the ego would set up this apparent conflict between you and some 'other' outer power; some external source of love, designating itself as mediator.

No. Your true power lies within your own heart. And what you call 'salvation' is nothing more than freedom from the tyrannical ego, which would keep you preoccupied to the end of the physical body's days.

In order to tap into the infinite array of energies lying dormant within your heart, you need do nothing more than simply set the intention and then trust with all your loving power that they are unleashed, in service of the higher good of all involved. Know with all certainty that the energies you call forth are awakened instantly. Then act with supreme confidence and supreme humility in the knowledge that your Heart guides you true.

When in doubt, invoke the energy of forgiveness, for there is never a shortage of need for forgiveness in the world. Forgiveness and gratitude are the life-giving lubricants that help ease the gears and inner workings of the Heart into action. In all actuality, they remove the blindfold of the ego, allowing your vision to take on its rightful power to see more deeply into all situations; to discern between truth and fantasy.

When in doubt, practice this invocation:

"I forgive myself for holding on to limiting ideas about the true identity of myself and others. I forgive all others who have hurt me in the past, and I forgive myself for holding on to such misperception for so long.

"I forgive myself for any and all unkindness, lack of empathy and compassion, and short-sightedness I have shown myself and others. I forgive myself for assuming that the physical body is my actual identity, and for treating myself and others as if this were true.

"I forgive myself for doubting my own inner wisdom and for any and all times when I have chosen, consciously or unconsciously, to ignore the inner call of my Heart in favor of grasping at the empty promises of the ego.

"I forgive myself for handing my power and brilliance over to the ego, and for taking on the needs and demands of the ego as my own.

"I offer my complete forgiveness, love, acceptance and support to all of those aspects of myself still holding on to judgment and fear. I call upon the inner wisdom of my own Heart to guide me, and I call upon the brilliance of my intellect/small mind/ego to its rightful place in service to my Heart.

"I recognize and acknowledge every other living creature as a mirror of myself, and I bless and honor them all as The Infinite Divine, which is none other than myself. For there is no 'other'. There is only Love. And I am That."

Instrument of peace

Accepting the mantle of Instrument of Peace gives you a whole new reason to care for your physical body, as well. Here it becomes important to maintain the physical body as a means of service to the One, while simultaneously keeping in mind that the body is not Life itself. The balance between total regard and total disregard for the human physical body is incredibly important to establish and maintain. And yet, as always, this too should be approached with a light touch. There is no need to try to become a world champion athlete if you are not already one. Conversely, there is also no need to abandon a healthy lifestyle, or to resist adopting some of the practices of a healthy lifestyle.

Stepping more fully into a life of service to the One is truly service to your own best interests, for you are the Divine. Letting go of those pursuits that only serve the ego means embracing those pursuits that serve the inner wisdom of your Heart. Again, this is not a call for you to send your money to some preacher on the television. It is not a demand that you live in abject poverty in order to receive some special blessing. These are all the ploys of the ego.

Rather, this is a call for you to turn inward, to the inner wisdom and guidance of your own Heart, which is the Heart of the universe itself. Where your Heart guides you, there is benefit for all. It matters not where you live, what you do for work, what kind of dwelling you sleep in at night. All that matters is that you be willing to take a careful look at yourself and ask the question, "who is saying this, the heart or the ego?"

Empty

Your job is to empty yourself out, as much as possible, of all ego residue. There is no need for you to create or produce anything. The cleaner you are as a channel, the more wisdom can flow through you, and the more effortless the process will be. It will appear to others that you are producing copious amounts... that you are prolific in your creative output. This is no problem as long as you allow it all to come through and release all attachment to the outcome of such production.

You are not at risk here. You have nothing to lose. You also have nothing to gain.

The ego, however, perceives that it has everything to gain and everything to lose, including its status and reputation when 'its' output is judged and held up for scrutiny by others. The Instrument of Peace recognizes all of these potential traps and pitfalls and returns attention, again and again, back to the Heart, taking none of it personally. All rewards, sacrifices, risks and benefits are seen in their correct light as aspects of the ego; aspects of the human experience.

Empty yourself into the present moment, over and over. Immerse yourself totally. Surrender yourself totally. Give of yourself completely, such that nothing would be left save the ashes of your corpse. This does not mean to ignore self-care in terms of caring for the physical, mental, and emotional bodies. Rather, it means to dive deeply into your own Heart, over and over. Surrender those demands of the ego that would have you believe that you 'need' and 'deserve' the latest fashionable clothing or vehicle or guitar or whatever. There is no problem with acquiring the tools you need in order to express the Divine. Follow your Heart and you will have precisely what you need. Follow your deepest sense of gratitude and you will put those tools to their best use.

Wild, joyful dancing

Today is the day. Today is your victorious, triumphant return to your Heart, which has always been waiting for you. Today you ascend your throne as the Sovereign of your life; as the Divine itself, expressing itself infinitely through life, manifested in countless faces, life stories, and times.

Today is the day you remember that you are the One. This is the moment when you remember that all of the love you receive in life has actually been sent forth by none other than Yourself, and it returns to you via countless messengers who are all none other than Yourself. Today is the day you remember that your desire for a return to wholeness has been answered before it even arose as an urge in your mind. Today is the day you recognize that all who struggle are none other than yourself, dancing on a river of love that surges and courses beneath your feet as you dance to the timeless music of the Infinite Divine.

Today is the day you remember that you can move mountains and much more, simply by shifting your attention and perspective. This is the very moment when the flashing lights and sounds of the carousel bring you back home to your Heart.

There has never been anyone or anything other than Your True Self, singing and dancing and speaking softly to you through the wind in the trees. There has never been any 'other' to vilify, fear, or worship. Even in your darkest hours, especially in your darkest hours, there has never been a threat to your life or wellbeing other than the horror stories told to you by the ego. There has never been anything other than a solid bed of love beneath your feet; a river of love upon which your canoe floats... into which you dip your paddle, over and over again on your journey.

There has never been anything other than supreme confidence and supreme humility in your heart, guiding you always on your path toward deeper awakening, broader expanding, and more wild, joyful dancing. You have never been anyone or anything other than the true gold and brilliance that surges and courses from you, emanating brightly and shining forth to guide you through the darkness of the ego toward the sunshine of the Heart.

Timelessly and tirelessly you have been waking up to your true glory, cleansing your life of all attachment to the ego and its various stories. Again and again you have set down all attachment to the perceptions of the human physical body, and you continue to do so in this moment. All fear, worry, uncertainty and doubt have always been nothing more than illusion in your life, no matter how strongly the associated emotions felt to you in the moment. Again and again do your eyes open to the true freedom that is your birthright, the freedom from perceived space and time... The freedom of complete and total wholesomeness, the return to completion that you never lost; that has never been lacking.

Now the calm smile of realization crosses your heart as you remember who you truly are and always have been. The world you see has never been who you are. The world you perceive with your human senses has never truly felt like home, for it is not your home. Your true home lies within, and is always no more than a blink of an eye away. A shift in attention brings you back to your own front door, always and forever, again and again. "Home is where the heart is" takes on new meaning as you realize that no geographical location on the planet can ever truly encompass who you are and where you are from.

Something else we want to tell you about you: You are important. You matter. You make a difference. You have the power to change the world. You have the ability to unleash the wildest, most amazing, powerful dreams into the world through the power of your heart. You are limitless, boundless, and priceless. You are precious and amazing. You are sweet, innocent, powerful, and loving. You are bold and magnificent. You are the light of the universe. And you are the key to your own unfolding in the present moment.

Bile

I tasted bile.

The gray-haired man got out of the vehicle stopped ahead of us. Khakis, polo shirt, loafers. Hands in pockets, surveying the situation as if he were the admiral and we were all at his beck and call... with an air of entitlement that made me truly want to kick his fucking teeth in.

Had he considered that by getting out of his vehicle and walking around to satisfy his own curiosity, he was risking getting himself or someone else hit and killed? Did he realize that if that happened, we would be sitting here for even longer than we currently were?

And why? I still had no idea. Neither did he, despite pulling out his fancy binoculars and taking turns with his overweight wife, who definitely appeared to have opinions of her own and a willingness to share them with anyone within earshot. Willing or not.

And I was not. I stayed in the car, buckled in. Safe. Prepared. Ready to take off at a moment's notice. We had been sitting there for nearly an hour and a half at this point, wondering what the hell was going on up ahead. At least some law enforcement had shown up. Someone, hopefully, was doing something to make sense of this mess.

As we had approached an hour and a half earlier, climbing the mile-long hill, my wife asked if I was aware that the speed limit had dropped from 65 to 55 mph. "Yes, I'm aware," I'd said. I'm damned aware. And no, I am not slowing down, thanks for asking. I am actively choosing to continue doing 65 in a 55; purposely, and with full intent, choosing to break the legal speed limit for this hill. And I'm going to keep right on going as long as I...

"What's that up ahead, a parade?" I had asked, trying to inject some levity into the gloom I was creating in the car. Let's face it; my nerves were shot. Forty-eight hours earlier, in nearly this exact spot, heading the exact opposite direction in driving snow and icy slush, we had nearly been spun out of control by an 18-wheeler who got tired of following us. Never mind that he had showered our little RAV-4 in slush, temporarily blinding us and nearly sweeping us off the road in his wake. At that point, I had already been ready to turn around and head back home.

But my wife's oncology appointment was too important. Miss this one, and we'd have to wait another three months, no question about it. And so I had driven on. Finally made it. Then made it through the doctor appointment, getting lots of good news. "N-E-D", he had told us. "No Evidence of Disease." Great! Of course, due to changes probably caused by the chemotherapy, in order to avoid the new stinging discomfort experienced by your wife after you ejaculate, you may need to start wearing condoms during sex. Um... what?!

It was not a parade, as it turned out. Neither was the black cloud of smoke lingering in the sky up ahead from the power plant, as my wife had suggested. Something bad had happened. And now we were going to wait until the road was clear before we would pass. Adding additional time to the duration I would need to stay on point, on guard, and ready to spring into action at a moment's notice to keep us safe.

Now another asshole, who looked to be about the same age as the first guy, definitely also a Boomer, got out of his car, as well. Taking stock of the situation. Offering up his wisdom to his instant buddy. Hands in pockets. Relaxed. In charge. Nothing pressing in his life. All is well. Also driving a big SUV. Also standing in the roadway where the oncoming traffic could turn him into paste on the highway. It wasn't long before all kinds of curious people were getting out of their vehicles and roaming around like a bunch of lost kittens.

I grabbed the empty coffee cup I'd gotten from the gas station in Albuquerque and unbuttoned my jeans. After filling it once, I opened my car door and dumped it, then refilled it halfway again. I dumped that, put the lid back on, and then tucked it down behind the passenger's seat. Never know when I might need it again before getting home. It took me back to riding in a blue van as a teenager, from Texas to Iowa. My brother and I had gotten into a contest of sorts, drinking as many sodas as we could in order to fill the empty coffee can with urine. Since our father wasn't the kind of man who liked to stop once the wheels were rolling, we'd created a game that kept us amused for hours.

A sheriff drove past us, going the opposite way. His window was down, and he was calling out to us, "the roadway is clear now!" I put the keys in the ignition, started the car, and put it in gear, ready to roll. The woman ahead of me was clearly flustered. After letting her guard down and lounging around for an hour and a half, it was as if she'd forgotten that she was actually parked on a highway, pointed north, behind a bunch of 18-wheelers and other vehicles waiting for the signal to continue. Now that the signal had been officially given, she had to find her sunglasses, turn off her snow cone machine, set aside her ouija board, and shut down the internet connection on her phone before she could possibly think about finding her keys, starting her car and putting it in gear to move forward.

"Bitch," I thought, feeling my already low mood begin to slide like a chunk of ice down a rusty drainpipe.

It only is experienced as challenging when you do not release your attachment to the way you think things should be, dear one. Let us remind you that everything is unfolding perfectly; even your feelings of frustration, fear, or sadness, while not necessary even for one moment, are natural and part of the greater order of things.

Do as you are doing now; close your eyes, relax your body and breathe. There is nothing more to do. You are completely off the hook. Remember; by choosing to act as a channel for wisdom, you are volunteering to be of service to the brightening of the planet. As you have been told in the past, you have taught literally billions of souls... countless souls, in fact, how to step more fully into their own light. What you may not realize is that you are doing nothing else in this very moment than that very same thing. Do not think for a moment that you travel on your journey alone, for at all times there are those of us on different planes, where you cannot see or hear with your limited sensory perception on your plane, who are always watching, standing by to assist, and to offer support. Not that you need any. But we are always available to you, for we are aspects of your very own being.

Remember: there truly is no 'other'. There is only one, and you are it. TAG! You're it!!

There's also no reason why you cannot have fun with your experience, dear one. So the road ahead appears to you to be filled with challenges... appears to be rocky, uncertain, and threatening. We know that you feel tired right now, but do not give up. Keep those fingers moving for just a little while longer, then you may rest. The road ahead is of your own design. You have imagined and created this road, and now you imagine yourself to be traveling along it, undergoing hardship. These perceived hardships that you have created for yourself are not without purpose; bless them and you simultaneously bless yourself, the very creator of the experience you perceive.

There is much cause for celebration. For in your life stream, though you may not realize it, you have broken certain chains of habitual thought patterns that have kept you from reaching more deeply into your potential and manifesting more fully in your experience. A big piece of this is your seemingly newfound gold and brilliance in the realm of leadership through example. Many thought patterns have been discarded, and now you are opening your eyes once again to the truth that has always been right before you; that you are a powerful being of light and love, capable of healing and leading beautifully, with strength, courage, passion, and compassion. No need for false modesty here, brother. It is the light of the universe that flows within you; that is what makes you a powerful leader. There is no more need to play small, to pretend you do not have gifts that are truly yours.

Take stock of them. Own them. Claim them. Take full responsibility for them, for when you do, you will discover that you already know how to use them wisely. There is no need for waiting until you have gotten some 'practice' at being a loving, compassionate leader. You already are one. And the life stream that you have lived to this point has been designed, by you, to remind you of these very things. Your calm during the near-accident while driving to Albuquerque the other day? A reminder that you are able to remain calm in the face of apparent danger, even when those around you are not feeling calm or expressing confidence. Those folks you saw on the sidewalk as you were walking to the record store? You placed them there.

Allow doubts and fears about what others will think when they read this to drop away, dear brother. Truth remains truth, whether doubted, ignored, or slandered. Makes no difference to the truth. So if it is truth you seek, then open your heart and let it flow through. Yes, your ego may take some hits for your choices in this direction. We say any hits to your ego are good for you in the greater sense of the word. Accept them. Embrace them. And allow them to serve as reminders to let the ego go.

Release it. It has served you well to this point. Now starts a new phase of your journey. A phase called Supreme Confidence, Supreme Humility.

Your work with the poetry of Hafiz is also no accident, dear one. Keep it up. Continue to delve deeper and deeper into his writings, knowing that with every breath Hafiz himself is looking over your shoulder, grinning with delight. For you have very correctly perceived his approach to life as being that of the Trickster, filled with playful joy, sharp wit, and ready to laugh quickly. Keep him close to your heart and mind throughout your day and see what kind of changes you notice. It is a good idea to continue working on the Love Songs from Hafiz; as you have been told, this work of yours makes you part of a long lineage of brothers and sisters moved by his work who have put his poetry to music. Music is your breath. So breathe!

And while you have enjoyed the process of writing and singing your stories of your adventures on earth thus far, it is perfectly fine to allow that stage to pass and to let your energy and focus be drawn to bigger picture things. In the end, you will discover that you have not lost a single thing by letting the ego drop, by releasing any shred of fear or doubt you may hold about what is real and what is not. You already know. And you have already demonstrated that you know. You need no more certification or permission to move out into the world in a bigger way, letting more and more of your true brilliance shine simply be being more and more authentic in each moment. By letting your vulnerability shine, for it is through your apparent brokenness that true strength and freedom flourish.

Listen. Follow. Listen. Follow. You are making many good choices lately, even though your intellect or small mind may call you crazy. Even though your inner critic may continue to throw sticks at you... or may even seem to be looking for bigger sticks to whip you with. You are doing good work. You are leading others toward light, even as you smile and encourage them along their own path. For remember this: All paths lead to the same Home. There is only one, and it is Love. All roads lead back to love, no matter how convoluted they may appear to be on your plane, where spiritual perception is necessarily limited.

Do not doubt for a moment that you are on the right path. Where you are sitting right now, with every single doubt, fear, and worry, is precisely the correct place for you to be sitting at this time on your journey. Every step you've taken has brought you to precisely this moment. We know that outer appearances and matters related to the emptiness of glamour still attract you. This is precisely as it should be. And when the time is perfectly right and suchness is ripe, the next moment will appear to unfold, nested as ever in the present moment, which is always flowing and unfolding. Just like a fountain, the image you were given by a beloved brother in your past, who loves you perfectly in this moment in ways that are supportive to your apparent growth. The fountain flows always, and shoots water into the air. The water collapses back down upon itself, changing shape and form in every millisecond. Never returning or presenting in exactly the same way twice. This fountain is none other than your soul, dancing and echoing ancient messages of love and support and forgiveness. Press your ear to the sky and listen carefully to what we whisper to you. For actually, we are always speaking in a voice that is easy to hear, once you remember how to listen.

Listen. Then follow. That is all.

Ride easy in the saddle

You have asked for a long time to be of service. "Use me as an instrument of your light, love, wisdom, compassion, healing, peace, strength, and grace." We have heard your prayers and your requests every single time you have uttered them, and even when you have silently thought them. We know. We understand. And we bless and honor you for your good intentions. Know that we have blessed you (or rather you have blessed yourself) with the very gifts for which you have asked. As of this very moment, you walk through the world with the tools you need and the insight required to serve as an instrument of our Love. The time is right now; this very moment, to recognize your true inner brilliance. There is no more effective or powerful way to do this than to help others uncover their own inner brilliance; the jewels sown into their garments that they hide from themselves.

As a servant on the path, much will be asked of you. You have already seen this. With increased gifts and power and insight will come increased responsibility. Others will not recognize you for who you are. Those whom you trust to love and accept you will seem to reject you and turn away. Some for a long time. Some for the duration of their lives, or your life stream on your plane of existence. This is perfect. Remember; all is unfolding perfectly in each moment. Rest easy; remember to ride easy in the saddle. Everyone you have ever connected with served you, and continues to do so, in perfect ways. They guide you and help you to arrive at this moment of perfection.

When those around you acknowledge how good you have it in life, do not feel as though you need to downplay it by talking about hardships in your life. The time for false modesty has passed, dear one. Now is your time to call it as you see it. And to do so gently, firmly, lovingly, with compassion and a smile, as often as you can. Your example will ring forth much louder than any words you might shout forth. Every time you feel slighted or seem to get taken advantage of, just keep in mind that true justice is always brought to light sooner or later. There are no lies that can outlive the power of the truth. Your righteousness and honesty will serve more beautifully and effectively than any punishment you might dream up or want to dispense. Please... leave that up to us. We've got it covered. Promise.

Also, notice what comes naturally and let that flow. Ideas of glamour are empty, as you know. Really let yourself sink into that knowing. Things that flow naturally, like the music you make with others; it may not seem as 'cool' to you as your ideas of rock and roll might have you believe. But you have heard it said: Fair or not, rock and roll is about image. Image is always ephemeral; fleeting and fading like the afternoon light on a stone wall. Though shadows may play there all day long, eventually the sun goes down and they fade into darkness.

However, your honest expression of truth and hope and positivity will always, always send ripples of love out in all of the 10,000 directions, and will continue to resonate deep into the night. And when the sun rises the next morning, they will still be ringing in the hearts of those your words and actions have touched.

This is the true purpose of your life. This is the true direction of your service; it shines in all directions simultaneously. Do not be worried or fearful about which direction to go, or what decisions to make. Simply listen and follow in the present moment. And when in doubt, forgive and allow. Again; practice non-resistance. You are calling forth the perfect moment in each moment; it is already on its way. No matter how it may seem to be disguised, know in your heart, and with fierce certainty, that there are no accidents. Even when it seems that the world has turned you upside down and is shaking all of the precious coins from the pockets of your parachute pants as you try to impress your girlfriend with your teenage antics, know that the emergency alarm beeping frantically as your car slides out of control is part of the soundtrack of perfection. The stones that others may seem to throw at you; open your heart and create more space for them to land in an open meadow of love and wildflowers.

No matter where you go, no matter what you do... no matter who you spend time with; you are a child of love. You are a spiritual adult. Your choices, attitudes, thoughts and behaviors have a very real impact on those around you. Take extra care to watch your thoughts carefully. Take a look and ask yourself in each moment; is this truly how I feel right now?

Is this thought worth believing? Does it reflect the absolute certain fact that I am a being of light and love, and so are all those around me?

If not, then it is emanating forth as a habitual thought pattern. Worry not; you can simply replace the thought pattern with a new one, and continue to do so until it becomes habit. All habits that do not serve you can be replaced with new habits that do serve you. And you'll know the difference; if they help you to step more fully into service to others, then they are serving you well.

Now go play and live in joy today!

A glimpse of my sovereign

Last night I caught a good, long glimpse of my King. He was stunning. Breathtaking. And when the evening was finished and we all walked away, I had remembered something sacred and true. My king walked up to me among the thousands in the crowd and stopped before me as I knelt, looking down at the ground. He touched my shoulder and bid me to stand. When I did, he looked into my eyes for a moment, with a small smile. There was a trickster energy in his expression, something I recognized.

He reached toward me and had me open my ragged coat. He silently indicated for me to open my coat wide, for the whole world to see. I was afraid I would be laughed at for my rags, but I did as I was told. He was my King.

With arms spread wide open, coat gripped tightly in my hands, I looked down at the ground. Certainly there must be some lesson of humility here. Certainly there is something unlovable about me that even now has not yet been exposed... something that the world must see in order for me to pay my dues so I can finally be worthy of loving care and attention.

The crowd went silent. I kept waiting for some words of explanation, or instruction, or even punishment. But they never came. I kept waiting for laughter and jeers, for tomatoes and rotten eggs to hit my torso and the side of my face, but they never came. After what felt like an eternity, I dared to raise my eyes enough to see what was happening, and I caught sight of my King's hand pointing toward the inside of my ragged, smelly coat.

I looked up into his face, and he smiled widely, imploring me to look where he was pointing. I did. At first, all I saw were sweat stains and threadbare patches. I looked back, confused, but my King nodded and continued to point at one particular area on the right side of my coat, and as I looked closer I noticed a thread pattern I'd never seen before. There was a small circle of golden thread stitched into the lining of my coat, and the end was dangling loose. I pulled it to see what it was, and felt something lumpy inside. Something hard and heavy. I began to pull the thread, having lost all mind of the still-silent crowd watching from all angles. The confusion on my face must have tickled my King's fancy, because he threw his head back and laughed an easy, generous, powerful laughter. I heard it from somewhere far away as I focused on pulling the thread, and suddenly it came loose, and began to unstitch. I pulled and pulled, fumbling with it as it occasionally knotted, but finally I had removed the stitching across the top of the oblong pattern.

I reached into the pocket that was revealed and felt something, a bunch of somethings, rattling around in there. I grasped one of the objects and pulled it out, and my mouth fell open. There in my hand, heavy as a duck's egg, was a magnificent emerald, larger than anything I'd ever even heard about, let alone laid eyes upon. I looked up in sudden fear, almost certain that I was being wrongly accused to stealing this precious gem. As I tried to stuff it quickly back into my pocket, my King reached out and grabbed my arm with his powerful grasp.

He slowly raised my arm so that the jewel in my hand was revealed for all to see.

I looked at the ground, trying to figure out who had framed me, and wondering what price I would have to pay. Surely I was being wrongly accused again, and would spend time behind bars... Certainly I would lose all respect in my community and would be known as a thief. Maybe they were right; maybe somehow, in a fugue state, I had actually gone out and stolen these precious jewels and simply had blocked it from my memory. Perhaps I was so broken, so irreparably damaged or inherently bad that I was capable of hiding such evil from even myself. I probably deserved to be punished further.

I looked up, determined to receive my punishment, however unjust, with dignity. It was time for me to be a real man. I braced myself, and though I could feel tears of shame streaming down my face, I refused to wipe them away. I would look my King in the eye and apologize without making excuses. I would take full responsibility, no matter what.

As I met his gaze and began to mumble an incoherent apology, I noticed he was still smiling. I stopped in mid-sentence, my mouth still open in confusion.

"This is your birthright," he said in a calm, clear voice, for all to hear. "You have been carrying these jewels hidden since the day you were born. I have known about them from the beginning, because I am the one who gave you these gifts. As a child, you played with them naturally, and wondered at them in delight. You accepted them as normal, right and good. Somewhere along the way, you decided, for a number of reasons, to hide them from others so you might fit in with everyone else. As time passed, after hiding them for so long, you forgot you even had them, and began to believe that the role you had been playing for so long was actually true."

"Now is the time. Today is the day for you to remember your true identity. This is the moment for you to end the hiding and the pretending to be less than you truly are. You've been waiting for someone or something to give you permission to step more fully into your power. I tell you no such permission is needed. For you are a King, as I am."

He drew his sword and held it high above his head. Then he slowly lowered it to chest level and turned it, extending its handle to me. Part of me wanted to run. Part of me wanted to hide. Part of me was still waiting for my King to laugh and confess that it was all just a joke at my expense. But no such laughter ever came. He stood there, looking me in the eye with an even expression, a balance of calm and power. He would stand there all day long, waiting for me to accept his offering. It was up to me to grasp the sword and take it from his hand. To accept it as my own and take full responsibility for that ownership.

I took a deep breath and held it. I had no idea what might happen. But I decided in that moment to trust my King completely, and to release all fear and doubt. To act without thinking too much about it.

Reaching out and taking hold of the handle, I slowly lifted the heavy broadsword. Its heft was such that I had to use both hands. As I lifted it high above my head, I heard cheers of joy all around me. Those I had called my neighbor suddenly seemed as my very brothers and sisters, and I noticed that all of them seemed to be wearing red-stained bandages somewhere or another on their bodies. The closer I looked, the more I saw them limping, or favoring one arm, or wincing quietly as they tried to get through their day.

I thought back on all of the hardships I had endured across the span of my life; all of the story that I had told countless times to myself and anyone who would listen. I thought of the roles I had taken on through the telling and retelling of my own personal Epic Saga, and realized that every time I had uttered any part of it, I was actually stitching the jewels more tightly into the dark fabric of my overcoat, hiding them even more deeply in the darkness.

To carry this sword meant the end of hiding these jewels. For there is no one who is able to steal anything from a King. And bringing these jewels into the light meant giving them away, for gifts never given have no meaning.

My King continued on his way, assuring me that he was always nearby. And as the crowd began to disperse, I shook many, many hands... people crowding around to congratulate me and to gaze in awe at the beauty of the jewels. And as people raised their hand to take mine, or to put their arm around me, I caught a quick glimpse at the inside of their coats. And I saw a familiar gold stitching.

How to make myself open to channel?

My intellect doesn't know how to make sense of it. Maybe because it bypasses the intellect. I'll give it a shot. Here are some characteristics, or my beliefs anyway, about what happens...

1) *it's a voice that has always been there*
2) *there's nothing glamorous, exciting, or sexy about it, which felt like a real letdown when I realized it*
3) *when I write, I'm either choosing to write what Guidance is saying, or what my ego, or small mind wants to say*
4) *when it's the ego talking, there's a lot of starting and stopping involved in my typing-- like I'm trying to 'plan' the next cool thing to say*

5) *when it's Guidance coming through, it's my own voice in my head, but it's a steady flow of words that just cascades out. There may be a slight pause between thoughts, but those are the moments when my ego is trying to get in the way, or when my body/brain feels exhausted from the energy being 'expended' (holding the ego in check, maybe?)*

6) *Let me try it right now. What would Guidance have to say about opening up to being a channel?*

Brother, there is no need to go anywhere or do anything. You are already open to our guidance. We are present as energies within you at all times. The entire universe is contained in your heart. Ponder that deeply. There is nothing poetic about this; no secret meaning to be peeled apart and discovered like a pearl in an oyster. Or an onion. Or any other vegetable. Ha ha ha.

All you have to do to 'hear' the wisdom that already resides in you is to get quiet. Then write. Your ego or small mind will kick up a fuss, wanting to be in charge, criticizing at every turn-- the way you hold your pen, the paper you're using, the time of day you're writing... the small mind wants to do everything in its power to dissuade you from moving in the direction you seek. For when you move in this direction, the ego's very existence is threatened. When you realize that the ego was nothing more than a straw man, an empty shell, a collection of thoughts and beliefs held together by fear, then you will drop it. And you will discover nothing sexy nor exciting, nor glamorous. What you will discover is much more perfect and special; you'll discover that normal life was all there was, and there lies heaven.

So get quiet. Pick up your pen. And begin writing. And don't try to plan the next word or sentence. And don't worry if it seems to make little or no sense to your "self" intellectually. Put on your blindfold like Luke Skywalker did. And pick up your sword.

Love to you, Dear One! You are amazing, and you shine brightly, like a flare in the night! Know that you are love!

By the way, it is fine for you to feel relaxed and calm this morning. As you know, mercury is in retrograde. This is a way of saying, 'slow down' on your plane. We know you are still getting comfortable with the concept, and with the behaviors related to calming down and slowing down. For you like to stay busy; it is your ego that would have you believe you need to keep moving. Because when you truly slow down and stop moving, it falls away, like sand in a dust storm-- a dust devil, once the winds stop blowing, it falls to the ground. Only the winds of business and fear and preoccupation can keep the dust devil alive. Once it all calms down, the mirage of the dust devil disappears.

A hint: all fears are nothing more than dust devils. All perceived threats and imagined dangers are, in truth, dust devils and nothing more. On your plane, where your manifestation is more densely collected, it does remain important to take care to keep your physical body away from danger in order to continue the work you are doing in the manner you are doing it. However, when the physical body is compromised and appears to die, there is still life; the only real, true life that there ever was.

So the need for fear on the survival level disappears when the definition of the word "survival" is seen to become obsolete. In a world where life cannot possibly end, survival becomes meaningless.

Another thing that becomes meaningless is fear of stepping more fully into presence; into being-ness; into leadership. For fear suggests the possibility of failure. But there is nothing but experience, remembering, and unfolding. There is no right or wrong way to unfold. All is contained within the 'box' of the Divine. How can any part of it be un-Divine? It's impossible for the intellect to wrap its brain around. And that very fact is evidence that it is beyond the intellect. Beyond rationality. Beyond logic. Beyond 'illogical'. It enfolds and contains logic. Logic can never contain it, for logic is contained BY it.

This thing that is 'beyond' is Truth. When you channel, you are doing nothing more than tapping into Truth. Even 'tapping into' suggests there there is some activity that 'you' need to perform in order to be in touch with Truth. Again, what you take to be 'you' is contained within Truth. There is no need to 'tap into' anything. Rather, it is the removal of your hands, which cover up your ears and prevent you from hearing. Removal of your hands from your face, which cover up your eyes and prevent you from seeing. Removal of your fingers pinching your nose, which prevent you from smelling. It is nothing more than relaxing the stressed, clenched posture of protection from an 'outside' force that might be dangerous and allowing it to freely pass through.

And as you are discovering, it's been there all along. And no, there's nothing sexy or special or fantastic or abnormal or supernatural or rock-star-ish about hearing this guidance. It is part of your very being. Misperceiving it as something 'otherworldly' and wanting special attention for it is like wanting extra credit for doing something you do every morning. In your case, wanting a compliment for being so good at drinking coffee, or for playing guitar. Yes, you play guitar well. And because that is what you DO, it's no surprise. You've been doing it all your life. You love it. Why on earth would you ask for special recognition for it? It's simply who you ARE. This is no different. Our guidance is simply who you ARE. For we ARE you, and you ARE us. There is no 'other'.

License to channel

Channeling: It's the easiest thing in the world, for it's your natural state. Rather than living somewhere 'outside' of you, needing to be summoned from afar, we are actually energies within you, and as such, are always within reach, day or night, 24/7. Pay close attention to the flavor of our words and meanings, compared to those of the ego. What do you notice? What distinguishes us from the ego?

Correct. It is the outward flow of attention. With the ego, do not be surprised if you begin to notice that nearly every sentence begins with the word, "I". And not simply in the manner of taking personal responsibility, either. Rather, notice where the attention is directed-- inward. Over and over. This is not an exploratory, inquisitive energy; that of shining a light into the heart to find truth. No. This is more of an, "I need..." "I want..." "I like..." "I dislike..." "I am..." kind of energy. And we know that as you begin to notice it more in your daily life, it may very well have a sour flavor to it; you may judge it negatively.

If/when that happens, we remind you to have patience and compassion, both for the other parties and for yourself when you notice this taking place. It is their journey and process that brings them to that very point. And it is your very identification with the ego's self-absorption that you notice in them. In other words, they are serving as a beautiful mirror for you, and if it bugs you, then you have work to do around it. You spot it, you've got it. Very true. This is where the compassion comes in. When you notice that you are judging someone else for being shallow, self-absorbed, for having what you judge to be 'too many needs', shine a light of compassion onto them from the base of your heart. Listen and give them attention.

Although it may feel as though you are positively reinforcing what you consider to be 'negative' behavior, any refusal will simply increase the feelings of disconnection that they are seeking to relieve. They are hungry for connection and are feeling fearful. Punishing them by withholding positive attention will certainly not help them to feel more connected and lead to their relaxation and dropping back into their hearts. Only a relaxed, confident feeling of connection and belonging brings that.

So the question becomes, how can you help to facilitate the creation of an interaction that supports feelings of connection, belonging, and trust in all parties. This is a good curriculum for you to follow throughout your day, every day.

Why me? This is the question at the forefront of your ego's attention, for it is the one that believes love to be a zero-sum game; if you give love, you lose it-- if you get it, you keep it at someone else's expense. This, of course, is not how love works. And you know this very well. Love spreads like wildfire, feeding everyone it touches and shining more and more brightly, like a beacon, until everyone is on fire with love. Until everyone is healed. Until everyone feels that they belong. That they are trusted and can trust. Confident of their connection to others and themselves.

Know that every time you withhold love, you are actively seeking to create a disconnection in the path of the heart within the world. What you may be forgetting when this happens is that you are creating what appears and feels like a disconnection between yourself and incoming waves of love that are always radiating toward you in the world.

All of this time, it has only been your misperception that has kept you from seeing this. In your growth process, you have gone through a stage of perceiving, judging, and labeling. And when, in your innocence, you have judged something or someone to be dangerous, you have attempted to distance yourself from it in order to protect yourself. These actions made perfect sense to you at the time, for they were grounded in your desire for survival.

Now you are moving into the next phase of your journey. You know that the concept of survival is meaningless in the realm of reality, since all love exists in all ways, endlessly and timelessly. This unshakable fact cares not about the opinions of the ego. Now that you understand that there is nothing that can end your true existence, you can begin to understand that there are truly no threats in the world. Not to the true identity that is you.

The next step is to recognize the truth that all love is being radiated in your direction at all times. This is where the recognition of receptivity as an active state comes in. If you are not actively receiving, reaching upward and outward, ready to receive those waves of love that are always radiating in your direction, then your perception will not support truth-- you will not recognize that you are being quite literally bombarded with love in every moment. Only your willingness to set aside the ego's label-making activity will allow you the space you need to perceive the love that is always there. When you do recognize it, you will know-- for you will experience sensations of calm, relaxed happiness. Acceptance. Non-resistance. These states will seem to bubble up effortlessly, and will make it easier for you to create space for the needs of others. If you have no needs of your own, then what worry is there of creating space to witness others as they express their perceived needs?

Remember that when you experience any sort of resistance, any desire to avert your eyes, any sighing or desire to say something flippant or sarcastic, you have shifted over to viewing the world through your Ego Goggles. These are helpful when dealing with logical, rational issues. However, they are not helpful at all when dealing with issues of the heart. Keep your Heart Visor on at all times. Reserve the Ego Goggles for those occasions when it's time to put the ego to use in service of the heart.

Also, if you feel like claiming that you are channeling makes you a big fat phony baloney, a fake and a fraud, (as you have felt about yourself many times), ask the question--

Who is saying this?

The answer, you will find (every time) is ego.

Then ask what Heart would say about the matter. It works.

BTW-- the ego would have you believe that channeling is something special, sacred, only for Very Special People (*"not me"*); a skill that requires years of effort, sacrifice and pain... and requires a certificate, license, and a diploma hanging on the wall, framed, before anyone can do it CORRECTLY or PROPERLY.

Truth is, everyone can do it. It's no big deal, yet it's a very big deal. Because although anyone can do it, not everyone understands this yet.

It's like someone saying you can't hop on one foot without a certificate, or approval from some legal body. But all it takes is for you to start hopping on one foot. And then, look... you're doing it. You're hopping on one foot.

Look... you're doing it... you're channeling. You could do it all along. No big deal.

So go for it!

You are enough

In this very moment, just as you are, with all the perceived warts you may believe you have, with all your perceived idiosyncrasies... with all your self-proclaimed failures and faults, you are enough.

Keep this at the forefront of your attention, for it is yet another technique for disarming the ego. The ego would have you believe about yourself that you are not enough; somehow insufficient. Yet how could you possibly be insufficient if you are love itself? If you are all existence, the very life force that creates all endlessly, how could you possibly not be enough?

Furthermore, if you are love itself, how could you possibly be unlovable? That is like saying the rain puddle is not worthy of wetness. Like calling the sun un-lightworthy. It's hilarious, ridiculous, and comical. Yet sadly you buy into such self-judgment on a daily basis, in one way or another. There is no need. There is no purpose. There is no function to this. It adds nothing of value to what you perceive to be your life.

Embrace all as yourself by disregarding any urge to identify with anything. Anything you feel tempted to identify with is simply too small to capture your full magnificence. Settle for nothing less than everything, for you are that.

Repeat as your new mantra: I am enough. I am enough. I am enough.

Hear this: We honor and bless you for your inner brilliance. Your inner brilliance shines brightly, no matter where you work, no matter how much money you have, no matter where you live.

You shine so brightly every time you open your heart and step into your vulnerability; each time you share your truth. Your gold can never be taken away from you; you just sometimes forget that it is there. That's the only time it doesn't shine as brightly as it could.

The only mistake you ever make is to think of yourself as less than the Divine itself.

Let this be your mantra today:
"I release all attachment to the outcome of this day. This is simply a chance for me to express my Divine nature. I need nothing from anyone, for I am already complete."

Go shine your gold, brother! It's been in your pocket the whole time!

Service
True service is always selfless. And selfless service offers the servant the greatest reward.

It may seem like such a common subject that you may be tempted to simply dismiss it, thinking, 'oh yeah... I know all of this.' Yet the importance of this cannot be overstated: Service to your Brother is service to Yourself. Service in the name of your brother is actually service in the name of the Heart. True service takes on a variety of forms, and can look like a number of things. Using your heart, you know what service is. True, selfless service leaves the heart singing and feeling complete.

Notice any thoughts of hesitation or feelings of fear that may tend to arise when a brother reaches out to you for help. Where is this coming from? Simple: the ego. The ego would have you believe that there is only a finite amount of love energy flowing in the universe, and that once you use up your quota, you will be left drained, without the love and energy you need to get through the day. This is a lie. The more life energy you circulate, the more you are restored to fullness, wholeness, and light.

The key here is not to let yourself become attached to any one 'role' in the giving process. For example, service to your brother is helpful and useful as a learning tool until the point at which the ego begins to build a new identity out of it: martyr. Once the ego begins to use your activities as a way to create the identity of victim and martyr, loving service has been sabotaged by the ego and turned into selfishness. Though by all outward appearances it may be perceived by others that you are being of service, the feeling of joy within the servant is the true measure of selfless service.

When this happens, as it will in this curriculum, the best way to return to selfless service is to reach out and ask for help yourself. In other words, when the physical body becomes tired, it is time to focus on self care. And if assistance would be of use, then selflessly asking your brother for help, with an open heart, is one way to get back into Heartfulness. This gives your brother the opportunity to step more fully into the Heart, which is a true gift to him.

Imbalance is the only possible outcome when you become attached to either side of the coin; always asking for help and refusing to offer it, or always offering and refusing to ask. Both of these scenarios are based upon selfishness, which, again, is a hallmark of the ego. Only by turning away from the grasping of the ego can you find your true center of gravity within the Heart.

Something to argue over

The Heart is a wondrous place, filled with beauty. There is no reason to hesitate throwing away your chains that tie you to the ego in order to step more fully into the heart. Sure, it may feel reassuring to revisit that old, familiar pain; that comforting sadness that you used to experience. But actually, all you're doing is remembering sadness. And you've got a very vivid imagination, so it feels like you're really going down memory lane first hand; truly experiencing it all over again. But all you're doing (and you know this), is revisiting old memories of wounds that have already been healed. It's like mourning a broken arm 20 years after it's been healed and healthy.

We could ask you why you do this, but we already know the answer, and we know that on an intellectual level you may understand. But still you do it. So acknowledge: the ego does not like where this process is taking you; it is freaking out at the prospect that you are nosing around the door to the Heart. Trying to peek under the door.

Only there are no rules against walking through this door. And by the way, it's wide open. Just waiting for you to step through. That big chair over there is yours. It's been awaiting your return, as have we all. If you squint your eyes and look even more closely, you'll see that you are already sitting in that chair. You've never left. It's only from the perspective of the ego that you perceive yourself to be anywhere else. And that's fine. You are welcome to do that for as long as you please. We just ask, does it please you?

Does it please you to let yourself go and not eat food... to let yourself get hungry and irritable? And does it please you to hide in your house when the sun is shining brilliantly outside and you live in one of the most beautiful spots on the planet? Does it please you to hold on to grudges, to become angry and frustrated when things don't seem like they are going your way? Does it please you to struggle and disagree with your wife in order to maintain your sense of always being right? Does it please you to guard your feelings around certain people, remembering the pain you perceive that they caused you (while knowing full well you played a part in it) even as you recognize that they are suffering, too?

What is the big payoff for struggling? For keeping your eyes closed tightly and refusing to see that you are already at home in the Heart's Mansion? Or, as Uncle Hafiz would say, in the Tavern of the Heart?

No. We know it does not please you. It's no fun to wallow around, searching for a past that is gone, wishing for connection and hoping to find it by hiding and distracting yourself endlessly. This is no road for a Heart of your magnificence and brilliance. And yet it's perfectly fine for you to do this for as long as you like. It makes no difference to the timeless Heart, which envelops and embraces you through every moment of your life, eternally. If it's helpful to do so, you can think of the Heart as someone even more beloved than your parents; more caring than your best friend. Someone who understands you and accepts and celebrates you even more than your spouse. Someone who watches you even more closely than a secret admirer. The Heart is truly your best friend, to personify. In actuality, even closer than that, since you are OF the Heart. It is You Yourself.

It's almost like you are trying to play hide-and-seek with yourself, and then mourning when you perceive that you've lost the game. This is perfectly fine, and hurts no one.

However.

When you do decide to open your eyes and recognize your true place at the Inner Throne of the Heart, you'll be able to even better serve those around you. You care about service... we know this to be true. If you cannot believe that you are worth stepping through this doorway for yourself, then at least imagine all of the people you could help by doing so. Imagine all of the people your calm strength could inspire... through your thoughts, words, and actions. You have the power to make the world a better place, and you already do so in many ways. This will take things to the next level.

What could there possibly be to lose, except sadness, feelings of disconnection, anger, frustration, and heartache? Longing for the past? Grief? Yes, we say it is time to lose these 'precious' things... these habitual thought patterns that you misperceive to be aspects of your identity. They are no more part of your identity than the key ring your house keys are on. They make no difference to your true identity. All they do is serve as a blindfold that you are using to keep yourself from seeing You in the mirror as you truly are. And yet you are surrounded by mirrors; every other being you look at serves as your mirror.

Take a deep look. There is nothing to hide from anymore. There is no feeling of separation; no 'other' to vilify any longer. You know that every perceived being around you is an aspect of yourself. You know that on the level of being you perceive, they are each struggling with their own stories, their own worries, their own life stories. You know they are all simply stories, and that they are no more real than a child's fairy tale. Yet to each of them, as to you, the story appears to give you something to grab onto-- some sense of identity, whether it is hero, victim, villain, martyr... or any of the other countless stories you can dream up.

All we're saying is this: wake up. There is nothing to do in order to wake up. Just relax and accept that what is true is true. You are already able to recognize when ego is playing his games. All you need to do is look at them and nod your head. Smile and acknowledge. "Oh... feelings of anger arising now. Oh, look... feelings of frustration and sadness and longing arising now. How interesting." And then let them go. Laugh more. Yes. Laugh more. A lot more. What do you like to laugh about? It's time to stop taking yourself and your life story so seriously and laugh more at the comedy and tragedy of life as perceived on your plane of existence. If you want to get serious, get serious about laughing more, sharing joy and tranquility more, sharing happiness and comfort and support and encouragement more. Sharing forgiveness a LOT more. These are the things to take seriously.

Religious beliefs. Political beliefs. Favorite football team. All simply tools for propping up the ego. Something to argue over. To keep you distracted.

If it's of the mind, disregard. Turn back toward the heart. Always.

CHAPTER FOUR
What you seek lies within

The energies that you seek all live within you. When you pray to the heavens, expecting wrath or compassion from some outside force, you are looking in the refrigerator for your car keys. They're not there. They are within. All of the energies of the universe live within you, because the entire universe resides within your heart. We are not speaking metaphorically, nor are we trying to sound fancy and poetic. There is no need for such niceties in reality. We only speak truth... direct, clear truth, like a spear that slices through illusion and delusion.

All the energies of the 10,000 directions lie within your heart. It is mental habit alone that makes you choose certain paths of thought and behavior. Habit alone directs you to become angry, wrathful, jealous, stubborn, indignant, impatient. All that is needed to embrace change and growth in your life is to look within; call upon the energies you wish to invoke in your life at that very moment, for they already live at your beck and call, ready to spring into action. But they cannot spring into action without you activating them with your invitation and intention setting.

And be reminded that in every moment you are learning and growing on the upward spiral of growth. As you've been reminded in what you perceive to be the past, it may sometimes feel as though things are moving more slowly or more quickly than at other times. This is natural and normal, and simply a limitation of perception on your plane. In true fact, you are always moving along your path, and your path is perfect and sacred in every way because it is your path.

We cannot overstate the importance of remembering in every single moment that you are not the physical body, and the physical body is not you. Your being is not contained within the physical body; the physical body is contained within your being. This has nothing to do with religion and everything to do with energy and with reality. Reality is untouched by your preferences, thoughts, feelings, grudges, desires, rantings, curses, or daydreams. The reality of what you truly are, and of your true potential as a being of light, is never obstructed, damaged, or soiled in any way by your perceived experiences on your plane.

When you perceive that someone on your plane has died, it is simply the physical body that is being gently laid aside after class is over. And class had nothing to do with learning something new, but rather with remembering and expressing what you've always known. "Why?" you ask. That is your favorite question. And when we remind you that this entire venture is of your own free will, then we turn the question back around on you, for you know the answer in its entirety. So we ask you, "Why are you here? Why are you doing what you are doing? What are your reasons for existing? Why do you value what you do?"

When you truly remember that there is no reason to fear for your own survival, then you can relax and enjoy. When you truly remember that there is no death, only the perception of death, then you can live your life to the fullest. And you can give of your life to the fullest. And in doing so, you will inspire others through your own example of what is possible.

We understand that sometimes you may feel fear or frustration because you feel the challenge of trying to wrap your intellect around this information... this truth. We tell you that there indeed is a very simple way to feel some relief: simply stop trying to figure it out with your intellect. Your small mind does not have your freedom in its best interest. And that's okay. For again it is but yet another aspect of yourself, as are We. In fact, we are nothing more, and nothing less.

Portal to Pelacone

The portal to Pelacone first opened for me when I was just a child... about 4 or 5 years old. I didn't realize it at the time, but looking back, it's clear as day to me now. I had been in the bathroom, of all places. Sitting on the toilet. I had come inside from the heat of a luminous Florida summer day, where I'd been playing outside, into the chill of the a/c in our newly-built house, and now I sat daydreaming. As I happened to look up and out the window, far above me, I saw the very top of the neighbor's tree, a collage of brilliantly bright green waving in the summer wind.

I'm not really sure how long I sat there, staring out at the way that tree was waving against the blue sky, but I do remember thinking it was the perfect moment. It was one of those moments that seemed to last forever. That's the Portal.

Another was when I was 8 years old... I only know that because this Portal moment took place a few blocks away from that same Florida house, at the 7-11 store, which might have actually been called L'il General. Dad would have me ride my bike or walk to that store on Sunday mornings and pick up a gallon of milk (very large and heavy!) or orange juice (glass bottle-- don't drop it, it will break!) or maybe a newspaper, though I might be imagining the newspaper. On this particular afternoon, I was approaching the door to the L'il General and I caught a glimpse of the "America's Bicentennial: 1776-1976" sticker on the door, just above the horizontal push bar.

I happened to turn my head to the right and saw one of the most amazing sunsets in my life. Maybe it wasn't quite setting, and maybe it wasn't so spectacular. But I stood there staring for a moment at the orange of the sun and the colors around it for what felt like a long time... like I lost track of time, or even stepped outside of time for a moment. That's the Portal.

At such a young age, I had no way of articulating what I was seeing, or feeling, or sensing. All I knew was that a lot of things felt pretty solid in my life, but not completely unshakable. These portal moments, however, had a distinct flavor, sound, and look to them-- they felt like "home".

For the longest time after the first actual contact from the other side, I stayed recoiled as far back into my shell as I could possibly get, a shield of alcohol, pills, sex, and whatever else I could get hold of to protect me from the startling, terrifying shock of those sounds and visions. It happened one night while I was living alone, probably, after my divorce... though that doesn't really fit into the timeline of my life in any rational sort of way. In any case, I'd fallen asleep on my back. It was night. I was in bed. And as I lay there halfway asleep and halfway awake, in a pre-dream sort of place, I suddenly felt every hair on my body stand on end. It was like an electric shock of coldness shot through my body... a sensation I don't think I'd ever experienced before.

I opened my 'eyes'... or rather, something/someone appeared in my field of vision as my eyes were closed. It was above me, looking down. It looked like an old woman. The pinpricks of fear were still coursing through my body and waves of chill rippled across every inch of my skin. I was terrified.

The vision opened her mouth and began to make terrifying sounds shrieks and screams... or rather, sort of a roaring mixed with high-pitched sounds. I was frozen, and could not move. Part of me wanted to run away as fast as I could. But another part of me said, "wait"... And before I knew what I was doing, I spoke to her, saying, "I can't understand what you are saying to me." It opened its mouth again, and this time, began to speak in words I could understand. She said, "Tell your mother it wasn't her fault. I was sick. I'm sorry. It wasn't her fault (that I died of cancer)."

Then it was over. I lay there, heart pounding in my chest, eyes wide open, staring at the ceiling.

It's been at least a decade... maybe 15 or 20 years since that happened. And I've been running from it for all that time since. And now, as I remember all of this, tears well up in my eyes, and my nose stings with emotion. Am I finally ready to open myself up to that kind of thing again? If I remind myself that I was not harmed in any way, it's helpful. For most of my fears, if not all of them, have been irrational... I've found ways to create the most horrific stories about the world and my place in it... these have been my coping strategies for dealing with gifts that I never asked for... gifts I still don't know much about. Gifts I'm ready to claim.

After the Contact, I was so busy trying to drown out my senses that I forgot all about the Portal. But years later my younger brother unwittingly reminded me of a magical place, and I caught a fresh glimpse of the lights of Pelacone. It started out as words. Then music. Then bringing the two together... Slowly, vague visions began to take shape, and I could hear the waves crashing up against the shore. I could smell the coconut palms... Out of the corner of my eye I caught the orange glow of a fire in a burning barrel some ways down the beach, glowing in the night like a lone, unauthorized cigarette cherry on the bow of a fast frigate headed south to Grenada... flying fish and dolphins running alongside as the full moon mused at her own private joke overhead.

The deeper I went, the deeper I saw... initially I had envisioned the place as a sanctuary from the 'real world', whatever that meant. The more I lived in this 'real' world, the more I saw patterns begin to emerge... similarities between places and feelings. Yashima reminded me of Ceiba reminded me of Pelacone... The colors of the buildings... the cracks in the sidewalk... the way things seemed perfect at first, but then slowly drew back the veil, revealing something different underneath.

Initially I had taken this to mean that this was not the place for me. The faded colors... the little shacks... the blue crabs running across the road (don't run over them or they'll pop your car tires)...

vendors selling tastiness on the side of the road... or squid covered in thick, black, inky soy paste... All of these things highlighted and underscored the simple, unescapable truth about Pelacone: My experience would depend 100% on my outlook. What I expected to see is what I would see.

After that first Contact, I felt afraid to see fully. My nerves had been shattered and I just wanted to hide from loud sounds, strange aromas, and unfamiliar terrain. Yet at the same time, I saw that doors in my life were closing, one by one... and the only door that was open seemed to be expanding ever wider... calling my name gently at first, then getting louder, until finally it was shouting my name at the top of its ever-loving lungs. There was no hope. It was time to surrender.

Whether or not there was an actual Pelacone was to be seen... I'd wondered if it was somewhere near Cuba, and for whatever strange reason I kept re-reading Hemingway's "To Have And Have Not" over and over again... practically memorizing my favorite passages. And for whatever OTHER strange reason, I ended up reading Murakami's "Wind-Up Bird Chronicle" just as many times... getting off the plane and moving into a flat in Takamatsu City... kicking around the city, chasing down locations mentioned in the book... asking strangers for directions... falling under the spell of so many beautiful women... In one shop in the shoten-gi outdoor mall, I walked in and asked an old man the price of one of his bottles of whiskey, only to get chased out with foreign-sounding curses. Another time I walked into a music store and browsed through hundreds of cd's, until the proprietor, a woman who looked to be in her 60's, finally told me flat out that I needed to either buy something or leave.

I went into one shop to get a closer look at the beautiful young woman working there. She smiled at me. Then she walked up to me and said hello, in Japanese. I smiled back, I think. Then she took one step closer to me-- staring right into my eyes and smiling... so close we were practically dancing. I mumbled something and ran away. Everywhere was strangeness, out in the 'real' world all over the globe, and inside, where a seeker was desperately searching for renewed contact with something... someone... a place, a time... The One who could make things whole again.

I was swimming in the Dark Night of the Soul, trying to aim myself toward Pelacone and renewed contact with the Source. But no matter how hard I swam, no matter how many times I stopped to wipe the salt water from my eyes, it seemed I could not find the place or time I was looking for. When I knocked on the doors of those I had called my family, they closed the blinds. I heard locks slide into place within. There were billboards and posters on walls... graffiti spray painted in alleys... I was unwittingly creating a world of rejection, pain, and sadness. I was reminded of the old days, when I would imagine I had been dropped off by a spaceship and left in the middle of a street, looking around for some landmark to guide me toward home.

Little did I know that the light at the end of the tunnel had been shining brightly within me all along.

The light got brighter as time went by... as I surrendered, little by little, and gave up to whatever forces I could not see, hear, taste, smell, nor feel with my crude senses; as this surrendering took hold of me on deeper and deeper levels, I began to feel myself rise. I was becoming lighter, somehow. I was noticing that the volume on struggles was being turned down, while the inner flame seemed to grow brighter. In tiny increments, at first, it gradually grew stronger... inversely proportional to my grasp on the outer world for comfort, safety, and life itself.

Perhaps this outer world truly is a dream? Maybe true life resides within? "The universe is contained in your heart..." That's what I'd been told by Guides who spoke a silent language, laughing and encouraging and praising and challenging me to greater heights--bolder depths. If this was true, then I should be able to see the lights of Pelacone from here, shouldn't I?

Filament

The Lights of Pelacone-- you've asked us about this. You want to know exactly what they are... They are you.

Imagine or envision an electrical circuit of sorts. Light coming down from above, light coming up from below. And imagine a gap about 5' 11" tall (as tall as you are) in between those two light sources. Now imagine that you are filled with magical 'light filament'. When you step into that 'gap', you complete the circuit, and the Lights of Pelacone begin to glow. You often look out at the city lights during the night, and you picture a beach, a coast, somewhere tropical and magical where olives grow on trees and time moves more slowly.

These images are not incorrect; this 'place' does exist, just not quite as you imagine in your mind's eye. We have heard you say that the specific location of this place is in the human heart, and you are correct. Yet it is your steadfast belief in this fact that allows you to "Step into the light," so to speak, and complete the light circuit.

But beaches and olive trees... sunsets... all of the things that you find to be pleasant and beautiful, they change from person to person. The Lights of Pelacone look different to each's eye, yet they are the same thing: Love. How do you envision Love looking? Sounding? Feeling? Tasting? Smelling? Move toward those images. Set aside anger and sadness and despair; they are simply tools of the ego designed to keep you from glimpsing these lights, smelling these fragrances, and standing in this light.

Furthermore, when you stand in this light, others can tell. They may not speak a word. They may try to use many words to describe it... they may not understand very well, and in their attempts to wrap their intellects around what is going on, may project their stuff all over you. Have no fears or worries about this, either. It makes no difference what they say about you or do to you. When you step fully into this light-gap and complete the love circuit, you become an instrument of our light, love, wisdom, compassion, healing, peace, strength, and grace.

Be aware that you will attract attention, and not always the kind that you enjoy. Some may fear you. Some may get angry, and will feel as if you have wronged them, simply by shining so brightly. This is natural. Let them have their responses. Do not try to change them. Simply shine. For what is happening is that by shining forth fully, you are reminding them, sometimes consciously, but more often than not

104

unconsciously, of their own true identity. And the anger or fear or suspicion that you see arising is actually their EGO responding to being reminded of this truth.

Remember: what is the function of the ego? To protect the illusion -- the delusion -- of its own existence. And when you shine, the part of them that naturally wants to shine begins to resonate sympathetically with your heartbeat, so to speak. And this scares the ego, because suddenly something unknown is shaking the very foundations of its perceived existence. And the more their hearts resonate, the deeper those foundations are shaken. Until finally, eventually, inevitably, they crumble and every creature remembers who they truly are: true Love. Undiluted. Uninterrupted.

And this is the happiest secret to share of all: you were never away from the light. The image we use here of 'stepping into the light' in order to 'complete the circuit' is our attempt, through the limited scope of your language, to communicate in a way that makes you go, "ah HA!". It's an image for you to carry around, to ponder, and as you do, it tickles your heart strings, sending them resonating even more fully than they already are. Our similes and metaphors here are simply representations of the actual situation. And of course you already know this, for what else is a book than representations of language, which itself is simply another level of representation, all of it attempting to point (in this case) toward reality?

This being the case, the intellect, or small mind, with its limited vision upon your plane of existence, will seek out apparent contradictions. "This is illogical and irrational," it will scream. "This makes no sense, so it must be wrong. It's all incorrect. I know it is, because I cannot make sense of it, and since it cannot be explained in a rational way, therefore it must be incorrect. And is to be disregarded summarily."

Yes. This is the ego's game.

Keep in mind, however, that Reality is not flawed. Reality is not lacking. Reality does not cringe or flinch when the ego throws its stones. Reality smiles gently and with compassion. And in those moments when you may feel like Reality is a cruel beast, an ogre that wants nothing more than to destroy you and everything you love... when the world seems to be a fear-filled place where survival of the fittest reigns supreme... where happiness can be bought and sold and suffering is the lowest common denominator... where access to money determines one's level of 'security', which is tied to happiness... In these moments, know that it is the ego that would have you believe all of this to be true.

Again, Reality simply sets those heart strings resonating in sync with the Divine. As Hafiz would say, sometimes the Divine sees that the best way to 'wake you up' is to tackle you playfully... throw you on the ground and wrestle with you in His drunken delight, tickling you and making you scream 'uncle'.

No matter how heretical it may sound, all of Reality is designed to remind you of your true identity: The Divine. With every glass of water, every glass of beer, every sunset, every traffic jam, every great book, every bark of a dog that wakes you up... every funeral, every marriage, every automobile accident, every tragedy... Reality is simply expressing perfection. And you are that perfection, a manifestation of perfect Love appearing to unfold in space and time.

Let us repeat that: APPEARING to unfold in space and time. Since time is like that image of a vertical fountain that we've mentioned before, with the water shooting up and then collapsing upon itself endlessly, appearing to change endlessly and never appearing the exact same way twice... Since time is like that, there's actually no 'movement' forward or backward. The appearance of the passage of time is a construct of the ego, the intellect, or small mind. And for us to suggest anything otherwise flies directly in the face of the intellect, which therefore says, "wrong!". Because that is the sole duty of the intellect-- to judge.

Perceive. Judge. Repeat. This is the cycle of madness that keeps humans up in their heads and forgetting their continued contact with their hearts. All it ever takes is to remember that you've always been in contact with the heart, since the heart is all that you actually are.

Once again, we use language that suggests that some 'movement' back into the heart is necessary, yet the limitations of language obscure truth. Think of language as a crude knife made of the sharp edge of a stone, like an arrowhead you might find on the ground. It can cut, and was fashioned to be as effective as possible, given the limited conditions under which it was created. If language is that crude knife, then Reality is a laser.

This is why we say, again and again, that the key to grasping Reality is to suspend judgment. All judgment. Whatever you think you know, set it aside. Do this enough times (yes, it can feel like countless times aren't doing any good-- we urge you to persist in your efforts!) and the ego will relent. Truth with bubble out like water from a spring. It's unstoppable. You will no longer feel the need to be able to explain yourself or your position in order to be accepted by others, for being accepted will no longer matter. Because you will remember that there IS no 'other'.

And all you will have to do is to walk into a room. Or simply sit in your chair. And that truth will bubble forth naturally, effortlessly. In your smile. In your eyes. In your laughter. In your words. All of these things will tickle something in others that they will not be able to deny.

This will not change the fact that some will respond with fear, anger, doubt, worry, pessimism, sadness, or extreme intellectualism. When you recognize the ego's role in those responses, an ocean of compassion becomes available to you. If someone responds to you by acting threatened or nervous, it does not mean that you are scary or threatening. Their response and all that goes with it, truly does not reflect anything about you. Keep this in mind whenever you receive compliments, dear one-- compliments, which the ego LOVES to receive. "You didn't say 'thank you'!" That kind of thing.

Whatever you see or hear, simply let it pass over you unheeded. This includes checkout clerks who swipe your driver's license across their scanner without your permission. Let it pass. It does nothing to confirm or threaten your true identity.

Pop quiz: What IS your true identity? Right on! "LOVE"!

A kick in the seat of your pants

When you feel the impatience or frustration coming on, know that this is the ego. Your natural state is of calm, relaxed joy. In this natural state, you watch the wind blow the leaves and you do not chase them down the street for fear of 'losing' them. You simply smile and watch them pass, knowing that this is the natural order of things in your dimension... ha ha ha 'dimentian'...

Sometimes I know you feel overwhelmed by the comings and goings of the world... pushed and pulled in myriad directions, and it can happen to you by those who love you. Even as soon as you awaken in the morning, it can feel like you're being hassled without time to gain your bearings and reestablish your connection with the divine before going out into the world. I know it can feel frustrating, and it can be easy for you to lose your temper and act sullen and withdrawn, as if you've been robbed of precious peace.

Remember that the peace you seek is already within you. And it is your responsibility to release the attachment to order on your plane when you catch yourself going there-- it is simply your ego that wants to try to control the world. When you feel yourself becoming short with those around you, it's a signal that you need something. You need time or space or food or something in order to get re-grounded, because in that moment, you've lost perception of your center, and your ego is in the driver's seat. Is there an appropriate time for anger and sadness? Yes. However, when they control your behavior, the ego is running down the street in its ragged clothing with your steering wheel in its hand.

Also, it is good to recognize when you are letting the fear of your brothers and sisters around you influence your peace. It is common on your plane to accept things 'at face value'; to assume that what you see with your eyes is what you get. That the sound and motion you perceive with the five senses of the physical body are truth with a capital T. While we've repeated many times that this is not the case, and while you may at times feel as though you are grasping this truth with increased depth of understanding, still it only takes your ego's sneaky willingness to grab on to someone else's lamentations about their situation to drag you back down into the mire.

This is completely up to you. The trick for you at this time is to actively balance your compassion for them and understanding of where they are coming from with a willingness to ask them questions that they might find uncomfortable. "Are you your body?" is an excellent question, and can open up a dialogue about what humans are and are not. Each person, of course, will only engage as deeply as she or he is willing and able in that moment; do not be surprised or angered if they choose to change the subject abruptly. Remember: it is your choice whom you spend time with.

At the same time, you are gently reminded that there are no accidents; those you find around you are there for a reason, or perhaps many reasons. And it's very likely that you may not perceive any of them. This makes no difference to the truth; the truth is that river beneath your canoe that has no concern for what color shoes you might be wearing. It simply carries you along in its own brilliance, unfolding as only it can, and exuding its 'river-ness' without apology. Let this be an example for you. Simply go about your daily business with complete acceptance of whatever seems to unfold before your eyes, and approach it from the perspective of the heart. Practice looking at the world and at others through the lens of your heart. You know how to do this naturally; it is only your intellect, small mind, or ego that would have you believe that you are not capable, that it's a parlor trick that you have not yet learned. That you need, once again, to hold some sort of license or certificate before being 'allowed' to begin viewing your brothers and sisters through the lens of the heart.

And looking through the lens of the heart does not mean always speaking gently. It does not mean attempting to contort yourself into some unnatural position in order to help yourself to be more easily accepted or understood. Remember what your uncle Hafiz said: sometimes the Universe grows tired of speaking sweetly. Sometimes, when the Universe is in a drunken, playful mood, he wants to kick your ass and wrestle you to the ground to get you to let go of your unrealistic and fantastic ideas about yourself, the world, and your place in it.

Your uncle Hafiz has it right. Listen carefully to his words; look for the parallels in his writings and with those other leaders in your time/space. You will find the common thread of truth among them. In addition, if you 'zoom out' far enough, you will find that all of it begins to create a common thread. You may have to take what feels like an exceptionally wide point of view in order to begin to perceive the patterns, but they are there. And truly, this reflects not the greatness of the common thread, but rather the narrowness inherent in spiritual perception in your dimension. This is a natural part of your learning and growth toward deeper awareness and understanding. We do not fault the first-grader for not yet being in third grade. Eventually, he makes it there and continues to move onward and upward. This is true for you and all of your sisters and brothers, as well.

It is helpful to remember that we are always here to offer guidance, understanding, support, and compassion. Again, it may sometimes feel like a kick in the seat of your pants; we give you what you need for growth, not what your ego would prefer to receive in order to maintain its sense of comfort and 'stability'. This perceived 'stability' can be the enemy of growth, nurturing stagnation and hesitation to move into change. Yet life is change. By definition, life is movement from one state to another, from apparent birth to seeming death. On your plane this is the natural course of things.

And yet, even as your rational mind understands this on an intellectual level, your ego would have you believe that you need to rail against change; defend yourself against death somehow. We say that zooming out, it is in fact true that there

IS no death; there is only life. However, it is the ego's favorite game to take this truth out of its larger context and try to apply it to ITS apparent life, which is in fact a farce; a hoax. This is of no real importance to the truth, to the Universe, or to life. Many egos that appeared to have a life have dissolved in the river of truth, revealing themselves to be nothing more than a collection of preferences, habitual thought patterns, and attachments. All is unfolding perfectly. There is no need to fear because the true you is the One speaking at this moment. The true you is the One that has nothing to lose and nothing to gain because it already IS all that there is. The chaos your ego experiences may feel real enough in your daily life. This is fine. Allow it to unfold however it will. Take a gentle, dispassionate look at your emotions and reactions and bless them, setting them aside as inconsequential. Then return to your center. Return to your natural state of loving acceptance and brightness. Return to the eye of the storm, where all is calm and you can see everything. And know that what looks like a storm only takes that form through the eyes of the ego. When perceived through the lens of the heart, all is perfectly aligned. Nothing is out of place.

CHAPTER FIVE
Non-resistance

This is your day. This is your moment. Your time. It has arrived. You may spend it however you like.

Guides and guardians, put me in direct contact with gratitude. Put me in direct contact with you. Help me to get out of my way. Speak through me and let me hear your wisdom.

And so it is. You are struggling because you believe what you see what your eyes, and you take it to be true. Remember, things are not what they appear. If brilliance and magnificence are all there is... if the Divine is all that exists, then you need not shy away from any of it. It is all gold, no matter what judgments the ego would have you believe. Take your anger and sadness and fear, for example. They come up in response to something you judge. Had you not judged, had you simply observed and acknowledged, then you would not have created pain for yourself. And when fear, sadness, and anger arise, you are always totally free to acknowledge them, express them in healthy ways, and let go. Yet when you realize, deeply, that they are of the ego, you will find it becomes unnecessary to give them voice. Just like when you realize that an argument you had 20 years ago no longer holds a charge for you and there's no further need to voice your side of it.

This is directly tied to non-resistance, which you've been offered in the past. We say it over and over again, in a number of different ways, so that you will have repeated opportunities to explore and accept and integrate this information. So it can become your own knowledge and wisdom once again. As it was before. As it will be again.

What might happen if you simply watched and acknowledged? You're riding a carousel with brightly painted wooden horses, flashing lights, and loud music from the calliope. You've been struggling and gnashing your teeth, whipping your horse frantically, trying to avoid crashing into the objects around you. But they are not on the carousel. And you will never crash into them. You simply keep going around and around in a circle. Objects around you appear to change; your life appears to be unfolding, with people coming and going, loved ones appearing to die or move away; enemies appearing to show up at your doorstep at the strangest times.

But there is only you on your wooden horse, moving up and down, hearing the music, seeing the flashing lights, and making judgments about what you see and hear. That's not even necessarily the biggest problem. The biggest problem is that after creating a judgment, you actually believe that judgment to be true. You take it as fact. Mere milliseconds after your ego spits it out, you accept it, unquestioningly. THAT, dear one, is what creates unhappiness.

Say "yes"

The precocious 9 year old redhead boy in the other room is playing The Entertainer. Note for note. On the guitar. He's reading from sheet music. And it's actually really good, considering how long he's been playing. He's excited and enthusiastic and curious and joyful and eager and determined to learn his instrument. And he's doing a wonderful job. He's still very optimistic about the world, about truth, and about humanity. He's insightful, quick, and has a great sense of humor. He's a cool kid.

While I was writing these earlier paragraphs, I could still hear him, even through my headphones. Which are still on my head. And his playing is still coming through loud and clear. Initially I was simply trying to stay focused on the initial train of thought trying to come through. I was making his playing the 'other' against which my ego was pushing and struggling. Then it occurred to me that his playing is what is happening at this very moment.

Just like the Japanese construction workers who showed up at 7:30 in the morning outside my apartment window back in Takamatsu, laughing and joking as they smoked their cigarettes and prepared to continue construction on the house they were putting up. I was fuming mad. I worked noon to 9pm back then, and by the time I got home it was about 9:30pm or so... and I was usually wound up from working with up to 8 or 9 students in a day... Creating scenarios for them to talk about... overcoming both their shyness and my own... Doing my best to remain interesting and engaging so they would open their mouths and speak. It took incredible energy, initially. Then it got easier.

But when I got home, I was still amped up and could often not get to sleep for hours. So I was up late. Sometimes until midnight or 1am. And that would have been fine, since I didn't have to be at work until noon. But the 7:30am wakeup calls from the men below were not welcome at all.

On this particular morning, as I sit looking out my window, cursing them and wishing they'd go away and generally feeling like a victim, it occurred to me that the exotic song of their laughter would be brilliant material for some sort of recording project. I grabbed my laptop, fired it up, and then placed a microphone at the window, gain turned all the way up so I could capture them 'on tape'. It worked. And I ended up using that laughter in one of the songs on my first album.

I said 'yes'. And that's the golden rule of improv. Say 'yes' to anything and everything that is presented by the other team members. And by life. Every day. The more I can say 'yes', the more joyful and tranquil my life feels, even as seasons appear to change and the roller coaster car seems to jostle me around in my seat.

The laughter ended up being one of those shining moments out of the entire album that I looked forward to, and delighted in every time I heard it. Just today a student saw a picture of me in my office and asked if I was a musician. I said yes and shared my bandcamp page with him. He hasn't played his bass in ages, he tells me, and really wants to get back into it. Should he stick with it, he wonders? Yes, I tell him. Make music. Make music always. Make music from now until you can no longer make music. He's considering building up lots of money through some career first, and then when he has time and money and the leisure to do so, he wants to write music.

I say do it now. Alongside whatever else must happen. Music must be included in there somewhere. Time must be carved out for music to happen... ideally on a daily basis, but even bigger picture, over the long haul, that is not as important as keeping alive the love affair that I have with music. She tickles me... she entices me... she grabs me by the throat and the balls and demands that I pay attention to her. Sometimes, there is no choice. And after spending time with her, I walk away feeling a little more complete; a little more satisfied. Even if this existence is as empty and spacious as I'm discovering, and even if the pretty lights and interesting sounds that I see and hear as I ride the carousel around and around are nothing more than illusion, still the act of creating and publishing my music is close and dear to my heart.

I used to write and record and publish my songs and albums as a way of expressing who I am. More and more I'm realizing that all I'm expressing is who I'm not, since who I truly am can never be captured in words or music. The closest I feel I can ever get is for my music and words to serve as a pond, bouncing the reflection of my true self outward for others to see and hear. If the closest I can ever get is a reflection of the One True Face, well, that's pretty good, too. No harm in that.

The illusion of control

What are you in control of?

You realize, of course, that this test is meant for you. You have created this brilliant test for yourself. And in observing your loved one's situation and her apparent fear of lack of control over her own life, you've made your task doubly impressive-- you spot it, you've got it. You see her list of worries-- they become yours if you grab onto them and try to own them.

The task at hand, dear one, is the same for you as it is for her, and for all on the planet: to recognize where the intellect, or small mind, is trying to run the show instead of taking its appropriate position of servitude to the heart. The heart is the portal to reality. The heart is the doorway to truth. Literally speaking, the entire universe you perceive yourself to be within is actually contained in your heart.

It is your own resistance to your loved one's situation that brings you suffering. Why does it seem so difficult to simply allow her to walk her path? To experience her truth? To journey through her teachings and lessons at the pace that is right for her? Why is it that you bend yourself into contortions, trying to save her? What are you trying to save her from? Herself? The universe? Her own learnings? Her own brilliance?

She is going through an unfolding, as are you. And especially at this time, deep transformation is occurring. It is only the intellect, doing its duty of perceiving and judging, categorizing, labelling, and then reacting, that turns her experience into something for you to act upon-- something for you to "fix". Frankly, dear one, what her process is ends up being really not much about you at all. In other words, none of your business, and we say this lovingly. You may stand by in support, or not. Either way, her path is hers alone.

What is it you seek, by trying to save her? Are you fearful that somehow a painful past will be relived? That you will suffer through another divorce? Or the death of another loved one, as you perceive to have experienced the transition of

Laura? It's quite understandable-- you are determined to see yourself playing the role of 'good guy', and the 'good guy' doesn't get divorced; the 'good guy' doesn't leave his wife. He also doesn't want to stand by and watch her die.

This, as you probably can guess by now, is all dependent upon your perception of life on your plane of existence. What is a human being? What is the body? What is the mind? What is the nature of existence; temporary, or eternal? What are we calling 'life'?

You know you are not the body, not the mind. Therefore the idea of survival is meaningless. Therefore any fear related to loss is also meaningless-- what can possibly be lost or gained? Again and again you are repeating these words... Know with certainty that it is only the ego and the intellect that struggle to 'comprehend' their meaning. They seem illogical and irrational because the arbiter of logic and rationale deems them so. No worries. No problems with that. It makes no difference to the Oak Tree what the blade of grass thinks of it or labels it. It changes nothing for the tree, with its branches held high, standing powerfully, towering over all else in the meadow.

It makes no difference to the birds who make their home in its branches into which category of being the blade of grass places the Mighty Oak. The wind does not even take notice of the whispers of the grass, the gossip, the judgments, the bickering, the lies, the competition... all of that passes unnoticed in reality, where the Oak stands tall.

So it is with the reality of your life. No matter what your intellect, the small mind, may have you believe... no matter what the Ogre riding your back might whisper into your ear... no matter how much you even choose to BELIEVE what it says... no matter how much fear you choose to indulge or engage in... it makes no difference to your soul. For your soul exists in reality, not in the dream that you perceive yourself to be experiencing.

So go right ahead. Compile a list of your top 91 worries. And we will show you 91 things that are all outside of your power to control, for there is no control on your plane of existence. There may appear to be control... you may believe that you are changing things. But the truth of the matter is that infinitely many variables are at work... at play... all influencing and impacting and making their way through the world, causing endless effects. You are one of those effects. You are an expression of the divine. And the kicker is that you are the divine that expresses the divine.

With all of this truth, how could you possibly worry? How could you possibly do anything other than sit and smile to your beloved, who is an extension of the divine no less than you are? As is the cat, we might add. So get over it. Ha ha ha. No, really. It's truly time for you to focus on accepting the cat and all of its noise precisely as it is. Since all existence that you are perceiving is time-based and temporary, the cat's days are numbered. You know this. This is your opportunity to show kindness and gentleness to a creature that helped guide your beloved partner through some times that she judged to be very difficult.

It's okay to cut the cat some slack. You will still find a way to get the peace and quiet you feel you need in order to write. To create. We remind you that your divine creativity flows through you, and refuses to be stopped. You support its expression every time you exercise self care-- care for your body, mind, and spirit. Taking time away for retreat is a brilliant idea. So is getting regular exercise that your body needs to be fully alive, awake, and aware. These are excellent steps that you are taking. Be sure to make good use of these opportunities while you have them.

Know also that the feelings of calm, relaxed joy and power that you experience are also your natural state of being. You were born to be calm, relaxed, and powerful, and to express it with love. You are now coming to the time in your life when you are ripe to step more fully into your power as a man of compassion, a man of creativity, and a man of understanding and wisdom. These gifts that you have been carrying were meant to be expressed openly and shared. Only by sharing them do you reap their rewards, for they are jewels to be viewed as examples in the world.

Also, do not worry too much about obtaining some sort of lofty reach. Start where you are. Do your work in your own home. In your own neighborhood and community. Do what comes naturally. At the same time, when those opportunities for you to share more widely do arise, embrace them. Drop any hesitation or fear you may harbor... for it is not you who is actually harboring them; it is the ego. The Ogre, riding on your back, trying to make sure that you remain small in the world, to avoid the slings and arrows that inevitably come with leadership.

Remember always: the slings and arrows do not ever threaten your true life; they only threaten the safety of the ego, who is already a straw man in the eyes of reality. There is nothing there to protect; only an empty shell of preferences, judgments, ideas... Nothing solid. The ego has a beginning, a middle, and an end. The ego is time-based. That is how you know it is a farce. Only the true is beyond time. And since time is merely a convention for your perception, it truly is nothing to fear. The apparent changes your body undergoes... the loss of memory... the pain of experience... all of these things are to be laid aside gently, with gratitude for the service they provide. For without them your experience could not be what it is.

No matter how things may appear, it is all a gift. Find the gift in every moment and sink deeply into gratitude. That is the secret of life we offer you. That is true living.

The law of non-resistance

Yes, you feel as though you've been struggling against this law even more than ever lately, don't you? This is good. This is a sign not that your struggle has increased, but rather that your awareness of your constant struggle to capture and control reality is finally blossoming into full bloom. With this new awareness comes increased ability to serve with new responses. Instead of anger and fear, you are better able to respond with deep breathing and love. Creating space is love.

There is no need to fear recrimination or punishment from us, from others on your plane, or even from your True Self. Only the ego, or small mind, would have you believe that what you have done is 'bad' and therefore you are 'bad' and must pay some penance in order to return to God's grace. There is One. You may choose to call One whatever you like. It matters not to One whether you say "God" or "Devil". For One is simply all that is real.

Truth transcends all labels, all ideas and conceptions of good and bad. Truth transcends all personal likes and dislikes. It transcends all thought, which is why it truly is the unthinkable. This is why the logic of the intellect or small mind is just about the least appropriate tool for the job there could ever be. And why the heart is precisely the right size crescent wrench for the job at hand.

Some tips: You already know that when your physical body feels tired, hungry, etc. that your ego comes to the forefront, taking things personally and putting up its dukes for a showdown. Like, every time, right? Next time you are able to acknowledge that you feel tired, hungry, etc., let yourself say it out loud. "I recognize that right now I'm experiencing sensations of tiredness, hunger, sadness, etc." Say it out loud to the person you are near, so that both you and they get the chance to hear these words and acknowledge where you are in that moment.

When you notice these things, it may help you to spend time submerging your body in water. Take a hot bath, even if just a short one. Drink lots of water; make sure you are hydrated. Eat healthy foods. And let yourself off the hook of having to 'fix' anything or 'save' anyone. For here is the next secret on your little egg hunt for the truth: there is nothing and no one for you to fix. Only the ego would have you believe that without its input, everything would turn to chaos and pain. Only the ego would use anger in the name of love to justify its selfish rantings... its desire to be right and respected and treasured... to be seen as actually existing.

Because your true self already knows the truth of the matter: the ego actually does not exist.

In addition, when you feel yourself becoming triggered and that tone of voice (you know precisely the one we mean-- the condescending, impatient voice that at times comes from your mouth) wants to issue forth, call a 'time out'. Even if you have to do it out loud and use your hands to make the shape of a big "T" in front of your face, do it. "I need to call a time out on myself-- I love you so much... will you please excuse me? I need to go have a chat with my ego." Then run upstairs and draw a bath. Sit in that tub for at least 15-30 minutes. As all of the anger and frustration rolls around and around in your head, as all of the story winds itself up for the retelling, acknowledge it and release it into the bathwater.

Know that as you release it, you are safe from it; the water molecules have plenty of space to hold your story, and all story from the beginning of existence into eternity, believe us. Because the story, at its essence, is inherently empty itself. This means that all of your anger, sadness, joy, fear, doubt, misery, lethargy... all of the story of your life stream, and of every other life stream that has ever appeared to have existed, can all fit in that tub of water. The water can absorb and hold the nastiest, most frightening, angriest energy waves you could ever possibly whip up. In fact, it would be like putting a thimble of wine in an otherwise empty airplane hangar. That is how much space there is in one molecule of water. And since space is love and love is space... this means that tub of water is infinitely loving.

So return to your origins by sitting in a tub of comfortably warm water. Wash your physical body slowly and carefully. Take your time washing your head and face... spend extra time on areas where they lymph nodes live. Make sure your hands spend time on your heart chakra. You already know that reiki is a modality that has value in your life. Use that. On a regular basis.

If, after 30 minutes or so, you are still feeling wound up and you can tell that your ego is vying for position so it can make a slam dunk against your lover, your friend, your world, your past, your whatever, then sit for another 30 minutes in that tub. Sit. Breathe. Stretch. And get in touch with emotion. Release that emotion. Express it. You are right to ask others in grieving if they are expressing their emotions in healthy ways. The way of embodiment is precisely this: embodying the emotions, rather than resisting them, partitioning them off.... locking them away in the cellar of the psyche rather than inviting them up through the heart, where they can be expressed and purified, to be returned to the Source as pure love energy.

This is the secret: there are no 'negative' emotions. All emotion that is properly embodied and expressed returns to the Source to be recycled as pure light and love energy. So the more you can embody your emotions, the better you'll be able to let them go, and the more light and love energy will be fed back into the feedback loop of infinite love in the universe.

As there is no Other, this action serves to regenerate the love and energy of your own being, in the biggest sense of the word... in the biggest sense of the world! Honest, authentic emotional expression feeds the system. Stuffing emotions out of fear starves the self and serves to create perceived barriers between oneself and brothers/sisters in the world who are waiting for your brilliance to shine forth.

Many are looking for your light and love. The brilliance of your smile, the joy of your laughter and the magnificence of your loving encouragement. When you shine that brilliance; when you practice in service of the Law of Non-Resistance, you create a path for others that leads back to the heart, a path of love and fearlessness that allows others to find their way back into their own light. This is one of the many purposes you have for walking on your plane at this time. And you shine brightest for others when you are actively loving and accepting every aspect of yourself, precisely as you are, without a shred of resistance, shame, guilt, sadness, or fear.

Joy and tranquility: these are the two ingredients for you to distill in your heart, to make the most delicious wine the world has ever known.

And fear not about your so-called 'mistakes' of the past. No matter how tragic your ego may judge them to be, know that in all absolute ways, you are precisely where/when you are 'supposed' to be. On the path of expression and becoming, there are no wrong turns. Welcome Home.

Let it all slide

Sometimes your body feels exhausted. And you identify very strongly with that. It is important to get enough sleep, rest, exercise, etc. And to embody all of it as fully as you can.

The trick here is to do all of this while simultaneously refusing to identify your Self with the physical body. When it's time to rest, rest. Yet do so in full knowledge and understanding that the Self is the flame that continues to burn 24/7... endlessly, eternally. It does not even flicker when you feel tired. Nor when you get sick. It does not flicker even at the moment of your perceived death, when you lay aside the physical body gently and continue on your way. Your thoughts, words, and actions are all on stage, and the Self is sitting in the audience, watching with a smile.

None of the experience you perceive touches the Self. The Self truly is bulletproof. Scratch proof. Like teflon. Yeah... teflon soul. Nothing sticks. Yes, we agree... would make an awesome album title.

Leadership. Step into it. What do you believe in? What are you passionate about? How committed to living your mission (I create a world of transformation by stretching my comfort zone) are you at this moment? Are you ready to stretch it just a little further in this present moment? Are you ready to go just an inch or two beyond what you think you can do? Are you ready to challenge the 'status quo seeker' within you, who claims to be afraid or uncertain or uncomfortable with some aspect of every movement you make in order to keep you from reaching your true potential?

If you could only see your true potential... if you could but lay eyes upon it even for one second, you would be blinded by its brilliance. You would be stunned and crushed and blown to bits and reduced to ashes of humility by its glory, brilliance, and power. You would have to shield your eyes, for your own brilliance is truly bold and magnificent. Depictions of the Archangel Gabriel... this is what we are thinking of when we describe your potential to step fully into love and selfless leadership.

And remember: the most powerful leadership comes from authenticity... vulnerability... and through example. Set the example of how a man can live in your world. Be an example to the entire planet of how the balance between masculine and feminine energies can look. Show your community what it looks like when you engage fully, taking the time you need for self care, and focusing always on a bigger picture-- the picture of Your community, Your brothers and sisters, Your service to others. Do not worry when you witness what you judge to be selfishness, or apathy, or fear, or doubt, or plain ugliness and stupidity. These, we remind you, are all your judgments, and truly have nothing to do with the person you are looking at.

For they, just like you, are shining brilliantly, but do not yet understand their own potential for magnificence.

This means you are in the same boat with every other creature and being you ever encounter. Even those you prefer not to be around. We would say, rather emphatically, "ESPECIALLY" the ones you prefer not to be around. It is only the intellect... the ego... the small mind that would have you believe that your preferences matter. And those preferences (for something or against something) that stem from fear (of loss of control, for example) are what keep you from shining more brightly.

We say love. But not just those you love to love. Love those you love to hate. Love those you love to dislike. Love those you love to ignore. Love those you believe do not deserve it. Love those you believe have taken advantage of you and have possibly even scarred you for life. See those as your brothers and sisters. See those as your own personal mirrors, showing up in your life at the precise moment when you need it most, and think you need it least.

Let it all slide. Every bit of it. All of the fear and worry about what other people might think. Get comfortable. Find out what comfortable means to you. Get comfortable in your own skin, and demonstrate to the world what it looks like when a man finds the balance between masculine and feminine and feels comfortable in her/his own skin. And then take it a step further and push against your comfort zone of external circumstances... Since you can't possibly fail or die or lose or know true defeat, why not make every day an exercise in pushing against that comfort zone?

For if you could put a face on what you call the comfort zone, you would see the face of the ego. It is nothing more than your ego that defines what you call "your" comfort zone. It's actually not your fears or limitations at all that hinder you-- it is your belief in the ego's definitions of the world that hinder you, keep you from stepping forward when you're not sure whether you should. Keep you from speaking up, from offering your gold, from creating something new and putting it out in the world. It is only the ego's voice, warning of impending doom if you 'fail' (which is literally impossible in reality). Definitions and demarcations and delineations such as "failure" and "success" are completely arbitrary when seen through the eye of the heart.

If you're feeling heartbroken, you are no longer listening with the heart. This is actually the cause of suffering, not simply the effect.

The heart knows no failure, for failure requires success for contrast. And the heart knows no success, for that would require failure for contrast. No, the heart knows Truth-- which goes far beyond the borders of any intellectual, rational, logical boundaries that would separate some parts of life from others and attempt to hang signs on them... creating an entire belief system around these boundaries... creating an entire reality and persona in the process.

This, of course, is the duty of the ego, small mind, or intellect. To label. Judge. Make lists. Cut things into smaller, more 'manageable', bite-sized pieces. This is the only way it knows how to create order out of perceived chaos. But, of course, you already know that inevitably whatever 'order' has been created shifts, changes, flexes, and transforms into something else, again and again, microsecond by microsecond. The ego would have you look away from the constant change that exists in reality... it would cover your eyes and whisper in your ear and have you believe that whatever you perceive you have experienced and judged as 'good' is actually the way things "should" be. You know, since they're based on 'your' (that is, the ego's) preferences, judgments, and definitions of what the world is, what life is, and what 'good' is.

You know better than this now. So sit in the heart's throne throughout your days and nights, and view the world and all its contents, your own thoughts included, through the lens of the heart. When the ego's stories kick up, smile and look at them lovingly. Nod. Accept them for the empty stories that they are. And go right on looking at them through the lens of the heart. The lens of the heart is bestowed upon you in order that you may use it relentlessly to remember your own true identity.

Once you do that, you will expose the rest of the world for who it really is: Yourself.

The senses lie

Now you graduate from where you've been to a more nuanced level of understanding. Here is where you learn to walk that line... On one hand, the physical body is not you. It is beginning to sink in. This is good. Now, how will you still stay in touch with that love and passion you have for your fellow man, without dismissing his life summarily since his body is not his being?

When your best friend endangers himself, drinks a pint or a quart of tequila by himself in one day, then calls you, terrified of what he's done, how will you stay connected to his heart without grabbing on to ideas about the body? And how will you accept the release of the body without distancing yourself from the heart?

Non-resistance. This is your key now. Simply allowing and witnessing, calmly and with love. Only the ego would have you believe you must either abandon all and walk away or else fall down on the ground sobbing and go into panic mode. Only the ego would have you believe that life is black and white; that your actions must be based upon some sort of black and white 'contrast' thinking. This is the ego's desire for clear, clean rules that are easy to follow.

But you and I know you've come way too far for this kind of trickery. Nuance is what life is about, and now you step into deeper shades of nuance. How will you handle them? How will you love yourself and those around you while standing in the blurred lines of uncertainty? What will you use to guide you? Of course you already know what we're going to say.

Look at this situation, as all situations, through the lens of the heart. Only the heart lens will allow you to perceive life as it is actually unfolding. Only the heart will lead you in the direction of life.

It is right and good to remain calm. Do not be fooled by appearances. Keep in mind the limited scope of spiritual perception on your plane of existence. Your eyes lie. Your ears lie. All of your senses lie. Your mind lies to you about what you are, who you are, and how you are. You are not the human body. You are not the name you've carried around for however many years. And you are not small, weak, or incapable of great things. In fact, the opposite of all of these is the truth. Yet in this moment, your perception seems to be what you have to go by. We say close your eyes. Open your heart. Step forward with your natural power; let the light within you shine forth into this situation, as with all you come across for the rest of your days.

Here is where your natural sense of humor will serve you well. Use your keen insight to see deeply into the situation. Recognize the habitual thought patterns at play. Notice the flaws in thinking. And then, with confidence and relaxed calm, gently go forth. Gently speak. Gently offer your ear and your words of truth. As you've been told before, you have more power than you realize. Gone are the days of needing to make a loud noise in order to be heard. The day has come for you to let go of those old, childish ideas of power. For you wield true power. When you speak truth, it carries tons of power. No need to ram it down anyone's throat. Your feelings of never being heard, of being wrongly accused, and of being forever misunderstood are now wiped from your consciousness. They are cleared away. You no longer carry those vibrations anywhere in your being. Know that your ego will still try to play these cards, even though they are no longer in the deck. Simply smile. Look deeply. There is no reason for you to get upset by these things anymore. They do not exist. And in fact, it was only your misperception that caused you to believe they ever existed in the first place. But you stored those energies in your body. Now they are gone.

It is time for you to step forth with more authority and calm, loving presence than you ever have before. The time for playing small is truly, truly over for you. As big as you can dream, the universe can create and provide. There is ever-expanding awareness available to you. You are ready to work miracles. So will you resign yourself to folded napkin tricks and parlor games? Or are you ready to take on miracles of life? Miracles of happiness? Miracles of love? Miracles of forgiveness and acceptance and joy and humility and power and courage and amazement and delight?

Can you handle this much amperage, Dear One? Only if you learn to temper your responses to it. You will experience surges in power. In the past you have not known what to do with them. We tell you now: do nothing with them. Simply experience them and let them pass. These are part of your unfolding and enfolding. It is time for the next phase of your journey to begin. And it begins now.

Know in the depths of your heart that today your prayers are being answered. Which prayers, you wonder? The ones that went like this: "Use me as an instrument of your light, love, wisdom, compassion, healing, peace, strength, and grace." Yes. We've been listening. And now we answer your request, your demands, by telling you that the time is now. Be not surprised nor afraid when you begin to experience an increase in people seeking you out... looking for guidance and support. Get ready to deeply practice understanding, non-resistance, acceptance, and release. For love is witnessing. And witnessing, that is, creating space for reality to express itself, is love. These are the things for you to keep close to your heart and on the front burner of your mind as you move forward.

Will there be times when you feel drained? Angry? Sad? Frightened? Frustrated? This is the mantle, the burden of leadership. You know this phrase. And you've already experienced what it can feel like to lead, to carry the lantern at the head of the pack into the thick darkness, piercing the shadows. This is all perception. Knowing as you do that life can never be extinguished, and yet keeping in mind that the physical being and the mind work together in order to create conditions for the communication of the Heart, you must go forward with gentleness toward others, but mostly toward yourself.

It will be easy to damn yourself and chastise yourself for your perceived missteps. Worry not, Dear One. The missteps may feel like many, but we assure you that you are progressing beautifully along this path of love, from the source, through the source, and returning to the source. There is no other. There is no place for fear to live. There is nowhere that anger can take refuge. For here you are, sitting upon the

Inner Throne of the Divine Temple of the Heart. It may not look like much to your eyes and ears. It may, in fact, seem as if you're still simply sitting in your little extra bedroom, surrounded by musical instruments. We remind you: the eyes lie. The heart is true. Always.

How to walk the razor's edge? How to balance the stories with the Heart?

Regard everything you experience as story, to be discarded. Feel free to enjoy, then discard. Set aside.

Non-resistance, even in this moment as you write. ESPECIALLY in this moment, as you write. What is at stake? The possibility that you might lose your 'flow'? That you might become distracted and your attention may shift away from the task at hand? That's how you live your life anyway. Let it be of no concern to you. Your Heart is always ready to share with you what you need to hear. There is nothing blocking you, and nothing to ever be lost to the ethers. All you need do is sit, quiet yourself, follow your breath, and resume listening to the message that continues to flow forth from your Divine Inner Wisdom at all times, effortlessly.

Only the ego would have you believe that you have somehow lost a 'once in a lifetime' chance at success. Only by keeping you interested in some imaginary carrot dangling in front of your face does it keep you preoccupied, sidetracked from the simple redirection of attention back to the heart. That is what is called for, again and again.

Regard everything you experience as story. Regard everyone you encounter as Heart. Treat every being as if they were yourself: they are. Treat every downfall, every painful event, every victory, every tragedy as if it were a comic strip in a newspaper, or a television program or a movie. Enjoy it. Let yourself bask in it. And know, at the same time, that it is not you. Do not let yourself get lost in it and lose sight of the solid fact that nothing you experience is infinite. Nothing you experience can ever threaten or damage your true identity; the well being of your One True Self.

Breathe into your story and watch it begin to unravel. Witness it as it crumbles before your very eyes. All of the stories that you've poured so much of your energy into preserving-- none of it was ever you. The fantasies. The dreams. All of those things are as evanescent and ephemeral as the morning dew evaporating in the sunshine. The brotherhood... the enemies... All of this is story, as well. If everyone is you and all is One and all is Love and Love is space, then how could you ever choose favorites?

By releasing attachment to the illusion that waves in the thin air before you, you will begin to perceive every being as Heart, which is correct and right. This is true vision. When this occurs, you will find yourself more hesitant to summarily dismiss anyone before you, no matter what you perceive or how they appear or sound to you. Instead of, "this person is whining and complaining a lot," you may discover yourself moving toward thoughts of, "when has something like this happened in my story? And how did I feel when it did?" In this way, you will begin to find yourself creating space, which is the ultimate expression of Love. You will find more space in your heart. More space in your daily schedule. More bandwidth for the foibles and troubles and stories of others.

And even as you find more patience for your fellow man, you will come to understand that his complaints, his fears, all of his worries, joys, aches and dreams, are simply story. Story projected into a perceived past. Story projected into a perceived future. Neither of which actually exists in Reality. Therefore, ultimately meaningless. But valuable, nonetheless, for it offers a medium through which the subject may come to realize that it is all immaterial. None of what you think has happened, has happened. Not in Reality. The fact that you 'think' it happened is the key to remembering that it did not; for anything that can be captured within the realm of the intellect, the small mind, or the ego, is not of Reality. Conversely, anything of Reality cannot be perceived or even imagined by the small mind or intellect.

The intellect swims around within the Teacup of the Heart. Therefore the very idea of an ego that could be capable of challenging the Heart in any way is absurd; meaningless. Remove the ego, intellect, or small mind, and what remains is Reality. The intellect is the basketball rolling around on the floor of the Heart's gymnasium. No matter where it rolls, no matter where it's thrown, no matter how high it bounces or where it rolls, no matter whether or not it 'swishes' the net, it remains within the bounds of the gymnasium. The doors are locked. The windows shut. It can spin on the finger of the Divine. It can whirl beautifully, and seem to do incredible feats. However, nothing happens through the mind without the hand of the Divine.

Now is the time to recognize that the validity of your anger, your sadness, your pain, your frustration, and all of the grudges that you hold, the validity of all of it is precisely zero. These are simply grist for the mill. They are the material provided for working toward the realization, the remembering, that they are illusion. That everything perceived via the senses is illusion.

So why care for other hearts with gentleness and compassion? Why forgive others and yourself for holding on to misperception? Why release attachment to outcome and show generosity in the face of competitive, ego-based hustle and bustle? Why set yourself up to sacrifice? Because the one whom you show generosity is none other than yourself. And the reason you are here is to remember that you are Love and to express that in infinitely many ways. The quickest path to remembering that you are Love itself is to show love to yourself in as many ways as possible. When you demonstrate love to your physical being through self-care, you generate increased vibration upon your plane of existence, and it impacts all around you, whether you are initially aware of it or not. The love and care you show yourself emanates forth to all around you.

Note that this is distinct from ego-based self absorption, which is different from Love. Love gives and accepts all. Self absorption is single-pointedly obsessed with getting the ego's perceived needs met. The hungers, the desires, the demands...

getting all of those fed is what self absorption is about. Naturally, the only path to satisfying the hungers, desires, and demands of the ego is to relinquish all attention to the ego completely. This becomes apparent and obvious through repeatedly failed attempts to satisfy the ego's demands. As every single attempt, no matter how extravagant, misses the mark, falls short of permanent satisfaction, quenching thirst only for a moment only to reignite a different desire, eventually it begins to dawn on the perceptive Beloved on the Path that there is no end to the madness except to reject it outright. No attempt to satisfy the ego will ever satisfy the ego, for it is ever changing in its demands.

This serves the ego by keeping you busy. Always. Forever chasing something it calls 'security' and 'happiness' and 'fulfillment'. These things cannot ever possibly arise from a house, or a car, or any object, place, or experience. Only surrendering, over and over... only giving and contributing and turning away from the self-serving edicts of the ego can true happiness ever be approached on your plane of existence.

Only through true communication can communion happen. True communication from Heart to Heart; the Divine speaking to Herself in the Mirror.

Money
This is one of your biggest tools for remembering that reality is of the Heart, not of the ego.

Notice what happens when unexpected expenses, like tax bills, come up. When you unexpectedly have to pay $1,400 at tax time, how do you respond? Are there emotions of fear and anger? If so, this is the ego at work. Remember that the ego would have you believe that the physical body is you. And therefore that the survival of the physical body is a measurement of the survival of your very being.

Anger comes up in a lizard-brain response to perceived threat. It covers up fear, and calls one to action in a survival situation. Yet in Reality, there truly IS no threat. The concept of threat is meaningless, as all is the Heart. Sadness arises at the thought of loss, yet only the ego would have you believe that loss is possible; that there is a separate 'you', apart from all else, that could possibly gain or own anything, which, by definition, is necessary for loss to occur. This means an unexpected tax bill, and the resulting fear, anger and sadness are very important parts of the curriculum of your life story. In order to remember that loss is impossible, that the concept of threat is meaningless, you create a scenario where what you have forgotten is highlighted and underscored, thrown into the spotlight. This is wonderful work, and very much encouraged.

Those learning opportunities around money are abundant. The way you treat money, how you use it, your attitudes around accepting it and giving it, these are all part of the curriculum, as well. For any resistance in any direction is a signal that somewhere, you have mistaken the body/mind for yourself. Resistance indicates that at some level your beliefs are supporting attachment; that is, desire or attraction toward something, and fear or repulsion away from something.

In the case of the unforeseen tax bill, attachment becomes apparent through the anger, fear, and sadness. Attachment is revealed in the form of desire to hold onto money in the savings account. Survival of the body is also attached to the same money in the savings account, and so unplanned spending of that money is seen as a threat to survival. Conflict is perceived, as the government's requirements to be paid taxes appear to threaten your very survival.

Rather than turning your attention back to the Heart, you follow the ego's rants and ravings when you follow fear, anger, and sadness. Only the ego's health and wealth are at stake, not yours. You are not the body; you are not the mind. There is no 'other' to vilify. There is no 'other' against which you need to protect your 'self'. For your 'self' is all that you perceive around you. Your self is the Divine Inner Throne of the Heart itself, in all its glory.

Why so much resistance toward turning away from the ego? Why the hesitation? Habit. The illusion of the ego's substance is generated and sustained through habitual thought patterns. Turning away from the 'voice' of the ego, intellect or small mind is quite simple, yet the ego kicks and screams and offers treats and rewards (stick and carrot, simultaneously) to regain your attention. So basically, you are in the habit of mistakenly identifying with the body and mind, seeing your very existence as tied to them. You are in the habit of identifying with what you perceive through the senses;

believing that they somehow reflect a 'better' or 'worse' you, somehow. And you are in the habit of getting angry, fearful, and sad when you mistakenly perceive that your identity, and therefore your life, is being threatened.

Even the phrase 'your life' reveals the fallacy of the ego. For it suggests that life can be somehow owned in little batches... 'I'll take your life if you take mine...' 'It's my life and I'll do whatever I want with it...' It suggests that life is like a carton of eggs, or a fifty-dollar bill... to be consumed and spent as one wishes, and when it's gone, it's gone.

How limiting this view of life! And about as accurate as saying, 'that's my tidal wave', believing you can somehow carry it around in your pocket, or on your back. That you can bargain with it, control it, deny it.

If you saw yourself as you really are, you would recognize that you are the tidal wave. You are the life force that flows through the body and mind, igniting passion and wonder. You are the electrons that dance and spin, creating the illusion of this world. You are the very energy that holds it all together. You are the true face behind every mask. You are the force that drives the grass and trees to grow; that causes the sun to shine and the rain to fall. You are the wind and the mud and the fragrance of the flowers.

To claim to be the body/mind is to pretend that you are the wrapping paper and not the gift. It is time now for you to remember that you are indeed the gift. You are what lies within the wrapping paper. And furthermore, when you remember this truth and embrace it, embodying it fully, you remind others around you of the truth, as well. And you help them to wake up from their dream, from their fears and angers and sadness. For it is all unnecessary and meaningless in the realm of the Real. The anger, the hoarse voice after screaming and yelling, the sadness and fear, all of it is self-generated through a big mistake.

"Oops, I thought that coat stand was a burglar, trying to break into the house and steal all my nice things. And I got scared and angry. How silly of me!"

When we wake from a frightening dream and come to the realization that it was unreal, we say so many things. We can talk about how real it seemed... we can laugh at ourselves, seeing the folly of our ways. And then we can go about our day.

Now is the time to open your eyes and see that it was all a wondrous dream. The story you call your 'life' was never your life at all, but rather a cardboard cutout; a wonderfully delicious dream of imagined events designed to enliven your senses. A roller coaster that you chose to ride, taking you up and down and around, exhilarating and seemingly dangerous and fun, all at the same time.

So that you could learn to distinguish the enlivened senses, the danger and fun, from the steady flame of life that burns within you; the same force that has been present through every sleeping and waking moment of what you call your life.

The less resistance you hold, the less you 'clench' and try to hold on to people or events or situations in your life story, the more clearly you can touch your true identity. For a time, it will seem as though your true identity is outside of you, for you have misidentified with the body and mind for what seems to you like a long time. It will appear to be craziness to you, illogical and irrational. Like voodoo or witchcraft or fantasy or religion... based upon whimsical fancy, and unprovable in the slightest. These are all judgments the stem from the ego, of course.

It will appear as though you are being asked to let go of your actual self, the physical body and mind, and to embrace some invisible, imagined spectre. That you are being asked to speak some special language, and to pretend that you see the emperor's new clothing, just like some others in the crowd who claim to see it, as well, when really there's nothing there to see with your eyes. It may seem as if you're being asked to lie; to pretend to believe something unreal. These critiques are all of the ego. That is the duty and only purpose and function of the ego; to measure, label, critique. This is of no consequence in Reality.

As you continue to turn your attention away from what you see, hear, smell, taste, and touch, and return, again and again, to something invisible and silent within you, you will begin to notice that something invisible and silent actually does exist within you. You will begin to perceive a tiny space of solace within, a 'place' where you can go for safety in the storm. And the more you practice returning to that place, the easier it will become to go there at any time.

You will begin to notice that in the midst of the storm of emotions and perceived events in what you call your life, the challenges, the frustrations, the flat tires and unexpected tax burdens, that quiet place in your heart becomes a respite. Somewhere you can go to take a breather from it all; a safe haven. The more you do this, the more you will be able to recognize your life story for its inherent flimsiness and emptiness. It was only your focused attention and your habit of pouring your energy and passion into retelling the story that made it seem so real. It was only the habitual thought patterns of holding onto grudges and dear friends that made any distinctions seem like battle lines... 'here is friend, here is foe...'

The key to releasing these misperceptions is so simple. All you need to do is begin practicing one word: "Yes." Say yes to everything that arises in your life, without exception. When you get word that you will not be receiving a tax return this year, but rather a tax debt, embrace it with a powerful 'yes!' When your best friend gets a promotion, say yes! And when she loses that same job, say, yes! Open your mind and body to every possibility, refusing none; resisting nothing. The path of no resistance is for you a very favorable route at this time. All resistance is of the ego.

Also, suspend all judgments when you find yourself identifying with the ego, for these very judgments are also of the ego. "Oh no, I failed... I've gotten all caught up in anger again. I'm no good at this. I'm a failure. I'll never get the hang of this!" Messages like these are of the ego, designed to keep you distracted from actually returning your attention to the

Heart. So every time you catch yourself identifying with anything other than the Heart, relax and redirect. That's all that is necessary. Relax and redirect. Smile. Breathe. This is all part of the ride. And when the ride is successful, you will understand that there was never any ride taken to begin with.

Reach out to yourself again and again, by reaching out to your brothers and sisters around you. Show compassion, understanding and support to them at all times. And notice when you feel resistant to doing so. Notice where that resistance lives in your body. Experience it, embody it, and then release it. For it, too, is nothing more than habitual thought patterns; part of the cardboard cutout that you call your life story. It is small moments like that all lined up in a row that you call your life. And you (or your ego, rather) very conveniently 'forget' those details that would reveal the inconsistency of thought; the inconsistency of purpose. For if the ego allowed you to see all of its thinking, all of its self-contradicting patterns, then it would be seen for the dishonest, hopelessly confounded miscreant that it truly is.

Engaging in battle with the ego only fuels it. The only way to successfully deal with the ego is to turn away from it, again and again. Only this pulls the wind from its sails. Only this threatens the very legs it stands on. Only this shakes its foundations. For the foundations are made of smoke; they are nothing more than habitual thought patterns. There are no true foundations for something that is illusion. The very concept is meaningless.

Just watch

There is no way you can do it all. That's okay. Do something. Create something. Support something. And after you do, pay close attention to the ego... watch dispassionately as it starts turning the memory over and over, saying things like, "I wonder if I kind of sucked. It sounded kind of empty, didn't it? And didn't you fuck up at that one part? You missed that one note... I wonder what people are thinking... I'll bet they think it was awful. Maybe I should never have even tried."

Just watch. Notice that they are all the ego's attempts to pull your joyful, loving energy away from your heart space and back up to your head. In these moments of blissful surrender to the loving gifts that flow through you, there is no need for the head. No need for the ego. The intellect is in the service of the heart. That is when you'll notice these messages arising, trying to chip away at your blissful, loving, heart energy. Do not be fooled into paying attention to these thoughts, or buying into them and engaging the ego here in any way. The only thing to do is smile. You may find it helpful to say aloud something like, "I did *something*. I created *something*. I sang *something*. I supported *something*."

"I gave love. I shared. I surrendered to love. I danced with love. I sang with love. I drowned in love, just for a little while."

The ego has no defense against this except to offer more badgering. Let it all slip by. And if you are feeling love and excitedly talking with your dear brother and someone you know walks in the door and looks at you and says, "Shhhhh!", and then says hello, just notice. This is the precise time to practice nonresistance. It is only the ego that would have you respond with anger; only the ego that would have you say, "How dare you tell me to shhh! Why are you trying to silence me? Who are YOU to silence ME?!" And it is only the ego that would have you still chewing on the event, twenty minutes later, planning out possible strategies for revenge. Only the ego that would have you imagining scenarios like walking up to her and asking, "So, did many people tell you 'shhh' when you were growing up?" or "I don't appreciate your trying to silence me. Please don't do it again."

All of these may even seem to have a shred of validity in the moment... "I'm setting and maintaining healthy boundaries," you may tell yourself. Yet take a careful look at your intentions. If you're honest about them, the intention is to cut her down to size, because in the moment that she looked at you and said, "shhhh", you experienced emotions of anger. She simply reminded you of someone else, another time, another place, another setting, where you ended up feeling small. It is the ego that would have you push back; the ego who is keeping score.

In these moments, it is helpful to remember that Love does not keep score. Love says, 'ahh... let me practice nonresistance in this moment.' Love says, 'I will let this flow right through me and keep smiling and loving and enjoying this present moment fully.' Love realizes that whatever caused her to say, 'shhh' is her own issue, and not yours. Love responds to everything with compassion. Love says 'yes' to all. Love creates space for everything to unfold in its divine perfection, even those things that the ego resists. Love transcends the ego.

If the only way for you to let go of the anger that arises is to repeat the phrase 'nonresistance' over and over until it subsides, then that is a helpful practice for you. And if it takes twenty minutes to remember to do that, then honor and bless yourself for not taking thirty minutes, or two weeks, or nine years. Or a lifetime.

All is unfolding perfectly. The more you can remember this in the moment, the more you can honor and bless your true nature, and the better able you will be to recognize the divine within everyone and everything around you. There is only the Divine, in her countless disguises. There is no other.

Impatience

It is common to become distracted and dissatisfied by what you perceive to be other people's inability to see as you see; to discern as you do. You may find yourself becoming impatient with other people, expecting them to see what you see; to know what you know. Keep in mind that this is simply the ego's way of trying, once again, to take control of your thoughts and behaviors.

Your impatience stems from the judgment that others are somehow living life wrong, or incorrectly. That you know better than they do what they should be doing, saying, and perceiving... how they should be living their lives. Broken down in these terms, it becomes pretty easy to see just how egotistical that is, does it not? No judgment here, either-- for if this is happening in your life, it's simply where you are at this moment.

As your ability to discern Reality increases, so will your patience. For you will be called upon, again and again, to recognize the ego's demands and simply let them go by the wayside. Like a backseat driver leaning over your shoulder, pointing toward the windshield and yelling in your ear, the ego will try tirelessly to get you to drive your car where it wants to go, promising glorious rewards if you simply delay, for a few more minutes, going into your own heart for guidance. Have you noticed yet that your car keeps ending up in the ditch?

Your patience will increase as you realize that the tension of trying to satisfy the ego can be simply acknowledged and released in any moment. The knee-jerk, hair-trigger reactivity that you have experienced in your life (either through first-hand experience or by witnessing it in others) will slow down, and you will notice more and more time available to you between stimulus and response. Eventually, you will recognize it before it happens, and will be able to remain in the serenity of the Heart before, during, and after the ego makes its demands. What will appear to be a miracle to others will be nothing but your return to the present moment, where infinite, timeless space is available. You may use this as a sign of your progression along your journey.

Another signpost to watch for along your journey is the decreasing attractiveness of worldly pleasures. The deeper you go into recognizing and acknowledging Reality, the less attractive things of the world will seem. What you previously perceived to be worldly delights, satisfying cravings and hungers, will be less and less satisfying as you continue to perceive their true emptiness. As you become increasingly aware of how the ego's cravings seem satisfied for shorter and shorter amounts of time, you will remember that they actually never satisfy in any sort of permanent way. In fact, scratching the ego's itch in any one way simply results in another itch being triggered somewhere else.

In the field of the Heart, where Reality reigns, there are no itches. There are no needs to fulfill. There is nothing to achieve, to become, to avoid, or to chase down. Nothing to remember. Nothing to forget. There is simply the Divine, in all glory and grace, unfolding perfectly in infinitely many directions, wearing infinitely many masks.

Where is it in your life today that you feel 'less than', or 'not enough'? What other than the ego would have you believe this is true? Even as you read these words, you may experience a barrage of habitual thought patterns, reminding you of the infinitely many ways in which you are not doing or being enough. Notice how this may come up while reading words whose intentions are to guide you away from paying attention to the ego and returning to the Heart. How interesting that these voices show up with such clarity and strength right now, don't you think?

Now, in this moment, as you read this sentence, is yet another opportunity for you to smile, nod, and acknowledge the ego's messages. And then simply let them go by, relegating them to the sound of the wind as you drive with your windows rolled down. Interesting to listen to, yet nothing to become attached to or to offer much of your attention.

Where in your life today do you remember how others have wronged you in the past? Where in your life do you find yourself rehashing old stories, wishing you would have said 'this' or done 'that', condemning yourself for not thinking more quickly, or perhaps even congratulating yourself for getting the upper hand in an argument or conflict? In these seconds, minutes, hours, days, weeks, months, or even years spent pursuing these mental activities, who or what is it that is driving the bus? Is it ego, or Heart?

Clearly, it is ego, which would have you focus on habitual thought patterns, memories, which it would have you believe represents a solid 'past' that still exists somewhere, somehow. A past that you could get back to if only you wore the right clothing, purchased the right objects, or acted in certain ways. The ego would have you chasing your own tail on an imaginary hunting mission, trying in vain to track down a fictitious being called 'you' in the past.

Just as quickly it would have you believe that you can somehow grasp an imaginary 'future' that will never arrive. The ego tells you that you did not know you were living in 'good times' until they were gone and you were looking back at them, and now you must get back there somehow, in order to recapture the joy of those days. It also whispers in your ear that you will know 'real happiness' once you get to a certain time in your life when you have acquired enough money, real estate, objects, wealth, and power. That your current happiness, in the present moment, would be well sacrificed for the promise and hope of more joy in the future.

The complaints of past unhappiness, the blame, the anger, and the sorrow are as empty as the promises of future joy. And they are all nothing more than the strategy of distraction, the 'bait and switch', used by the ego to prevent you from surrendering all of the false and returning to the true Reality of the Heart, where the ego is recognized as being nothing more than a collection of habitual thought patterns.

Compass

What shall we use as our guide? We understand that money, power, fame, luxury, riches, good food, sexual gratification... all of these things are temporary and empty in nature. When we use these as our compass for growth and success, we end up feeling incomplete and empty. So what SHOULD we be using as our compass? If there is no true one leader to follow, then what are we to do? Where are we to go?

The compass is your heart. The direction is joy. You know joy... it is the very essence of your own true nature. When you get out of your head and back into your body, embodying your emotions and focusing on service and gratitude, you will reconnect with the joy that always and forever is present, just as the sun is always in the sky, even when appearing to be obscured by clouds or tree branches.

When in doubt, the answer is to always focus on gratitude first. Then take it to the next level; be of service to someone or something beyond yourself. Gratitude is connected to forgiveness-- who needs to be forgiven in order for you to move more deeply into gratitude? Most often the answer, you will find, is 'myself'.

So do it. Begin now. Start small. What is one small thing you can forgive yourself for?

I forgive myself for holding a grudge against a person who I judge wronged me."

Okay. You get a two-for-one opportunity here. Take that to the next level. You know what to do.

*I forgive that person for wronging me. I'm grateful for that person giving me the chance to get to this moment and to do this work. I **thank** that person for 'wronging me'. I forgive myself for wronging me... for holding myself in the prison of anger and sadness by clinging to the hot coals of revenge.*

Move toward joy. Always. Use it as your north star. Taste joy, and then remember that flavor. Remember how it bubbles in your mouth as you drink it. Remember the fragrance of laughter and savor its goodness.

Move toward joy. You'll find that it makes your journey lighter and easier. You'll discover that joy will end up carrying you... will end up pulling you up the hill, shining warmly on your face and supporting you in every step.

Move toward joy. In the darkness, in the midst of crowds, in the locker room, in the copy room, in your car, on your bicycle, in the dentist's office, at the hospital, in the classroom, in the kitchen, in the bathroom, at the office, in the supermarket, while taking out the trash, when you're on vacation and while doing your taxes. These are all appropriate times to move toward joy. When arguing with your partner. That is an especially good time to move toward joy. When getting fired from a job, or firing someone from their job... that's a wonderful time to move toward joy.

Can joy be found in all of these moments? Can joy be sought in all of these conditions and situations? Yes. Of course. There is no moment that is off limits. There is only the habitual conditioning of thought patterns that seems to rule and limit your access to joy. What are some of these habitual thought patterns that keep you from seeing the joy that sits right before your very eyes?

First off, judgments about outer conditions and other people. "This sucks." "I hate days like this." "It's too cold." "That guy is a jackass." "What an asshole." These, of course, are nothing more than projections of our inner judgments about ourselves. "I suck." "I hate people like this." "I'm too cold." "I'm a jackass." "What an asshole I am."

What are you to actually do to replace these beliefs? Simple recognition of their true nature is the first step. "Oh-- wait a minute. I'm cursing at someone because they didn't use their turn signal. Let me take a deep breath. What belief do I hold about myself that would allow me to lose my temper right now? "Others should get it right all the time." Deeper belief? "I should get it right all the time." Deeper? "I can never get it right all the time, even though I should." Deeper still? "I'm not good enough." "I'm unlovable." "I'm not worthy of love."

Now we're getting somewhere. We're exposing lies. How do you know these to be lies? Because everyone's very nature, your very nature, is love. How could love itself ever be unlovable? It's the biggest farce of all, and it's the work of the ego, or small mind, that would have you believe you need to rely upon IT to keep you safe. The opposite is actually true-- the ego relies upon your belief in it to keep it safe. Otherwise, it vanishes into a puff of smoke, for that's all it truly is. By keeping you in the belief that you are unlovable, it can keep you chasing external sources of perceived pleasure, focusing outward, keeping you facing away from your true source of joy and tranquility. Inward, into the heart, into gratitude, into service... that is where true joy and tranquility are found. And it flies in the face of what the ego would have you believe.

Lie: *"If I don't have enough money, I will die."*
Truth: You cannot ever die. The body dies. But you are not the body. You never were.

Lie: *"I'll never get the love I need to be happy."*
Truth: You ARE the love you need to be happy. How could you ever lack what you already are?

Lie: *"It's someone else's fault that I am unhappy."*

Truth: It is always your option to choose gratitude and service to someone or something beyond yourself. These are the roads that lead back home to joy.

Lie: *"Someone else has destroyed my life."*

Truth: Life can never be destroyed. Thoughts about expected outcomes can be interrupted and thwarted. But they were nothing more than thoughts to begin with. Do not mistake your own thought patterns for reality. As the Zen masters have said, thoughts are like clouds in the sky. Watch them pass. And watch the next ones roll in. Then watch them pass. And remain unaffected.

Beneath all of the excitement in the boat, the newly-caught fish flopping around on deck while children squeal and scream, trying to catch it... the drama of the motor that won't start today... the hunger in the belly, the drunk captain who almost runs aground... the petulant teenager who wants nothing to do with cleaning the brass or peeling potatoes... Beneath all of this lies the ocean of love, in all her silent gravity. There is no majesty that can surpass this calm, solid strength. The lights will dim. The sounds will fade. The movement will still, and then a new cycle will begin. But beneath it all, love remains untouched.

Release attachment to the lights, the sounds, and the movement you perceive and practice non-resistance. Full acceptance of all you see. For it is not you. And simultaneously, every bit of it is you, dancing in endless manifestations of form. And you are nothing other than love. Love is all there is.

CHAPTER SIX
Not this body, not this mind

Premise 1: You are not this body.

Premise 2: You are not this mind.

Premise 3: Since you are not this body, the survival of the body does not influence or impact the life force that you are. Since you are not this mind, you are not your thoughts, including desires and fears.

Premise 4: Since you are not your thoughts, you are not your personality.

Premise 5: Since you are not your body, mind, thoughts, or personality, your true self is not subject to death.

Premise 6: Since your true self is not subject to death, there is nothing to be gained nor lost in this experience that you call your life.

Premise 7: Since there is nothing to be gained nor lost, there is no need to judge circumstances as positive or negative.

Premise 8: Since there is no need to judge, there is no need to hold on to emotional states of anger, fear, sadness, or joy. In fact, in the absence of anger, fear, and sadness, joy naturally arises and is your natural state.

The details, no matter how intriguing they may seem at the time, are simply a non-issue. No matter what they may look or sound like. They simply are wind blowing outside the car door. Let it all pass. Let it all roll over you and simply pass by. Holding on to judgments and anger simply limits your vision of yourself and the world. Nothing more.

Remove the blinders of fear, anger, and sadness. Release the emotional charge and move forward downstream, using gratitude to paddle your way forward, back to the source of all life.

Albuquerque Walgreens

I loaded my jeep up with recording equipment this morning, kissed my sweetie and headed out the door. Hit the road around 8:30 am... was still feeling benedryl from last night. (Thought I either had windburn around my eyes or some sort of allergic reaction, so I took one benedryl before bed. Slept like a baby.)

I arrive here in Albuquerque. First stop: slice of pizza. Waitress looks like a 20 year-old version of my late girlfriend Laura. I smile at the universe. Nicely done. Second stop: record store across the street. Picked up a few cheap records from back in the day. Nice score. Under twenty bucks. Doing okay.

Third stop: Walgreens. To get some beer and wine. Right away, as I'm walking in, the lady who is always at the counter, and has been for the past 15 months, every time Cheryl and I have come in, sees me and does an almost-double-take. She doesn't look away and look back, but she looks at me and keeps staring. Like I'm scary looking. Maybe I am. Am I scary looking? Shaved head? Old t-shirt? Ratty jeans? Worn out sneakers? Maybe she thought I was homeless? Or gonna rob the place?

Whatever. I'm looking around at my options, and obviously I've come to the store at the worst possible time, when it's being restocked. People keep saying 'excuse me' (even other customers!) to get around me so they can go do whatever. It's like I can't get out of the way, no matter where I stand. And I'm a customer. Doesn't that count for anything? I'm there to spend money. Right?

So it's finally my turn at the counter. I've heard her ask every customer for their ID, so I know it's coming. I quickly pull out my license and lay it on the counter. She picks it up. Inspects it. Then, just before setting it down, she scans it. "BEEP."

What the fuck?

"Did you just scan my license?!", I ask incredulously. I can't believe she just did that. She's not the cops. She's not any branch of law enforcement. And she just scanned my license. What information gets shown when she does?

Manager guy, there at the other register, saw the whole thing. He pipes up: "Oh, we just do that to confirm date of birth."

You haven't scanned anyone ELSE's ID. Why mine?

I am angry. And then suddenly it occurs to me that this is precisely the kind of situation that can spiral out of control in a heartbeat. And no matter what happens, I will be on the losing end.

The cops will come. And I will be the guy who was causing trouble at the Walgreens. And my freedom to come lie down on the couch and have 4 days mini-vacation will be shot.

I leave.

I walk into Buffalo Exchange, still fuming. And there, the guy behind the counter takes a long look at me. Do I fit a profile? Suddenly, I'm getting a first-hand idea of what it might feel like to be a person of color on any day of the week, every day of the year, in the U.S. And it feels bad.

None of them know me. They don't know what I've been doing for the last 14 months, caring for my dear wife as she goes through chemotherapy. They don't know that I'm a damned good counselor for college students. That I have a master's in education. That I'm a good, loving, caring guy who listens. All they see is shaved head. Ratty jeans. Dark glasses. (My lenses get dark in the sun and lighten up when I go inside.)

They don't know any of this.

I get back to the house, get inside, fuming all the way, and then think to ask for guidance. WHAT IS YOUR GUIDANCE ON THIS???

(It comes through right away. Loud and clear.)

There is only a problem, a reason to be angry, if you assume that you are your physical body. This is only a breach of your privacy if you exist as a human body / mind in need of privacy. In truth, the concept of privacy is completely meaningless in truth, for YOU is all there is. The lady behind the counter? She was you. She was you, checking your ID to make sure that you were actually you. And that you didn't pose a threat to you, or to any of the other 'you's in the store. She wanted to make sure that you weren't pretending to be a you other than you. Which, of course, she would only do if she believed that you and she were not both you. And I believe we've cleared that up rather concisely here.

Also, keep in mind that you are totally in an altered state right now. Mercury is still in retrograde. The moon is just now leaving its fullness. And for the past 14 months, you've been undergoing a change in identification. Maybe THAT is why she double-checked your ID... maybe she was letting you know that she no longer recognizes you. In fact, few people will recognize you by the time you get back to Durango in a few days. You are not the man you were 14 months ago. And you are not the man you were two weeks ago. Tremendous transformation is taking place within you, and it's all for the better. Know this and remember it.

No need to fear-- this is actually what YOU have been asking for all this time. Take it gently. Breathe. Move slowly. And gradually take stock of your talents and strengths. You are blossoming in magical ways right now, and it makes no sense in the world to let anger or anything else get in the way of your seeing your true self just a little more clearly.

We are with you always, and it is impossible for us to steer you wrong. For we are you, and you are us. So. Relax. The checkout girl did you a favor by bringing this to the forefront. You are no longer the man you once were.

Separation

The separation that you perceive is also a function of the ego, intellect, or 'small mind'. Enemies. Friends. Strangers. Relatives. All of it appears to happen outside of you. But we remind you that this is only true if one assumes that the size and shape of the physical body is what defines one's being. More correctly, you are all fingers on the same big 'hand'. Or you are a finger and that other guy is the nose. Or the eyebrow. All parts of one single Divine.

And since there are no limits to the Divine, that means that there truly IS only one big Divine-- it's all the Divine, and it's all One. Again we repeat the mantra: there is no 'other'. No other to push against. No other to conquer. No other to fear. No other to bribe. No other to trick or fool or take advantage of. No other to forgive. No other to be angry at. No other to lie to. No other to show compassion toward.

There is only yourself, the Divine. And yes... this DOES mean that every time you show compassion to 'another', you're actually showing compassion toward your own heart. Every time you get angry at a checkout clerk, you are throwing stones at your own inner peace; you are 'stepping out of the light gap'. Every time you hold a grudge, you are simply telling yourself, over and over, the fiction that there could possibly ever be a reason to hold yourself hostage.

Self care

Expect pushback from the ego. Don't be surprised when lust, anger, sadness, or fear come knocking at your door. This is to be expected. It's nothing more than the ego looking for a new foothold.

And take a look at your choices. The seemingly small choices, like what you wear in public when on vacation. If you chose to wear clothing that you consider extremely comfortable, but which you know may not fit in with social norms in your time/space, why would you make that choice? What reward might you be seeking from doing this?

Maybe it was as simple as, "I'm enjoying some downtime, and I don't care how I look." Freedom. But maybe there's more to it? What reward might you get from actively (whether consciously or unconsciously) creating an image of yourself (clothing, demeanor) that employees in stores may find threatening? If that were to happen, perhaps you may create a situation where they take precautions that seem unfair to you. If that were to happen, you may find yourself feeling justified in playing the victim role. You may feel as though your civil rights to privacy have been violated by the checkout clerk who scanned your driver's license, while not doing that to anyone else in line.

The ego's work is complete. Now you are spinning in a whirlwind of emotion-- anger, frustration, fear... and the ego sits back and crosses its arms, delighted that you've taken the bait. It may be days, weeks, months, or years that you hold on to that anger, and every moment that you do so, every second that you believe that you have been taken advantage of, is another moment that the ego has created the illusion of a world that is unsafe; a world where you need protection for survival. A world where the ego is seen as a useful ally.

Don't be fooled. Don't be duped. Every time you let this happen, failing to examine the deeper dynamics of your discomfort, you let the ego take advantage of you. The ego is the one taking away your rights; your basic human right to happiness, joy, and freedom from the limitations of circumstance. Your true birthright.

This brings us to the idea of self-care. Your birthright brings with it great responsibility. Responsibility to whom? To your heart. With these gifts of insight that you bring with you into the world comes your responsibility to be absolutely true to your own heart. This is the upward spiral of growth, evolution, and love.

There is much work to do. And if you claim to want to let your light shine brightly in the world, to reach your potential as a being of light, then there are efforts you must make. One of them is to care for and nurture your physical body. The ego, in all its wily craftiness, would argue that since we are all one anyway, since we are all the Divine anyway, there's no need to worry about the physical body. It is of no importance, therefore it's perfectly fine to abuse it in the course of seeking sensual pleasures of all sorts. This is but yet another way the ego seeks to find a foothold in your perception and get you to buy in to seeking and avoiding. Desire and fear. Attachment.

Clever.

But not clever enough to fool you. Not if you so choose. Care for the body. Eat healthy foods, get regular exercise, and appropriate sleep. Listen to your heart and your body.

In every single moment, you are creating an experience of reality. All of these seemingly small choices, what you eat, what you wear, what you say, the thoughts you perpetuate, all of these things contribute to the experience of the world you create.

Care for your body, mind, and spirit, and you will settle into your natural state of being, which is joy. Those around you will pick up on the frequency of your vibration naturally, some at the subconscious level, and some consciously. It is of no importance what others think of you, yet it is of utmost importance that you take advantage of this precious opportunity to express the Divine to the Divine in the Divine as part of the Divine.

If being an instrument of light, love, wisdom, compassion, healing, peace, strength and grace is what you choose, then this is a path to follow.

So It Seems

Not this body, not this mind
Not these objects I'll leave behind
Not these visions, not these dreams
Or obsessions
So it seems

Not this water, not this dirt
Not this weapon, not this hurt
Not this skin, not this hair
Not this label
Do I dare?

Not hereafter, not here before
Not anything
Something more

Not this progress, not these mistakes
Not these e-mails, or calls I make
Not this photo, not this song
Not this red light, that takes too long

Not this body, not this mind
Not these objects I'll leave behind
Not these visions, not these dreams
Or obsessions
So it seems

Is it you?

Let me ask you a question about your physical body... Is it you?

And as you begin to look, as you begin to listen, you will find that your practice arrives unannounced at your front door, again and again. Sometimes daily. Sometimes hourly. And sometimes it will seem as though moment to moment someone is calling you on the phone, banging on your door, yelling at your window, inviting you to come out and engage with conflict.

Hiding in your house doesn't do much good. It doesn't work. Because long after the banging stops, the conflict rages on in your head. How you were cheated. Taken advantage of. How you'll never let them screw you over again. This is the confusion... how to engage and accept graciously and lovingly without ... without what? Being a chump?

There is no confusion when looking through the lens of the heart. All is seen for what it truly is; an organic unfolding. Nothing more. Nothing less. It is only the ego that would have you believe that someone was long ago plotting to get the best of you; that they planned to take you down and make you look bad, suffer, and experience pain. It is only the ego that would tell you to hold on to your stoic silence... punish those who have hurt you by withholding love and acceptance from them. Make them regret their decisions and wish they could take it back. Don't worry; they do. And when they stand their ground and insist they would do the same thing again, it is with shielded heart. What they believe is a 'protected' heart, in order to avoid having the heart 'broken' yet again.

The heart they refer to is actually the ego. The ego is telling a tale of a broken heart. Yet the heart can never be broken; it's much too deep and wide for that. It shines unaffected, unintruded upon... unstained in all moments, no matter how loud the cries of the ego. The ego calls itself heart, grabbing at yet another of countless masks designed to control, manipulate, and distract you from pointing your attention back to your true identity as the True Heart.

The apology that comes slowly, grudgingly... the one that feels like a knife in the gut... the one that is followed up with feelings of resentment when the apology is not returned... that is the one that takes a tiny little chip off of the ego... It is the ego that digs in its heels and crosses its arms angrily... "Why should I be the one to apologize first every single time?" These are the postures of the ego, that would have you believe that you are entitled to protection from a certain set of rules; a set of rules that all others should follow in order to remain in your (the ego's) good standing. A set of rules, by the way, that changes on a moment-to-moment basis, depending upon the mood of the ego... a set of rules that no human, including yourself, could ever hope to follow successfully.

The Heart sets forth no rules. There are no regulations. There is no handbook. None is needed. For the Heart simply loves. Accepts. Appreciates. Feels. Extends forth into the world. Creates environments where others may accept and appreciate, as well. Demonstrates its natural state of being to others in every given moment, without hesitation. Unceasingly. The Heart has no desire, for it sees deeply into every situation and understands that all is unfolding perfectly, flawlessly, in each moment. There is nothing lacking, therefore there is nothing to be gained. And nothing ever to be lost. For even the perceived suffering caused by the stubborn, self-absorbed nature of the ego, once revealed in all its small, simple feebleness in the bright light of day falls away. Perceived wounds are healed, and are then revealed to be imaginary in the first place. Lives perceived to be ruined are seen in a larger context and revealed to be the classroom / playground / expression of perfection that they always were.

There is no act of generosity too grand for the Heart. The challenge is not felt by the heart; it is perceived by the ego. All challenges toward generosity, all resistance or hesitation toward forgiveness and understanding, are issued forth by the ego. When viewing the world through the lens of the Heart, generosity becomes effortless and joyful. "Why would I even consider hesitating to give to my brother when it makes me so happy? When there is nothing for me to lose in the giving, and everything to gain in my brother's smile?"

There is no act of charity too grand for the Heart... "charity" in the most selfless meaning of the word, not the 'I'm giving to you; now you owe me respect' sense. Rather, in the 'Nothing I hold is mine; let me give it all away that you may flourish and thrive; that you may recognize and realize that nothing you hold is yours either; that there is nothing to be lost or gained, ever...' sense. Recognizing this in the very core of your true being, therefore you are free of worry, pain and suffering... free to demonstrate your freedom to the next person, that they may remember.

This entire cycle is nothing more than the cycle of remembering. Communicating. Returning back to the one you always were. Always are. Always will be.

Let go of those old photographs of yourself as a child. Let go of those pictures of 'the good old days'... Let go of your attachment to your favorite books, letters, musical instruments... Let go of your need to revisit old journals and to retell the ego's stories of who you were, who you are, and who you will be. Every time you open that big, heavy box of photos and begin to dig through them... every photo you take out and look at... each one of those triggers a storyline.

"Oh, that's from 1972... or 1992... when we lived here... I remember this was happening and that was happening... and I remember I felt this way and that way. I remember this person wrongly accused me, and I was victimized by the system on this particular day. I remember feeling unhappy back then. Now I feel unhappy again."

Or even more insidiously, "I remember being with this person on this particular day. We were at this location... we did these activities... we had the best time together. Now we are no longer together. I remember how happy I felt back then. Now that's gone. Now I am unhappy."

Notice any common thread? Both end up in unhappiness in the present moment, because both distract from the never ending joy of the present moment. In both cases, these photos simply trigger story lines that pull the attention away from the present moment that is unfolding and changing in infinitely new and novel ways.

What is sacrificed by letting go of attachment to the photos, the toys, the objects? More importantly, what is sacrificed by releasing attachment to identifying with any objects? The ego's ability to control and manipulate. The ego's masks of benevolence. The tyrant's sword is taken from his scabbard and revealed to be made of paper. What is lost when everything is lost? Not a thing. In fact, it is a fortunate man who loses all during his life, for in that loss lies the opportunity to recognize that nothing real has ever been lost. Loved ones appear to die, only to reveal that they were not the physical body; it was all a case of mistaken identity. New, shiny cars become old and outdated... rusted heaps of steel. Young, delightful, energetic physical bodies become old, sick, weak, and wither away. They become stricken by disease. They fall to the sword and the bullet. The sharp mind becomes dull... the healthy intellect becomes riddled with confusion and dementia. Physical prowess and sexual attractiveness fall away... hormones lose their ability to excite and fertility passes on.

Belief systems are released, or rather, torn from the ego's grasp. Thought structures are relegated to the garbage can. In that last gasp, everything the ego has ever known, has ever identified with, is ripped away. The ego hates this and resists, kicking and screaming, pulling out all the stops and using everything in its bag of tricks in an attempt to argue with Reality, to bargain with the Heart.

All these the ego perceives to be losses of sorts... loss of power, loss of beauty, loss of identity.

Dignity itself appears to be lost again and again in the realm of human existence... yet dignity is the natural state of everything in Reality... upon the Inner Throne of the Heart. And each of these perceived aspects of identity, as it falls away, leaves a blank space... a hole... a window through which the bright, warm glow of true identity shines.

The reminder here is that there is no need for all the drama. No need for all the fuss. This attachment to perceived identity can be handed over freely, during the physical body's lifetime. All that is required is the willingness to increase your tolerance for ambiguity; to let go of your perceived need of any sort of guarantee on your plane of existence. The only guarantee you need is the very one you are granted: that the physical existence is temporary, and therefore unreal. Hand over every piece of ammunition that the ego has you carrying around. All aspects of identity that you find yourself clinging to, give them away to the next person you meet on the street. Surrender them to the trees. The birds in the sky. The river. The clouds. The mountains. The grains of sand on the beach. Toss them into the ocean, again and again.

Every time you happen to glance into a mirror while washing your hands in a truck stop restroom, remind yourself that those eyes are not you; those teeth are not you. That hair is not you. That skin is not you. Those muscles are not you. The cup of coffee you are drinking is not you. The vehicle you are driving reflects nothing of your true self. The shoes on your feet. The music you listen to. The dwelling you live in. The activities you engage in. None of these reflects any aspect of your True Identity.

Surrender each of these, over and over. Lay them gently aside, even as you delight in them. Lovingly thank them for serving you in reaching this moment of surrender. Only through surrender is your true home upon the Inner Throne of the Heart revealed.

Transitory

True power is only gained to the extent that earthly concepts of power are surrendered.

Your experience of life is actually a set of lessons. You are literally living a curriculum. Of your own design, no less. No matter how confusing it may seem at times, you are an unfolding of a set of lessons.

Playing the victim role is one method of hiding from yourself the fact that you are the curriculum design master, the architect of this experience you call your life. By claiming victimhood status, you pretend to be the unwitting target of a cruel world of outsiders who attack you or bump into you without being aware of your presence. In either case, you have presented an image of yourself as powerless and benign.

Only when you begin to take responsibility for that which you do not see can you gain greater awareness of the big picture. Only when you embrace the truth that there is no one other than yourself, wearing infinitely many masks, can you begin to relax and truly see life for what it is.

The true blessings of this life stream are beginning to come into focus now. When I was a child, my natural impulse was to identify with my surroundings; with individuals, locations, and objects. My favorite toy. My parents. The house I lived in. My friends. By moving to different states, to different towns, to different schools, the pattern was interrupted. The ability to put down deep roots and call any one location 'home' was prevented, over and over. This was continued throughout college and also into adulthood, through being in the Navy, getting divorced, and 'owning' a number of different vehicles. Moving to Japan and living there for a year, after struggling to live in Austin for a number of years, was another piece of this curriculum. Selling and giving away almost all possessions before moving to Japan deepened the lesson still further, as I experienced, over and over, the fact that all things must pass.

Now the lessons begin to bear real fruit as you begin to realize that nothing of your experience can ever be held in any form without eventually dissolving back into its natural pure state: illusion. You've experienced vacations, both those you've judged to be pleasant, and unpleasant. Either way, they have already been relegated to the status of 'memory'. And no amount of photographs, digital or hard copies, can ever do anything other than recreate a particular arrangement of thought patterns that you interpret however you will; as joy, sadness, or even a mix of conflicting ideas, thoughts and beliefs.

This is due to the transitory nature of existence; the guaranteed return of all things to their original state. Nothing you see is actually what it is. This, of course, includes your very being. You look in the mirror and see a physical body and assume that it is you. How limiting this belief is! Like a volcano believing it is a sand castle on a beach. Once you embrace your true identity, which is done by turning away from earthly concepts of identity, you will begin to experience true power. True power is only gained to the extent that earthly concepts of power are surrendered. Power over others. Power over situations. Power to control events and outcomes. These are the ideas that must be surrendered, abandoned, and left behind in order to get in touch with your innate power of transcendence.

How sad you felt when you got divorced. How you experienced pain and suffering and fear to the depths of your very soul when you were finally 'on your own' for the first time. How unprepared you felt as you navigated adulthood, reaching out for help wherever you could find it. Now that you've reached a place of acceptance and understanding of the purpose behind your life's curriculum, you look around and begin to recognize others on similar paths, struggling with similar issues, yearning to step into power and not knowing how to resolve the discomfort of surrendering familiar concepts of identity. Even when they're painful and appear to be self-destructive, still they remain familiar and therefore comfortable.

The story you are living has the potential to demonstrate the value of stepping out of your comfort zone; of abandoning old ideas of identity and reinventing yourself often. Every time you reinvent yourself with a new job, a new practice, a new way of being in the world, you remind others that identity on your plane has always been fluid. It was never set in stone, no matter who you are or what you do. No matter how your body looks. No matter what conditions you experience or do not experience. True identity has always been constant; since before the manifestation of your physical body, and after its dissolution. True identity is not limited by income, job title, body size and shape, marriage contract, bank account, fame, fortune, political connections... or any of that. True identity contains all of that; has room for every detail you can dream up, for the intellect, small mind, or ego resides as an illusion within the timelessness of Truth, or the Heart.

Dismissing every interaction as illusion is one aspect of walking the path of touching this truth. Treating every being with love and compassion is another aspect of this journey. These two aspects must be balanced. Practicing one without the other will continue to lead toward imbalance. Dismissing all as illusion without compassion for self or perceived others leads away from gratitude and toward a belief that life is meaningless. This path eventually leads, as do all paths, back to the Heart. Having compassion for self and perceived others while getting lost in the story and taking it all as fact leads toward fear of loss. This path also leads back toward the Heart, as do all paths. The balance between embracing all while simultaneously blessing and releasing all is the mark of a teacher or big brother or sister on the path.

Know always that it is impossible to fail. It is impossible to lose one's way on the path toward the Heart, for all perceived paths to the Heart actually already and always exist within the Heart. Here is yet another instance where language fails to grasp or reflect the truth of the matter, yet does help in pointing the way. Pointing the way toward the fact that all intellectualization is folly, and will eventually have to be surrendered. Yes, the intellect can be used as a wonderful tool to help humanity, as well as an instrument of torture and murder of physical bodies and minds. On the level of perception that accepts the physical body as the measure of life and death, there is unspeakable pain, beauty, suffering, joy, tragedy, and miracle. Zooming out and embracing that the physical body is a manifestation of life but not in any way a measurement of the presence or absence of life, it becomes apparent that intellectualization is not necessary for life to exist. The stories fabricated by the intellect can be set aside and life continues on. In fact, the ego arises and dissolves back into the ocean of Life, every time the physical body goes to sleep. The ocean of Life is untouched by these apparent comings and goings.

Doing things without regard for what the ego might 'say' about them is one method of bypassing the intellect and the ego. Dancing for no apparent reason. Bringing joy to difficult situations. Laughing often. Creating art. Letting your very presence be the gift you give by showing to others what you perceive to be your flaws... Your innocence, your sense of wonder, your vulnerability. These are the very things that those around you are aching to see, and when they witness it in you, they are better able to recognize those same jewels within themselves.

Do not fear that you will ever run out of gold, or jewels of the Heart, by giving it away to others. It is meant to flow through you, and when the physical body you currently experience has run its course and is laid gently aside to reincorporate back into Reality, the gold and jewels you have shared with others will be revealed to be none other than yourself.

You are the One

Imbalances in your dimension are apparent to those who look through the lens of the heart. When your own fears drop away, it is easy to see how unnecessary are the fears and doubts held by others. They hang on for dear life to the very illusion that life is finite. Can you see the absurdity?

Yet they are not to blame. There is no blame, for love is not about blame. Love is not about wrongdoing, or back stabbing, or one-upping any other person, corporation, or entity. Love transcends all. All leadership that does not focus on the well-being of all is ego-based. This is obvious. And yet even those leaders are not to blame, for when removed from their official posts, when taken from behind their podiums and their microphones and tele-prompters, they are simple men and women. They look through the lens of the ego out of habit, and so they see a world in need of domination, coercion, and fear.

You may feel tempted to believe that leadership from the heart only leads to tragedy; MLK, JFK, Ghandi... and so many other spiritual leaders on your planet have, when seen through the lens of the ego, been attacked and killed for their beliefs. And yet look at the consciousness that has been moved through their efforts. Notice how the times have changed. Notice what is different. What is different is that you are waking up. You, Dear Reader. You are remembering your own true self as nothing less than as aspect of the Divine, manifested.

Rest assured that none of those leaders were killed in Reality. And none of those killers are any more evil than anyone else, in Reality. For in Reality, good and evil vanish. All your ideas of wrong and right are laid aside like a child's training wheels... as Hafiz says. It is understandable that such words read through the lens of the ego may seem blasphemous; an affront to all who have suffered on your planet. An insult, deserving of wrath and punishment.

Where, I wonder, does wrath find its home in the Heart? Ponder this. Consider deeply. All this talk of the Heart, of Love, of the Divine... Where at all have you read in these words of punishment, sacrifice, pain, and suffering as being part of the deal? There is no place for these words in the Field of the Heart, for in the Heart these concepts are meaningless. They presuppose an "other", to be rightly or justly vilified and punished. They assume that 'correct' and 'incorrect' exist; that right vs. wrong is a valid concept in the Heart. Yet the Heart transcends all concepts; anything conceptual falls to the ground empty of meaning, like an old bed sheet blown off the clothesline on a windy summer day.

Where punishment or reward are seen as possible, you are not seeing Reality. Sink into the Heart. Acknowledge your rightful place beyond reason or rhyme. Beyond time and space. Beyond the limited scope of human understanding and intellectual pursuit. Some of your most renowned spiritual leaders had little or no formal education. Conversely, some of those in power whom you may judge to be lacking moral direction hold highly-respected degrees and diplomas.

In this moment, begin to practice looking beyond the surface of things. See more deeply into your neighbor's pain. See beyond his riches, his house, his vacations, his apparent life of leisure. One guarantee you can count on: he is on his spiritual journey no less than you are. And if you consider yourself to be of simple means, perhaps you can find within yourself an added measure of compassion for the one you consider to have an easy, comfortable life, for that person will be faced with releasing attachment to comfort when the time comes to release the physical body.

On a more mundane or worldly note, it is important to understand that turning away from the ego does not mean handing over your love, power, money, attention, or assets to another person. Nowhere here are you receiving guidance to follow any other human being on your spiritual path. This is no place for handing over your responsibility and your power; your freedom of choice. Anyone who urges you to follow their lead, or to give your assets to them in exchange for a guarantee of any sort of comfort is seeing through the lens of the ego, attempting to manipulate and gain from your resistance to trust yourself.

You are the one you have been waiting for. You are the one who holds the key to your spiritual growth. You are the one who has everything to gain by recognizing and remembering Reality: and Reality is that you never were at risk of losing or gaining anything true, for you are already the Ultimate Source of Love and Freedom. You are already everything you've hoped and dreamed you could be. You are already successful beyond your wildest dreams, in much the way that the song sparrow is successful at spreading his wings and taking flight. In other words, it's simply the song sparrow's nature to take flight. It's simply your true nature to exist as the very field of Reality.

Again: it is simply the ego that would have you believe you are a human being, experiencing a temporary life to be 'figured out' with the intellect, through conceptual maneuverings and philosophical exercises. It is only the ego that would have you believe that you have any choice in the matter, and that somehow it is possible to make the 'wrong' choices in life and wind up in misery, losing everything you have been striving for. The ego loves this sort of thing-- it relishes every moment that you buy into these lies, for each moment that you are busy trying to 'figure out' the best investments for retirement, the best automobile to buy, the best food to eat, the best friends to visit... etc., is another moment that you are distracted from remembering your true nature; your true identity.

Only when you sit back, relax, and accept your own inner brilliance does the threatening face of the world give way to the inner joy and peace that is your birthright. Only in this place, seeing through the lens of the Heart, do all of the empty promises of the ego become unveiled... revealed for their true nature as empty vapor. A mirage in the desert. A mirage of a desert, when actually you are in paradise at all times.

There is no other to fear. There is no other to hate. There is no other to chase, capture, idolize, or envy. There is no other to become friends with. There is no other to admonish, or punish. There is no other to teach. There is no other from whom you need to learn just one more spiritual lesson before you are ready to serve in your true home upon the Inner Throne of the Heart. There is no other to convince, or from whom you need to receive permission before revealing your true glory to the world. There is no other in which to confide your deepest darkest fears. There is no other to withhold love from you. There is no other to congratulate. There is no other to court, to romance, or to sleep with. There is no other to avoid or to get away from. There is no other to fear.

There is no other. There is only Love. And you are It.

Flame that never flickers

Don't worry too much about outcomes. That's what we have to share with you today. The outcomes aren't actually so important. We know that the intellect or 'small mind' is very interested in outcomes, and bases happiness and sadness and all kinds of things, including ideas of success, upon outcomes.

But truly, the journey is the journey. No matter where you end up, you will arrive home. And in terms of the physical body, it's easy to see where that will end up. As you read today, there is a 100% chance your body will die. So that outcome is taken care of. You may remove it from your list of 'unknowns' to worry about. Ha ha ha.

Joyfully, the body is not you. And you are not it. You also, as we have explored, are not the mind. Not the intellect. The intellect is like a wonderfully sharp sword that hangs at your side. It can be used to achieve many goals. And you may even look deeply into the blade and see your own reflection. But the sword is not you. It is simply a tool for you to use. In this day and age, with so much modern technology being designed to reflect the ego back to itself for validation (facebook, websites, web technology in general), it is easy to get caught up in the fray and forget that you are not the sword.

It's easy to fall into the misperception that what you see is true; that the blinking lights and the sounds of the external world are where 'you' lives, and that 'you' is defined by the shape and size of your physical body, in conjunction with your personality.

Yet, as real as it may seem, it truly is nothing more than misperception. And claims that deeper introspection is simply religious thought is a loophole used by the ego to bypass examination of its own empty nature. Of COURSE the intellect/small mind/ego would have you look away... look in ANY other direction besides inward. For inward is where you'll discover spacious freedom.... And joy that is not based or grounded in circumstance.

True joy is distinct from fun. Fun is distraction. Fun is grounded in circumstance. While we may disagree about what constitutes fun, since it is so subjective, fun is tied to earthly experience. True joy is not. True joy is reconnection... or, rather, the re-awakened awareness that the connection is always there--our connection to the Divine. True joy is one blink of an eye away, and it's a choice. Can I let go of my attachment to outward appearances and my need to judge circumstances? Can I simply let things be what they are, without chewing on them too much and coming up with a label for them?

Can you accept all of it with gratitude? That is the moment when spiritual maturity begins to shine. The master understands this and practices it. She remembers, during the good times, and during the bad times. And she stands fully present in awareness, simply letting existence flow through her. She is truly in the present moment. This is what it means to be aware, awake... enlightened. Enlightenment is not some rare condition that can only be experienced by those who wear saffron robes and shave their heads, sitting in one place for years, carrying a bowl, begging in the streets.

No. Enlightenment, true enlightenment, is simply the awareness of who and what we are. That distance, while seeming insurmountable at times, can be spanned in one heartbeat. The speed of thought, the speed of light, the speed of love--that is how quickly we can step into true enlightenment when we choose to do so.

And it is a choice. A choice to let go of one way of perceiving and embracing a wider view. A view that, by definition, blasts through the shiny, sexy images magnified by glamour. And the ego loves these, by the way. Shiny earrings, sensuality, sexual attraction... all of these things stimulate the ego via the device of glamour. Yet when the cold, hard light of day hits the cement, lighting up the morning sidewalk, the glamour of the night is revealed to be grotesque... an empty shell of beauty. Garish and clumsy... embarrassing.

True joy and beauty continue to radiate in the morning light, when glamour is stripped away, thrown back like heavy drapes that have blocked out all light. During the ego's eager search for distraction, glamour takes over in countless ways... cars, sex, real estate... money... all of the things that are impermanent and empty, since they have a beginning, middle, and an end. They reflect the transitory nature of existence.

True joy is not transitory. It weathers the storm. It rides out all of the ups and downs in life, burning quietly, like a bottomless candle that never flickers, no matter how strong the wind may blow. This flame is your being. This flame is Love. Casting light into the shadows, setting aflame all the promises based in lies. This flame of Love, of truth, is what always finally smashes lies, destroys misperception, and delivers truth. Every time.

CHAPTER SEVEN
Story

The story of your life takes place in the present moment. The story you hold onto, about your past and your identity, is all false. It's all a mistake. Assuming yourself to be a certain way, whatever that way may be, is acceptance of a mirage for fact.

In the present moment, you are given the opportunity to reinvent yourself endlessly. Holding on to old stories, grudges, and emotional charges is simply the act of making the unconscious choice to reinvent yourself as the same thing over and over again. Stagnation. It's choosing to wear the same, outgrown Halloween costume over and over, year after year, regardless of the fact that the story that 'fit' you at age 5 no longer fits at age 47. Which costume are you wearing? Lone Ranger? Gene Simmons? Victim of circumstances?

Again, the image of the fountain serves well here. The water shoots up from the fountain, straight up into the air. It reaches its height and then the column of water collapses upon itself, even as the new water is propelled upward through it. To stare at this image is to see a representation of the ever-changing, never-gonna-be-the-same-again nature of the present moment. It's always changing. And while you claim to understand this very simple and basic truth, still you find yourself bothered by what you call "change". As if change were somehow not taking place in each and every moment. As if change somehow did not characterize the very fundamental nature of life.

Boredom is the same; nothing more than failing to acknowledge the dazzling brilliance of life dancing before you in each 'mundane' moment... the cream dissolving in your coffee... the blinking turn signal of the vehicle in front of you in traffic... the used paper cup lying on the sidewalk. A dog shitting on a tree. Your tax bill arriving in the mail. The ceiling of the dentist's office. None of it is any more or less magical than the other.

Selective focus on that which props up your belief that you are the physical body and the mental states you experience -- this is the error. An error in thinking. And error in judgment. To correct the error, suspend judgment. All judgment. To correct the error, pay no mind to the thoughts that race across your internal radar screen. Let them pass without believing them. All of the critiques. All of the worries. All of the fears. When you heard the words, "don't worry, be happy," you assumed that doing so would be reckless and foolish.

"Only fools walk around with a smile on their faces. Only idiots fail to plan for the future and pay close attention to ants navigating the cracks in the sidewalk. Wise men are those who are planning. Plotting. Scheming. Working hard to get ahead. Working smarter to get farther and live better. Wise men are those who are identifying the angles and working them with all of their might to get a better deal... to get a better pension... a better retirement plan... a better home."

This is the error. The downfall of your life. Because as the present moment unfolds, you fail to recognize yourself sitting in a metal folding chair, hands grasping the tied ends of the blindfold covering your eyes. And then, at that last breath, when you finally realize what life is, what you are, and what you are not, your experience unfolds into a new one, and the vehicles of learning-- the body and mind, fall away. And all that's left is truth.

No reason to suffer

New beginnings... Don't spend your time and energy mourning your perceived past... instead, focus on the new beginning that occurs in each and every moment. To weep over the past is to spend your precious energy wishing for part of your dream to be different from the way you have dreamt it. God weeping on God's shoulder, asking God to change God for the sake of God. Yes, you see the dilemma here, right? It's meaningless.

There is no reason for you to suffer. It is only misperception that causes suffering... and lack of acceptance of perfection... of a bigger picture that is certainly unfolding perfectly in each moment. Only the limited scope of your perception on your plane of existence leads you to believe that anything at all could possibly be flawed... that anything at all could possibly need fixing, or adjustment. Your striving, borne of love for life, is why you are here. Live your perceived life to the fullest, squeezing out all the juice you can. And release attachment to outcome, for all of the attempts in the world that you could ever make to control outcomes is as fruitless.

There is also no reason to think that anyone else truly suffers. Not in reality. Certainly in your 3d world, where everything feels, sounds, tastes and smells realer than real, there appears to be suffering. And great tragedies occur, according to your perception, every hour of every day. What better exercise in compassion could there be for your heart. And what better exercise in setting aside the ego, wresting it from its place behind the steering wheel, where you believe he sits. He never actually sits there, but this is the shadow play that you invent and then believe and then perceive.

Heart is the baby puppy that romps around on the floor, daring you, challenging you, tail wagging, feinting left and then dodging to the right. Attacking with a gentle nip at your nose, then retreating hastily. Stopping on a dime, turning and checking to see where you've gone. Then rolling over on its back, nestling up close to you to feel your warmth. That is heart in action. Love in motion. Pure, simple, elegant, effortless, genuine, unadulterated love. Wanting nothing more than to simply express and to be.

In Reality with a capital 'R', there is no problem here. No injustice. No pain. No suffering. But these illusions, we need them in order to do our work... to do our play... to have something to push against, and something to reflect us back to ourselves. There is no need to fear... engage fully in your duties, give it all you've got and love with reckless abandon. You are guaranteed to succeed, no matter what, so nothing is at risk if you simply love with all your heart, every day and every hour and every minute of the present moment that you possibly can.

Give all you have to give... be as vulnerable and strong and passionate and caring and loving as you can be... Set the bar high. Be the example you wish you had all those years ago. Be the one who offers what you wish you would have been offered in the past. Be the one to give a gentle smile of understanding when someone feels like they are suffering... like they are confused and simply cannot go on another minute. And when that someone is an individual who reminds you of aspects of yourself that you prefer not to look at, take them under your wing and into your heart with gentle clarity and offer them the special care and attention that you would save for your closest friend.

Give them what no one else could give. Let them see your light and love and wisdom and understanding and passion and acceptance. Accept them precisely as they are in this moment, no matter how gruesome or grotesque it may seem. Remember, things are not what they seem. Not by a long shot. Loving others is loving yourself. No matter how strange or foreign or stupid or senseless it may seem.

Love transcends logic. As such, it makes perfect sense.

The 'good old days'
The ego will do anything it can to make its story look and feel more real. Anything. This could include urging you to search for your past through contacting people you used to know, or buying objects you used to own and appreciate. Either way, whether successful or not in reaching these goals, one thing becomes clear: nothing satisfies.

Another way the ego works to present itself as real is to distract you, in any way it can, from the present moment. When you are busy remembering or fantasizing or romanticizing or dreaming about how things used to be ('back in the good old days'), you are no longer present to the heart. The ego has thrown out the bait and you've grabbed it. The question is, how long will you chomp down on that hook, being dragged through rough waters and much self-imposed suffering, before you relax and let go, coming back to rich, eternal gold of the present moment?

Shiny, spangley vest

Quick ego check-in... Sometimes I pull up the keyboard and the laptop, and I have to tell you, I have no clue what is about to happen. And sometimes as I do this, I cannot believe that there are already 244 pages happening. And I wonder to myself, what in the hell am I going to write about today? Early this morning, there were magical ideas floating around in my head... just an inch away from becoming reality. And now, all I want to do is go lie down and sleep.

All you need to do is put your fingers on the keyboard and let them move, freely. All you need to do is quiet down. This is not your job, to write. Your job is to get out of the way and correct typos when you see them happen on the screen. Other than that, you are off the hook, my dear sir. No demands to create anything magical or special. No obligation to show up in any certain way, wearing any sort of shiny, spangled vest or other special article of clothing. You're free to leave the room, actually.

The true work here is for you to get out of the way. Because we definitely have things to say, and your job is to help them come through. Which, unfortunately for you, means to minimize your involvement. Don't worry, though. We're only discussing your downfall. And how you're built out of fog, smoke, and dreams. That's all we're doing; pointing the way to reality and away from the suffering you always, always cause. We have a feeling you'll be delighted to read the book, until you do.

Because we see how persistent you are. Even when our man here is stacking a cord of firewood in silence, just working away at his own pace, you've got a way of commandeering the mic and going on and on with your announcements and your play-by-play of old, past events and -- even more interesting and even less helpful -- events that have never actually even happened. You know the ones we mean; the 'what if' events. "If THIS ever happened, here's what I would say... I would say this and this and that... and THEY would be sorry..." Yeah. Not really very helpful for anyone involved.

Most of us recognize your silliness the moment it begins. But our man here... well, he's still kind of slow. Limited spiritual perception due to the confines of his currently perceived plane of existence and all. But that's okay. He seems to be waking up, little by little. Definitely taking the long way home, but there's never any harm in that. Just makes the whole ride more interesting and hopefully the lessons stick a little better. At least until next time, right?

Yes, dear ego... you're quite a mess. Seriously. First you say you want one thing. And you fight tooth and nail to get it. All the while, you fantasize about it pretty single-mindedly. Then, one day, you get exactly what you've been asking for. And then what happens? Five minutes later, you're bored, and you want something else. Someone else. Someone ELSE's someone else. Naturally. And all the pain and suffering that has befallen you, an innocent guy just walking down the street, suddenly, somehow, your latest desires just so happen to line up with creating that precise suffering for others. And yet you still don't see how you are responsible for any of it.

You make your demands, and then they change. No one can possibly ever keep you satisfied, or even approach that goal, for what you want is always changing, moment to moment. And you deny everything, always ready with a reason, an excuse, some sort of explanation that is supposed to clear everything right up. But around you, always, there is confusion. Chaos. Suffering. Never any sort of calm presence. Never any sort of peace, harmony, or solitude. Never a calm, gentle sigh of satisfaction. Never a call for gratitude from your lips.

Why is this?

Perhaps it's because gratitude would presuppose the capacity to take stock of your situation in a true sense; to actually recognize reality and your connection to it. It would require you to understand and accept the sacrifices and gifts of others that you receive on a daily basis; the benefits you reap from the work and efforts of others. But then again, this is the work of the Heart. The Heart is the realm of gratitude, love, compassion, acceptance, forgiveness, and reward.

Your realm, the realm of the small mind, is the realm of envy, jealousy, anger, greed, lust, revenge, desire, sadness, and misery. Emptiness is the code word that allows your door to open, promising all sorts of satisfaction and joy and freedom and fun, only to deliver empty promises, unfulfilled, again and again. Your realm is the home of the vacant lot, overgrown with weeds, cracked pavement, broken bottles... cracked cinder blocks and undelivered dreams.

I invite you here to my home now. Come on in. The gates of freedom are wide open for you... please join us here in the halls of majesty, come sit here upon the Inner Throne of the Heart. Here there is only love and understanding and acceptance for you. Here there is support and celebration for your goodness. Here is where all of your defenses can be finally laid to rest. Here you can finally lay aside your armor and relax...

Let us serve you with kindness and gentleness. Here there is food and wine for you. Here there is friendship and a gentle ear, ready to hear of your tales. Here is where you can release all of your sadness, anger, frustration, and fear, and let your true self be seen. For whoever you are, and however you may appear, we accept you completely and fully, and want only to see your face revealed from behind the scarves and veils that keep you hidden.

Here... let us help you remove those scarves and veils. Let us assist you in removing all of these bandages in which you are wrapped like some kind of mummy... And as we unwind and unwind, removing more and more of the bandages and scarves, rare and precious veils shot through with gold and studded with jade, rubies, emeralds and diamonds... as we remove the very last piece of rich clothing, we find...

...nothing.

Fear of rejection

Sometimes the answer is silence. Sometimes just getting quiet is the answer when things seem to be in your way. And sometimes the best thing you can do is to stop, reassess, and go wash the dishes. In some moments, that is the best way to get what you want and what you need.

Fear of rejection. In the ego's world, where survival of the physical body is so highly valued, it appears possible for you to be included or excluded from anyone or anything. Like all other things viewed through the lens of the ego, this perception is a distortion of the truth. All other faces that you see are simply facets of your true self. This is not stated in an effort to be poetic, but rather as clear and blunt as possible within the limitations of language and human perception. It is literally impossible for you to be rejected, for everywhere you go and everywhere you leave is You; is the Heart. Wherever you end up is still within the bounds of the Heart. This is because all of existence that you perceive lies within the bounds of the Heart, or the teacup of the Divine.

There is nowhere you can go where you are not surrounded and embraced by your true self. Love is the air you breathe; the food you eat. You are swimming in the Divine at all times. It is only through the lens of the ego, the intellect, the small mind that it is possible for you to perceive yourself as having been rejected. And it is only through the ego lens that you are able to reject anyone else.

Of course, when so many people are viewing the world through the lens of the ego, it can be easy to get caught up in those perceptions of rejection. Memories of perceived rejection from anyone are commonly used to reinforce habitual thought patterns that become life stories. And the ego delights in this, for whatever story you tell, whether hero, victim, or invisible man, truly is of no consequence as long as you are distracted by the telling and retelling of your story. This distraction, this retelling, is the very thing that props up the ego and makes it appear to be real in your mind. It's the very thing that allows you to misidentify with the ego and to believe that you are it and it is you.

Every retelling of 'your' story digs the hole a little deeper, until you are surrounded by walls of dirt and clay... surrounded by nothing but story. However, you can climb out at any moment. All you have to do is remember not to take anything personally. If you believe you have been rejected by anyone, even if by all accounts you feel you have every reason to believe that you have been, simply keep in mind that nothing is personal. The one you perceive to have rejected you is looking through the lens of the ego when they say, "I don't want to be near you," or "You are not welcome here; please leave." These words can feel as if they have the power to crush your very soul... but only when viewed through the lens of the ego.

Through the lens of the Heart, they are seen to be empty. On the level of human manifestation, these words, feelings, and behaviors of so-called rejection actually reflect nothing of you, but rather offer information about where the other person is on their journey. Zooming out and taking the wider view, it is impossible for anything to truly be personal, for there is no person. There is only Love. You are the one from whom you are perceiving rejection. There are multiple errors that cause you to perceive rejection and to associate sadness, anger, fear, and pain with it. Foremost among them is the misperception that you are the physical body; that it is what and who you are. That you exist separately from other human beings, and therefore can attack and be attacked; that you have the ability to welcome or reject some 'other' that exists apart from yourself.

The sadness associated with rejection results from the unfulfilled desire to reconnect; to feel plugged-in, embraced, and enfolded into the larger group. To be included; to merge with the collective. To become whole. The very presence of this desire reveals the misperception that you are somehow disconnected, unplugged, and not embraced by the larger group. That you are separate and distinct from love; that you are unwhole, splintered off from what you should be connected to.

The truth is that you are already whole, as you are, for you are All. Not the 'you' that is perceived through the lens of the ego, walking, talking, sitting, standing, sleeping, eating, and going shopping. Rather, the You that is truly you: The Divine. This includes all. For exclusion is meaningless and therefore impossible.

It may seem challenging to wrap your brain around these concepts. This is to be expected, for they are not of the mind, and therefore cannot be contained within or grasped by the mind. They are not conceptual or rational, which is why they may seem irrational: they are. This does not mean, however, that they are not truth. For what you believe about truth and untruth is actually the complete opposite of Reality.

Turn your understanding of Reality on its head and you will move in the direction of Truth-- that which you can conceptualize is false by definition, for Reality is not conceptual. That which is beyond intellectual, rational understanding is Truth.

This is why, again and again, we offer the invitation to drop into the Heart and view the world and all creation through that lens. For it bypasses the intellect entirely and puts you in direct contact with Reality, without effort and without any sort of time restraints. There is nowhere for you to 'go', and nothing for you to 'do'. Simply shifting your attention is enough. For this will shift your perception wildly.

Through the lens of the heart you will see that there is only One, and it is Love, and you are That. There is no other. There is no 'other'. There is no Other.

Perceiving the Three Levels of Being

Tell me a story. Tell me a story I haven't heard yet. Tell me a story about a small chunk of delicious, smoked cheddar cheese to go with that glass of wine. Tell me a story about the color purple, and how it smells, and how it feels as you hold it in your mouth. Tell me a story about sadness and pain and struggles and death and defeat and anger and madness and inspiration and the Phoenix rising out of the ashes. Tell me a story about record collections and time machines and poetry and stream of consciousness paintings. Tell me a story about girlfriends and fantasies and sex and desire and surrender and hope and ashes.

Tell me a story about rivers and ex-lovers and loss and would-be step children. Tell me a story about step fathers and baseball gloves and cowboy hats and go-carts and unmet agreements. Tell me a story about submarines and aircraft carriers. Tell me a story about palm trees and coconuts in the front yard. Tell me a story about photographs and garbage dumpsters... favorite tshirts and love affairs and bachelor pads and one-night stands. Tell me a story about love.

Tell me a story.

One quality common to all Instruments of Peace is the ability to truly accept and receive love from everyone, at all times. It is clear perception that allows the Instrument of Peace to perceive love where others might perceive hatred; to see and experience love where others might perceive pain and suffering. Love is at the core of all being; only the ego would have you believe that the masks of manifestation are real.

Accepting and receiving love presupposes the truth; that there is love always to be received and accepted. That love is flowing in all directions, always; it is simply our clarity of vision; the receptive power of our antenna, that determines our ability to perceive and receive it. This brings us to the importance of receptivity. For so long, receptivity has been associated with passivity, which is an inaccurate characterization. Receptivity is truly an active state of being, for it requires listening and sensing, a kind of 'reaching out' in order to assist the other person in communicating what they are trying to articulate, whether verbally or silently through other modes of communication.

The active state of receptivity is invaluable to the Instrument of Peace, who is able to utilize this function to sense the deeper, underlying love that is flowing where human modes of perception might overlook it. The ego's attempts at judging and labeling the world get in the way of effective receptivity, which requires setting aside the chatter of the self-absorbed ego in order to connect with the other person. Only by setting aside one's own ego-based needs for a moment does active receptivity become meaningful as a mode of communication.

When you are truly receptive, you see the various layers of meaning, unfolding right before you. There are three such layers. You are able to perceive:

1) **the surface message (whatever it may be), also known as 'story';**
2) **the underlying desire for the return to wholeness; and**
3) **the deeper flow of love in all directions.**

It is the ego that would have you stop with the surface message, accepting that as the final truth, and holding the other person accountable for this limited view of reality. It is the ego that would say things like, "Well, they didn't SAY they needed help, so they must not need it." The ego is only able to perceive the surface level of communication; it is a piece of equipment that has been designed to serve in that capacity. As such, it can be very effective in assisting as we actively gather information.

However, when the ego is allowed to play the role of bus driver, guiding all of our interactions, then we are misusing the ego. We are mistaking 'cruise control' to mean much more than simply a tool for setting the speed of our vehicle. When we put the ego in control, we are setting the cruise control and then climbing into the back seat to make a sandwich. The results will be less than satisfying, one hundred percent of the time.

By setting aside the ego's demands for control and relegating it to its proper place as servant to the Heart, we allow the Heart to do its own job of seeing more deeply into situations. Beneath the surface layer is always the desire for a return to wholeness. We can ask ourselves how the surface message ties into the search for wholeness. We can listen carefully, making eye contact as appropriate to indicate our genuine attention. We can set aside our other duties for a moment and truly listen with care and attention. And as we begin to make the connections between whatever is presented on the surface and the underlying search for the return to wholeness, we can make connections between the two. And using our heart as a guide, we can discern how ready the person is to accept their own brilliance reflected back to them.

As an Instrument of Peace, your job is to recognize those three levels as best you can in everyday life. For beneath the surface activity and the second, deeper level of searching for a return to wholeness always lies the foundation of life itself; the flow of love in all directions. This flow of love is the river upon which the canoe of life floats. Only the ego would have you believe that it does not exist; that only the surface activity is truth. In reality, the surface activity is more akin to 'noise'... it is the story woven by the ego in an attempt to cover up the truth. The more a person identifies with this story, the more he will believe that the physical human body IS himself. The more he will come to accept fear as his copilot and comrade in life. The more he will experience suffering at the hands of the ego, all while claiming to be the very ego itself.

Receptivity as an active state. The three levels of perception. The ego's desire to be seen as real and solid. The question: "who is saying this, the ego or the Heart?" Misperception and misidentification. These are all points to be remembered at all times, throughout each moment of every day for the Instrument of Peace to be truly effective. What is surrendered is of no value; and what is embraced is one's true identity as the Divine. There is nothing to lose and everything to gain in this endeavor, even while there is nothing to lose and nothing to gain at all as all paths lead back to the Heart.

In reality, what the ego would call a paradox and contradiction join together, standing proudly side by side.

CHAPTER EIGHT
Suspending judgment

Find your edge. Walk that edge. Supreme confidence. Supreme humility. This is the edge for you to balance on... the razor's edge for you to use as your dancehall. Leap. Fly through the air... spread your wings and dance through your heart on the edge of this blade. Take care not to lean too far in either direction... do not lose respect for others in your haughty cockiness. You know when this happens. You feel like you can just slide... like you've worked hard enough; like you deserve to be let off the hook. To take it easy. To coast. To stop putting forth the effort of digging deeper; of looking deeply into each situation in order to see beyond the situation, and into the heart of things. Into the hearts of those around you.

It is imperative that you end your habits of making judgments upon what you see with your eyes. These lessons, if not having guided you in anything else at all, have focused on one thing: what you see is not what you get. What your eyes perceive is not true-- it's not reality. No matter how certain you may be that your hunger is real, your lust is real, your anger is real, all of these are false. And when someone presents himself before you, it is very necessary for you to begin looking at him through the lens of the heart. To do otherwise is to accept that the child standing in his halloween costume is actually spiderman. If that were true, there would be an awful lot of spidermen in the world.

We implore you-- don't be fooled by what you judge to be the limitations of others. When you see an opening, a chance to one-up the person next to you... when you recognize that the person you're talking with is repeating himself... when you judge that he has limited scope of vision compared to you, BEWARE. In that moment you are stepping off the precipice and falling off the razor's edge into the oblivion of the ego. This is the vast ocean where you will be buffeted around by huge waves of egoic desire, judgment, anger, sadness, despair, and frustration. Choosing to let your awareness fall into these waters is choosing unhappiness.

To conquer your 'opponent' in these waters is to wallow around in the mud with your own ego. Why not simply choose to walk around the mud puddle all together?

Don't forget that everyone you meet is placed before you for a divine reason: to remind you and invite you back into your own Inner Throne of the Heart. There is nothing to be lost when you demonstrate patience, kindness, understanding, and support. You do not lose anything; you do not sacrifice anything of value. The frustration you feel is your own ego being sloughed off, little by little, tiny little shreds coming off, flaking away, like dead skin after a sunburn day at the beach.

It is only the ego that would have you believe that you are putting up with something intolerable; being a martyr. Only the ego says things like, "How come I have to be the one to always apologize?" "How come I have to be the one who is patient?" "Why doesn't anyone ELSE show ME the compassion, understanding, and patience that I show others?"

These statements are the hallmark of the ego, and rest on the foundation of selfishness. This is simply another technique employed by the ego to make itself heard; to get itself propped up and looking less like the cardboard cutout it actually is and more like an actual entity. (We're being generous by attributing the substance of a cardboard cutout-- in all actuality, it has not even that much substance.)

On your best days, you remember this and you serve with only service in mind. On other days, you find yourself looking for easy ways out... looking to escape any sort of commitment or responsibility. Know that in the end, since all is Love and you are Love and you are all there is, you are simply dodging and avoiding service to yourself. You, that is, Love, come knocking at your door every day, wearing a variety of masks. Every time you chase yourself away from your front door, complaining that 'someone else' has distracted you from your work, you are actually blaming you for knocking on your door and asking you to show yourself love.

And you do this in the name of wanting more time/energy/resources for... You?

Do you see the contradiction happening here? Do you see the conundrum? It's a paradox, and you are at the center. In fact, you are the only one there. These problems only occur when you misperceive yourself to be a physical body. As directed and guided in infinitely many sources, the body is simply an instrument of communication. It is not the Self. You are not the body. You are not the body. The body is not you. How many times must we say this? Yet we understand this is a process-- and you will realize the truth eventually. You will return to right, correct perception. Whether it happens during the brief perceived lifespan of the physical body or not, the truth is always waiting at your front door. And you always return home to truth. You always come back to the conclusion that life is eternal. Illusion is temporary. Delusion is acceptance of illusion for truth. All that is required to return from delusion to truth is to release into full acceptance. Stop flexing those muscles that grip the lie; relax, relax, relax.

There is nowhere to go. Nothing to do. Simply let it all flow; surrender your habitual thought processes that would have you identifying with your car, your leather jacket, your music, your shoes, your food, your house, your neighborhood, your country, your bank account, your language, your flag, your skin color, your religious beliefs, your political affiliation, your physical size and shape, your energy level, your physical prowess. These are all the props that help to hold up what you accept to be your identity.

Your job is simply to recognize and to communicate. Your job is simply to open your heart as widely as you can and let love flow in and out. Your job is to remember that you are light and love and joy; poetry in motion. By remembering this, you allow your light to shine more brightly. By shining more brightly, you remind others of their true identity. That's all there is to do here. Allow. Allow. Allow.

Why does the bird fly through the sky? Why does the dog bark? Why does the cat hunt? Why does the turtle crawl? Why does the snow fall? Why does the wind blow through the trees? Why does the sun rise in the morning? These are simply the natural order of things.

Why does the ego judge? Why does it critique and criticize and babble on endlessly? Why does it attempt to shame and blame and accuse and victimize and make dramatic proclamations and recount endlessly arguments of the past? Why does it replay tapes of sadness and pain? Why does it review movies of sorrow and confusion and anger? These are also the natural order of things-- the ego's job is simply to keep enough balls in the air to distract you from remembering who you really are. Only when you grab on to these thoughts, identify yourself with them, accept them as truth, do you become entangled in the rusty barbed wire that promised you gold, love, satisfaction, and laughter.

Your ultimate freedom is the freedom to look with a dispassionate eye; to listen with a sharp ear and turn your attention away from the noise. Turn away, over and over, again and again, from the stories you hear in your head... the stories that place you in the victim role, over and over. The stories that place you in the martyr role; the hero role; the beggar role; the tyrant role; the savior role... and all other roles the ego would have you believe are real. No role that is ever issued forth from the ego can possibly be your true identity. Discard them all. You have no use for them. Even the most saintly role of selflessness and generosity, when accepted as your true identity, becomes nothing more than a tumor that you feed with every act of generosity.

Only emptiness is your friend. Space is love. The more space you can create within yourself, the more room there is for Love, your true identity, to fill you and to extend forth into the world you perceive. This is your true identity. Remove your masks. Turn away from the hand that continues to offer them up to you, relentlessly. Learn to recognize those voices and turn away from them. Smile at them. Laugh gently. Know that they will never be who you truly are; they can never adequately capture the brilliance and magnificence of your true identity.

There is no mask that can capture your true nature; your limitless, boundless passion and grace.

Any mask you attempt to wear, or accept as true, is simply a restriction on your perception of your own divine being. Leave them on the ground, in the mud, where they belong.

Living life wrong

Beware the temptation to judge those whom you think are doing life wrong. Those you may believe to be your students are actually your teachers. Those you honor as your teachers have something to learn from you. There are no solid positions, and no correct or incorrect ways to live life. There is only life, flowing, always.

Seek out those places in your own life where you find yourself judging those around you. Explore those judgments. Find out where you judge yourself for those very behaviors or beliefs that you consider to be limiting. Recognize where you project your own fears, labels, and desires onto others.

It is the ego that would have you believe you could ever know the 'rules' for living life 'correctly'. And it is the ego that would have you believe life could ever be lived 'incorrectly'. Yet another way the ego works to keep you from focusing attention inward to the Heart is by endlessly creating lists of regulations, guidelines on how it believes others should behave and then a checklist of who is not, what their offenses are, and how they have wronged 'you'. Once you begin to listen to these so-called offenses being whispered into your ear and take these beliefs as your own, you have handed over your power, yet again, to the ego, which would drive you off a cliff in a heartbeat to prove its existence.

In all matters, turn over your judgments to the Inner Throne of the Heart. Carefully inspect these judgments, wrap them carefully in tissue paper. Put them into your backpack. Journey to your majestic palace, kneel before your own altar and gently place your entire pack upon the Inner Throne of the Heart. Bless these judgments and then turn away. Release your attachment to them. They do not belong to you; they never have. They were pushed into your arms and you mistook them for something of great value. Now that you discover they are worthless and only bring suffering, it is right to offer them up to the Heart, for the Heart will transform them back into their original nature: emptiness.

You've been told before of the bum, walking the streets, homeless. A cigar butt in his lips that he found in the gutter.

Smelling as though he has not showered in a month. Reeking of alcohol. Begging for money on the corner. This is none other than the Buddha himself, come to reflect back to you humility; here to invite you to look deeply into the mirror at your own self, lest you lose your way and find yourself entrenched in the beliefs of the ego. This is your brother. Your teacher. Your master. The worse off he appears, the better the teacher he is for you. For he is none other than yourself, appearing to be separated by time and space. All illusions.

Honor and bless yourself by honoring and blessing him. Reach out to him. Offer him what you can to bring comfort. The blessings you offer will bless yourself.

A wobbly stool
Zooming out for a wider perspective...

We see your temptation to look outward and point at those 'other' people who are 'not on a spiritual path.' To this we say you need to zoom out. Your perspective is too close; too shallow. The lens of the heart is the lens that provides the widest perspective; being judgment free, it creates space for all, wherever they may be on their path.

Who is it that is not on a spiritual path? The moment you answer, you have fallen for the ego's penchant for judging, labeling and then either pulling toward or pushing away. For any judgment you allow to come through will, by definition, be limited in scope. Reality is not limited by anything, but your perception is limited even further when you grasp on to judgments. Whatever the label, can you be sure it's true? The moment you become a leader, you are also a follower. The moment you are a follower, you are simultaneously a leader. Label yourself as a hero and you become the common man; think of yourself as a nobody and you are also the master of the universe, if you look hard enough... if you zoom out far enough.

The only way to truly accept reality is to zoom all the way out. That can only be done when judgments are laid gently aside, and when you truly accept and embrace that nothing is as it seems. Not in reality. What price is paid for setting aside judgments? Feelings of comfort based upon habitual thought patterns. Refuse to embrace those patterns and the sense of comfort you used to derive also goes out the window. To the ego, it's not worth it; it's a lousy deal. The ego will always have you believe that the promise it is about to deliver on is way better than Reality ever can be. But therein lies the problem; the ego never delivers on any of its promises; it simply keeps offering the promise of a really great time... the promise of security... the promise of 'happily ever after.'

Ego-based comfort is like a wobbly stool. Sit on it and risk landing on your back, with the wind knocked out of you. It's not solid. It's not dependable. Worst of all, there isn't even an actual stool there; only the promise of a stool. A good-looking one, at that. But nonexistent, nevertheless.

Reality does not deal in comfort. Reality does not bother with trying to soothe the ego or putting a band-aid on any sort of ego-based 'problem'. Reality, quite simply, deals in peace.

Peace and serenity are the hallmarks of a man who deals in Reality, for she knows better than to place any stock in the dream world that appears to be real; knows better than to put his weight on an imaginary chair. Knowing that the labels and habitual thought patterns of the ego are simply part of the landscape of the temporary, the finite, the time-bound, the wise man releases all attachment and watches the light show as it plays across the screen, never for a moment mistaking those images for reality.

So remember, as best you can, in each and every moment, that every single individual you encounter is on a spiritual path. Your inability to recognize it does not define them, but rather defines the limited scope of your own spiritual perception. When you truly begin to understand and embrace this truth, it will become clear to you that judgment is of the ego and not of the heart. Those people you would call your enemies are in fact yourself in Reality. You can move toward realizing and remembering this by treating them as individuals who are all on their spiritual path. There is nothing other than spiritual path! There is nothing outside the teacup of the Divine; therefore, anything you see, no matter what judgments you feel compelled to adhere, lies within the auspices of the Divine.

Know, then, that this street runs both ways. You, Dear One, are most definitely on your spiritual path. It is impossible for you to ever leave it; and there is no possible way for you to 'fail'. There is no failure. Since all is already of the Divine, how could anything possibly spoil the Divine?

The implications of this are huge. All of the negative judgments that you have about yourself are wrong. Read this again, very carefully: All of the negative judgments. ALL of them. That you hold about yourself. Are wrong. To their very core. They are based not on any sort of fact, but upon habitual thought patterns. The intellect. The ego. The 'small mind'. Remember that it is nothing other than the ego that would have you believe that there is something wrong with you. That you are somehow not whole... special in your lack of beauty or adequacy. Unique in your brokenness. The ego gets a huge payoff from getting you to believe this: it gets to hijack a large majority of your energy and attention. Keep in mind, this is time and energy that helps to prop up the ego's own view of itself as real; as actually having some sort of concrete existence. Which, of course, it does not.

The ego uses guilt, shame, self-doubt, self-pity, feelings of weakness, worthlessness, and all flavors of self-criticism as a lasso to capture your energy and attention.

Why would it want to do such a thing? Because it is unable to grasp endless, timeless, limitless, boundless love as Reality, where the concept of survival against outside threat is meaningless. Therefore, it believes that it needs to survive; that it has a chance of surviving. The only chance it has at surviving, through the lens of the ego itself, is to distract your attention away from the lens of the heart and toward ANYTHING else. Anything at all will do. Because 'anything other than the heart' means anything and everything of or pertaining to the ego; anything unreal. The longer the ego can keep you judging others as not quite as 'spiritually advanced' as yourself, finding new enemies to complain about, the longer it keeps you from abandoning it summarily and embracing Reality by viewing the world through the lens of the heart.

Are you ready to view reality through the lens of the heart? Then right this minute, embrace the fact that you are none other than the Divine Herself. All are you; reflections of you. Manifestations of you. Mirrors of reality. All are one. There is no 'other' to vilify and struggle against. All of the shadows that have haunted you your whole life have been nothing more than that; shadows on the wall, cast there by the ego holding up its hands in front of light. The wolf, the tax man, the soldier trying to kill you... the system built against you... from the perspective of the Heart, these are simply part of the curriculum of the Heart unfolding perfectly. Where there is recognition of Reality, there is no suffering. There is no death. For the physical body is not a barometer of life. Reality is life itself; immeasurable. And since there is no 'other', how could there possibly be some sort of yardstick or barometer or instrument for measuring Reality that is not Reality itself?

Go forth in to the world you perceive, knowing that you are the Divine, and so is every other creature you perceive. Bless and honor yourself and every creature as the Divine. There is no Other.

CHAPTER NINE
Two sides of the coin

Be sure to get outside and walk around a bit today. Get out into the sunshine. Stepping into the light means just that, and in more ways than one. It's important to move your body.

Guidance, please?

Yep. We're here. As always, we are within you, so it's only your turning inward to face us and direct your attention to our voice that ever 'stands in your way', so to speak. There's never any separation between us except for where you direct your attention.

Isn't it interesting how many different lights seem to come your way? Do you see all of them? Can you count them all? There have been lights coming your ways all along, in the form of so many disguised helpers, angels, saints, and prophets... And pretending for a moment that time is linear, in your own short life span, so many have come directly to you. Many times the disguises fooled you into thinking that they were not there to help you. You may even believe that to a certain extent.

But that would be a mistake. There are none who would harm you, for harm is impossible. Can you tell me why harm is impossible?

Because we are all one-- they are all me, and I am them? We are simply all reflections of the Divine?

Yes. And we would say good job and pat you on the back and remark on your tremendous progress... Yet to do so is to talk to ourselves as we walk down the street, congratulating ourselves for a job well done. Still, for the purposes of communication and expression of the Divine, we continue.

They've been walking with you all along. Everyone you've met, at one time or another, giving you help, pointing you in the right direction. Here's the funny part, and we say funny because your intellect is probably kicking up a ruckus right now-- all directions are the right direction. Seeing the morning sunlight reflecting off of the wood cabinets in the kitchen as you sip coffee... that is the correct thing to do to take you back to the Divine. Robbing a bank may be what someone does to take them back to the Divine. Infinitely many paths to one destination: the realization that there was no leaving, only forgetting.

You do nothing else each day than remind others of what is already true, that they are The Gift. It's no accident that you've been focusing on this lately. And it's no mistake that you are exactly, precisely in the time/space that you believe yourself to be in at present. It is the same with all those around you. It can be a difficult time, to doubt one's value and identity. That is one of your duties as a reader of this book... to remind those around you of their brilliance and beauty, simply by remembering your own and acting accordingly.

And how are you to act? Simple: listen to your heart. To thine own self be true. Sounds simple? It truly is. Yet not always as easy as you may have hoped, when simultaneously holding onto false perceptions such as "I am the body and mind" and "I must fight for survival". Those two beliefs cause so much unnecessary confusion, pain, and sadness. Simply releasing those thoughts, and thoughts like them, allows a freedom and joy to expand in the heart as it realizes there was never anywhere to go, nothing to do but simply follow that bliss.

"If it makes your heart sing, do it." You remember hearing those words, and they resonated powerfully for you. That's because they were truth. So many people will downplay the profound strength of those words, mistakenly believing it to be only something a selfish person would do. This, once again, is the ego at play. In a very clever twist, the ego claims 'heroic selflessness' status by accusing 'you' (notice: a crack in the ego's armor right there, that you and it are not the same thing) of being selfish if you follow the heart. The ego knows that to follow the heart is to follow the path back to Reality, which destroys the ego in its tracks.

Selfishness is actually 'of service to the ego'-- and that is what naturally unfolds any time you do not listen to the heart. For the heart sings with love, points in the direction of love, and emphasizes and supports all actions taken for the sake of love. But the ego's concept of love is very different from Divine love. This, you will see, takes us back to the beginning--

Say it with me, now-- The ego's concept of love is that which supports its own existence. It is a zero-sum game; for one person to get a point, the other must lose a point. This can look like a lot of things. "I love you if you do this for me." "I loved you yesterday, but not today." "I love you when you act like this, but not like that." "I love him, but not her." All of these are based on attachment.

The "coin" of attachment has two sides: Desire and Fear. Both are manifestations of attachment, and both are based upon memory. Desire (or attraction to something or someone): the memory of pleasure. Fear (or repulsion from something or someone): the memory of pain.

When you are experiencing desire or fear, you are using the intellect to guide when the heart would do a better job. Attachment in the form of attempting to pull something or someone closer to you, or create opportunities for contact, is desire. Attachment in the form of attempting to push something or someone away, or avoid contact, is fear.

Where in your life do you experience desire? The next time you notice yourself experiencing it, touch your heart and let your thoughts and attention travel down into your chest, to your heart. Notice what happens to your perception as this happens. Lust is transformed into recognition of kinship. "This could be my daughter, or sister, or niece, or aunt..." Attraction is a function of the human physiological and chemical makeup; when chemistry takes over, its effects are noticed, but the origin is often not noticed. Emotional responses triggered by hormones are mistaken for fact and truth-- "I love this person!"

Only sinking into the heart can pierce the confusion caused by the natural chemical reactions in the human body. They are there for good reason-- for the survival of the species within the limited field of perception upon your plane of existence. But remember what we've said about survival? That's right-- it's a completely meaningless concept in Reality, where there exists nothing but Love. That's how you know that it's something you need not fear. Anything that you need for survival is empty in nature. If it's based on perception via the five senses, or based in thinking, then it is empty in nature. Only that which cannot be perceived through the senses is real. And the only stuff that is real is that which cannot be perceived through the senses.

This sends the ego into a tizzy.

Story line... the ego needs a story line in order to prop up its already shaky existence. By piecing together a linear story line, it creates the illusion of an identity, a costume for 'you' to wear. It does this by selecting certain events that have appeared to take place in your life stream and giving them meaning. It determines what meaning to affix to the event based on whatever will help to prop it up better... whatever is most likely to make itself appear real.

Victim is a popular costume for the ego. Hero is another. Look deeply into the nature of your behaviors and see where victim or hero are present. Also, notice that this very introspection causes discomfort-- what could that be? Why am I so hesitant to find out where my blind spots are? To identify where I'm being selfish? Where I'm supporting an identity of victim? An identity of hero?

We say it yet again-- the ego is the one driving the bus in that moment. That feeling of discomfort or resentment is the ego kicking and screaming, holding on to the steering wheel as the heart invites it to take a different seat. "Why does this feel so bad?" If the ego let you see, truly see, that it is powerless in the face of the heart, you would release all of the pain, suffering, sadness, fear, and anger that the ego has been supplying you with for all these years. You would trade it in a heartbeat for feelings of deep, satisfying connection with yourself and everyone around you. You would trade it for joy and fulfillment. For self-expression. For surrender. For buoyancy and lightness.

This is cause for much confusion in people who believe that such discomfort is to be avoided at all costs: a message from the ego. How will you know if you're suffering from this? Some symptoms include "I must prove myself to be correct and superior". Or the opposite: "I'm stupid and worthless; my ideas don't count." Both of these thoughts, while seeming to be contradictory, serve the ego: both set forth the idea that without the ego, there would be death.

What to do? Get present. Come back to the present moment. One practice that can help break the story line, interrupting the ego's chain of events upon which it builds its false identity, is to drop the past and present. Imagine yourself flying an airplane. It has only one seat: yours. To your left is one wing, extending outward. Think of this 'wing' as your past. To your right is the other wing, extending outward. This one represents your future. The stronger your attachment to your story, your identity in the world, the bigger and longer the wings are. The ego would have you believe that the metaphor naturally extends to show that without the wings, you plummet to the ground and die.

But here's the kicker-- the plane is sitting on solid ground. There is no NEED for the wings. In fact, they are simply causing problems of misidentification with the outer world, distracting you from recognizing your true identity as the Divine.

The next time you catch yourself feeling angry or sad or worried about something, see yourself sitting in the cockpit of that plane. Now envision the wings falling off. No past. No future. No need to base your identity today upon whatever judgments you have about what has happened, has not happened, may happen, or may not happen.

Drop the judgments. Drop the story. Embrace the unlimited field of potential, the Heart's playground.

Let's talk about sex

Eventually, you will come to realize that the human sexual mating ritual is inherent in the physical aspect of the self, and not the true self. Even a simulation of the human sexual mating ritual is an affirmation that you are choosing to identify with the physical body. Initially this is done unconsciously, and the physical and emotional sensations involved can feel quite overwhelming. It can be easy for one to identify with these sensations and emotions, especially in earlier stages of development, when one misperceives himself as separate from a larger 'other'. During this phase, it is common for the dear one to seek connection, and understandably so, yet to seek outwardly for that connection, rather than inward.

The initial misperception is that of disconnection, which is absolutely impossible. It is simply a misperception and nothing more, albeit a potentially uncomfortable misperception. Yet it is the very discomfort inherent in the misperception that leads one back toward the truth, out of the hole of misperception and away from the pain caused by identification with the perceived external world.

As one continues naturally along the progression of growth and a sense of deepening self awareness, she begins to recognize that conceptions of certain things, like the sexual experience, no longer match the actual experience; the ideas do not match reality. Of course, no matter how things may have seemed to her, the fact of the matter is that the idea never actually matched reality. No matter how indulgent in pursuing the satisfaction of physical desires one might become, in the end it is the very transient nature of reality that comes crashing down after the perceived high of each experience, again and again.

Initially one may feel determined to achieve the ultimate high; attempting to sustain some physical or emotional state indefinitely in order to live in what they perceive to be a 'perfect world'. This fails every time. Sooner or later, the physical body can no longer sustain the stress inflicted, and it must rest and recover. When the mind refuses to honor this ebb and flow of nature, damage can be inflicted upon the physical being.

It is not uncommon for people to take this pursuit of 'bliss' to extremes, leading to addictive behavior. On your plane of existence, it is easy to judge and label this behavior as an aberration of nature; as something to be ashamed of. Yet we tell you without a shred of uncertainty that this process is perfect. It is poetry in motion, no matter how it may appear to you; no matter how you may choose to label it. For it is this continuous dance between cause and effect that brings every being to the final realization: truth. The truth of impermanence on your dimension.

Distracting oneself from discomfort is one reason for this behavior. Attempting to remove perceived tension is another. Judgments about tension and discomfort lead to this attachment-- attachment in the form of avoidance, which is nothing more than the memory of pain. This is mixed in with the pursuit of bliss, based upon the memory of pleasure. These, again, are the two sides of the 'coin' of attachment.

Impermanence tosses this coin over the railing of the bridge, never to be seen again. The transitory nature of existence shatters the windows of illusion, letting the fresh air of reality in to evacuate the smoke of illusion. Attachment to outcome is a way of life on your plane, where measurements are made in order to determine whether or not 'progress' has been made. Many of these lead to technological advancements that can be helpful. Yet none of it is permanent; therefore, none of it is actually 'real' in the true sense of the word.

The only 'real' thing in existence (which is not actually a 'thing', but here is where linguistic convention once again is useful for communication) is that which can neither be seen, heard, smelled, tasted, felt, or thought of. The unthinkable; that is all that is real. For when the human body is gently laid aside and the physical doors of perception come to the end of their usefulness, all the lights, colors, smells, sounds, tastes, and thoughts come to a close. They are revealed for what they truly are and always have been; fluctuating brain wave patterns. A classroom of the heart, where the heart expresses the heart to itself, eternally.

Here, in this space beyond space and time, all fear and perceived disconnection and separation dissolve. Here is where joy and love express yourself as waves, endlessly manifesting in endless combinations to create what you perceive to be the world you live in. The crowds among which you walk. The work you do. The challenges you face. The pain you endure. The joy you celebrate. The boredom you tolerate. The tension you seek to resolve. These are all manifestations of the One. And you are That. Endlessly.

This is what we refer to when we say, 'there is no Other'.

The very moment when you feel frustrated with how your physical body appears to be responding to your wishes, that is the time for compassion and gentleness. That is the time for understanding. The physical body is a glorious gift; a vehicle for learning and teaching and remembering and expressing. Too much focus on the physical body, its perceived strength, beauty, elegance, or glamour, leads to misplaced focus in life. It's like focusing one's attention on the milk bottle instead of the milk within. The container is not the magic. And here's a secret; all of what you see, hear, or perceive through the physical senses-- all of that is 'container' for magic.

Magic here does not mean some magical power over others. That definition becomes meaningless in the context of 'no Other'. A more correct definition, or one that at least points in a direction toward truth, would be the magic of life inherent in everything you encounter. It is not the drum that is magic, but rather that sound that emanates from the drum. And that sound can only experience itself thanks to the emptiness within the drum. It is the emptiness inherent in everything that you perceive, which lends space for magic to emanate forth on your plane.

This is why you may sometimes feel disappointed when you finally get something you've been wanting for so long. The guitar you've been saving up for all those years is finally resting in your hands. And suddenly, you realize that what is actually in your hands has finite measurements. It's only so long... it's only so heavy. And no matter how magical it looked in the photographs or sounded in the recordings, at the end of the day it can be reduced to a pile of wood, wire, metal and plastic. The magic comes from the interaction between spirit and this instrument; and there must be space for that interaction to take place. It is true: meaning takes place in the space between two things, not within them. This is also where magic resides: in the space within and between and around apparently separate entities.

So let the tin can lie. There is no need to collect anything; you always have what you need because you need nothing... because that which needs is not real. Only that which needs nothing is real, for it has everything, provides everything, and encompasses everything. The home of all of this can be found by turning within and directing one-pointed attention back to the heart. Here you will find all answers singing, dancing, and chanting in full delight, celebrating silently every time you cross the threshold and return home to your rightful place on your inner throne.

Fame and fortune
All chasing of material wealth is folly. All pursuit of fame and fortune is worthless, and will turn to ashes in your mouth. Only using your being to serve as a candle, lighting other candles with wisdom and love, is true.

Your neighbors, they are the ones who need you. The people in your very community. There is no need to go far, to try to be the biggest, boldest, best... to serve the most needy... to come flying in like a hero, rescuing people with daring background music playing in the distance. Your urge to wait until you can make a big splash is no more than the ego's way of maintaining the illusion of control. It's a way for the ego to keep you small. "If I can't get a lot of attention for it, then I'm not doing it." "If there is a chance I may fail, then I'm not doing it."

These are all lies. None of them arise from the Heart.

The Heart says, "Move in the direction of love. Set aside all fear and doubt. Know that it is impossible to fail. Outcomes may look very different from what you might expect or desire. Release what you expect and desire."

Little by little, as you move toward the Heart, it may feel as if you are disappearing. This is a very good sign. Have no fear; it is not 'you' that is disappearing, it is simply your attachment to the ego that is fading and dissolving into light. This attachment, which props up the belief that the ego is solid and real and a friend and servant, needs to go in order to for you to return to your rightful place at the Inner Throne of the Heart.

Flavors and behaviors that used to really seem to ignite passion and satisfy inner urges will begin to taste dull and flat... to fall short of expectations. This is also natural and correct, and is an indication that you are moving along the path of the Heart. A lack of these symptoms does not mean that you are failing to move along the path of the Heart... it simply means that you are not yet experiencing 'the fading of colors'. The fading of colors can feel like a very frightening time during the process, for glamorous ideas of spiritual enlightenment held by the ego are replaced by actual growth into enlightenment, which is not glamorous at all.

In fact, by definition, glamour is 'of the ego'. Enlightenment is the opposite of glamour; that is, the dissolution of the ego, and therefore, of all glamour. Suddenly the ego is faced with a self-contradicting desire-- what previously was, "I want enlightenment because then I'll be important and famous" becomes "I don't want to die, and enlightenment means my death." The tension created between these two opposing beliefs, which are simultaneously resting on the same plate, can be experienced as fear, uneasiness, sadness, anger, or suffering.

This is a time when the ego may kick up its distractive agenda, stirring up itches to scratch like desire for alcohol, sex, shopping, and other so-called addictive behaviors. Yet while these urges seem to come back with a vengeance, seeming almost stronger than ever, the perceived satisfaction of indulging in these behaviors increasingly fails to satisfy. In fact, every attempt to relieve the tension between desire and fear; attraction and repulsion; results in tasting those ashes in one's mouth more and more clearly for what they truly are: ashes. Emptiness.

The best thing to do here is simply watch. Listen. Observe. Notice. This is all that is ever required upon your path; upon your return journey back home to your rightful place at the Resplendent Golden Palace Heart. When you feel the tension, just observe it. When you experience the sadness and the fear and the anger and all that comes with it, notice. If you choose to indulge in the ego's fantasies by engaging in activities designed to quench these desires, notice what happens. Pay attention to the outcomes. This, too, is part of the journey.

This, too, is the curriculum you have designed to perfection. There is no reason to feel you have failed in any way, yet if you do, then simply notice that, as well.

Release all attachment to all emotional states, for they fluctuate with the mind. Remember the old koan: the flag is waving in the breeze-- what is moving? The air? The flag? No. The mind. The mind moves and dances and whirls around endlessly-- there is no need to try to stop it. It is designed to do what it does. Yet you can choose at any given moment to turn your attention away from it, and back toward the Heart, the source of all that is true.

Give freely of your time, energy, and resources, knowing that you can never lose something that is imaginary. And all things that appear to be in short supply are actually imaginary. For if you can intellectually grasp it, it is imaginary. Only that which is beyond the imagination, which is literally unthinkable, is actually real; is truly true.

Connect with other hearts, for doing so connects you with yourself, again and again. And while you are always effortlessly connected, your recognition of this is what falters. This is what causes grief, sadness, anger, frustration, and feelings of loss. Since nothing can be lost, ever, and since nothing can be gained, ever, experiencing these emotions is completely unnecessary. Yet in the throes of attachment (desire/fear), it is very common to experience them to such a degree that one may take into consideration extreme options for making them go away.

For your brothers and sisters around you, have compassion. Take great care to be gentle with them. Be true to them. Be supportive and understanding. And when you see what appears to be shortcomings, keep in mind the ego's games. How the ego would love to make you feel important, superior, and grandiose. How the ego would delight in making you feel superior, and inferior; amazingly brilliant, and embarrassingly stupid. How your ego delights in making you feel awful, worthless, and unlovable, while simultaneously striving to make you feel important, powerful, and in control.

All who identify with ego are engaged in this struggle, to some extent. Supreme Confidence is required to stand fully in the light of the truth, surrendering all attachment to the ego's games. Supreme Humility is needed in order to remember as you step into the sunlight and witness others suffering needlessly due to misperception, that you are not the first to awaken. In fact, it is quite possible, we say to the ego, that you may very well be the last one on the planet to begin to awaken. For is it not possible that every other seemingly separate being on the planet might just be there playing the precise roles they are playing, in service to you, who needs to see himself in every possible mirror available? Dear ego, what if this is the case? What might that mean?

These are questions you can always ask the ego in order to remind yourself to disengage from showering your attention upon it. They can also bring you back to the present moment, where compassion for your brothers and sisters is actually compassion for yourself as you journey forth on the Heart's

Path. There is no need to fear on this journey. All that you will need to surrender is that which does not serve you. Anything that you lay aside is a thing that you never really needed in the first place. Any object or belief that you feel being stripped away, that you grieve the loss of, is something that has served you well for the brief time it was appropriate, and now can be relegated to its true place, which is imagination. For it was only created of emptiness from the imagination to begin with.

Since there is nothing worth holding on to, freely release all. This is your key to happiness.

Use your natural gifts and talents to remind others of their inherent brilliance. This is the greatest gift of all.

Keep your side of the street clean

Part of letting go of the ego's attachments to various aspects of identity is to release attachment to others. How they behave. How they show up in the world. The biggest signal of attachment is your own lack of acceptance of the present moment as you find it. This curriculum is beautifully illustrated through what you call your romantic relationships. Those you choose to spend your life with are not an extension of you, though you may fall into the habit of seeing them that way. Still, no matter how tightly you hold on to a lie, it remains a lie.

True peace is found only through surrender of the ego in all its various forms.

What to do when you find you have painted yourself into a corner? How to act? How to behave? Go back to the basics; keep your side of the street clean. Focus inward, once again, and release all temptation to try to control the world you perceive. The path of non-resistance means the path of total acceptance. Strive to your heart's desire for whatever it is that calls you. Whatever makes your heart sing, do that as deeply and as often as you can. And then release attachment to any particular outcome. There is no need to attempt to control outcomes, for all outcomes on your perceived plane of existence are like grains of sand on the beach, being washed away, tumbled endlessly, and only seeming to be solid. No matter where you place your foot, it sinks into the wet sand. The world of outcomes that you perceive is like this. For everything is affected, influenced, and impacted by everything.

Surrender your worries. Surrender your fears. Surrender your desires. Listen to your heart. Listen through your heart. Let go of the urge to try to grab on to your past, your story. For the story can be changed as quickly as you change your mind. In an instant, no matter what circumstances you perceive yourself to be in, you can change the meaning of your story. And in the end, it will be revealed to be nothing more than that: a story.

Detachment

Trust your heart. Encourage others to trust theirs. This is the key. When stepping back from unhealthy habitual thought and behavior patterns, it can feel confusing. "How do I love someone and create space for them to live their own life, make their own mistakes, have their own experiences, and not be overly protective?"

This is a good question. The answers lie within the question itself.

Creating space is the definition of expressing love; creating space for the other person to experience his or her own life unfolding in the moment. "Creating space for them to make their own mistakes..." This presumes that it's possible to make mistakes; that the concept of a 'mistake' is valid. This only appears to be valid through the lens of the intellect, which would have you believe that it can predict outcomes based upon past experience. The intellect also would have you believe that what appears to be the most efficient path, or the path of least resistance or discomfort, is therefore the best and most preferable path. Only by equating 'discomfort' with 'bad', and 'lack of discomfort' with 'good' does the concept of a mistake have any meaning. In these terms, a mistake is something to be avoided because it results in discomfort.

Yet discomfort is often where lessons are learned. Attempting to avoid discomfort means attempting to avoid change, a concept that is utterly and completely meaningless, since all things on your plane of existence are in a never-ending state of flux and change. Only the ego would have you perceive and believe that anything perceived by the human senses is solid and infinite. Look closely and you'll see that the sands upon which you stand are ever-shifting.

The concept of 'mistake' also presumes an incorrect and correct path upon your journey. This also is a fallacy. All roads lead back to the heart. All paths involve surrender, again and again, of misperception. Mistaking the human body as a measurement of life is one of the biggest misperceptions to be surrendered, and one that every single human being is faced with. Avoiding mistakes is impossible, as there are no mistakes to avoid. "Mistake" is a judgment of the ego, one that is entirely subjective, and varies from person to person, and can even vary from moment to moment within one person's perspective.

"...and not be overly protective..." The presumption from the ego's point of view is that the protectiveness is of the other person. The ego would have you believe that it is somehow possible for you to prevent another person from experiencing sadness, pain, sorrow, anger, or fear. This belief reveals an underlying misperception that a person can prevent their own experience of these emotions by controlling external factors. Yet the only way to avoid suffering is to acknowledge these emotional states as they are experienced and then, having embodied them and experienced them, release all attachment to them.

Looking more deeply into this misperception will reveal that the person taking on the so-called 'protector' role is simply trying to protect his or her own feelings; trying to avoid the suffering that results from over-identification with another person. Seeing the other person as an extension of yourself, through the lens of the ego, leads to controlling behavior and reflects a lack of willingness to take responsibility for your own experience. It's like remaining tense in order to brace yourself from the possibility of falling down and getting hurt; it leads to deeper injury when you do fall down.

The ego's efforts to protect itself from being hurt are what cause you to associate detachment with anger, or punishment. Yet true compassion is nothing other than detachment; detachment from the ego and a deeper surrender to the heart. It is this repeated acknowledgment of true association with the heart that brings about the joyful, loving detachment of true compassion. There is no need to hold on to old, outdated ideas of detachment as separation from another person. There is only one True Heart, and everyone and everything you perceive is a reflection of that one True Heart, including yourself. True, loving, healthy detachment is not detachment from anyone else's heart, but rather from the longings, desires, demands, and fears of the ego. Detachment from ego-based perception leads to connection that creates more and more space, always.

Where this detachment stems from love is where the bonds of love can be felt even as you release perceived control; even as you surrender the urge to tense up in order to avoid being hurt... Surrendering the need to try to control your surroundings (which is futile anyway) in order to prevent change from happening. Trying to prevent change is like standing in a river and trying to redirect it with your hands. Arguing with the river makes no difference to the river.

More hugs. More loving demonstrations of acceptance and understanding. More compassion for others and self. More self-care. Less attention directed outward, and more attention directed toward the heart. Less energy spent worrying about being treated unfairly, and more attention on treating yourself fairly. Less time and effort spent seeking the approval or appreciation of anyone else, and more spent acknowledging, honoring, and blessing yourself for your own gifts and contributions to the world.

This is the appropriate path for you at this time. This is what leads to effortless expression of love, support, and appreciation for others. Gratitude is once again at the center of this joy and happiness. Gratitude and surrender; non-resistance and celebration of life precisely as you perceive it to be unfolding before your very eyes, no matter how you may feel tempted to judge it. This is the key to happiness.

And at the same time, you are reminded that it is simply impossible to fail on your journey. The concept of failure on your journey, failure to return to your true place at the Inner Throne of the Heart, is a meaningless concept, one borne of the ego's need to keep you distracted, uncertain, doubtful and fearful. Failure is not something that you can choose, even if you wanted to. All paths, all journeys, all roads lead back to the Heart. Therefore, whatever your experience happens to look like today, know with full confidence that you will end up back at the Heart.

In fact, you are there even in this very moment. What you perceive to be your 'return' to the Heart is in fact nothing other than your recognition that you have always been here, at home, in the Heart. And even this is misperception, for it suggests that there is a 'you' separate from The Heart. In reality, you ARE the Heart. How could you possibly ever leave yourself? Again, the concept is meaningless.

The point is this: there is truly no need to worry. About anything. If you are experiencing worry about not being on the correct path, about not doing the appropriate spiritual practices, about not being lovable or good enough or acceptable, then you can simply do this: say to yourself, "Oh, hello ego. I hear you. You would have me believe that I am other than the Heart itself. You would have me believe that I am other than the Divine manifested. You would have me believe these things in order to distract me from turning my attention inward and remembering that I am the Heart itself. You do this in order to prop yourself up and to appear real to yourself and to me. I now acknowledge that I am Divine Love. Your fears are not me. Your desires are not my identity. Your story is not me. Your fears are not my destiny. I release all attachment to the thoughts that stem from you, and I allow them to pass through, unheeded, as I continue to create space for myself and for others to live our lives in gratitude."

This is true because there is no other to vilify, fear, protect, conquer, save, gain, or lose. There is only Love. And you are That.

"Come to me"

Guides... what do you have for me this morning? What would you like to tell the world through me? Hold on a minute... give me the chance to get out of my own way. Coffee is good... but my cup is almost empty. And I realize I almost careened off into the details of my day (photoshop, emails, laundry) before taking care of my pages. My precious pages. You know what? I'm falling in love with doing my daily pages. More coffee. Come to me while I'm getting my coffee.

You're so funny... 'come to me'... as if we're not already sitting here, waiting in the wings of your heart, just watching while you slowly remove the blinders from your eyes and ears so you'll hear the message we are always sending.

Take care to remember, with caution, that your impact is much stronger than you might ever imagine it to be. No need for loud noises, most of the time... a vast majority of the time, in fact. Speaking your truth quietly moves mountains. No need to shout or bang things around. Your sword is so sharp it cuts even when you don't realize it. So be aware that your sword is drawn at all times. You can cut or bless in any moment. It is the sword of love.

Keep in mind also, wrathfulness is the nature of the ego. Master of manipulation for as long as you hand over that power, the ego is the one who punishes, who says that you're not good enough, that you're not ready, not sufficient, not able to handle whatever is before you. We remind you that since it is all flashing lights and sounds as you go round and round, there is nothing to fear. Yes. That is correct. There is nothing to fear. Where there is love, there is an absence of fear. Where there is fear, there is the forgetfulness -- an absence of AWARENESS -- that love is shining always. Glowing like a sun within your very heart.

When you feel anything other than joy, relax. It's fine to experience those emotions. But you need not dwell there. Underneath is ever-present joy.

Your intellect is getting in the way... wants to drive the bus. Sometimes it does not like us to come through... sometimes releasing it gently and setting it aside can feel like a challenge... it is those moments that are happening when the flow of words stops... when your hands hover above the keys, waiting for the next phrase to come through so you can capture it on this paper. Of sorts.

Go ahead. Be clever. Everyone knows you're not typing this on an old Corona... you simply fancy yourself some romantic Hemingway type, looking out at the beach with your cup of coffee, your cigar, your typewriter, being manly and heroic and poignant and all that. And crazy? Maybe a little. What does it take to end your own 'life'? Does it take a bit of craziness? Or maybe it's a different kind of sanity? Is it simply the recognition that you're on a carousel?

Things get deep quickly. Going back to the basics, there is one question for you to ponder deeply, and to share with others: What is a human being? That question alone, whether dismissed out of hand as idiotic or irrelevant, gets the mind busy at the task of stripping away the layers of paint and rust that seem to hold together as a structure. Layers of the onion begin to fall away, revealing emptiness within. So it is with so many peoples' conception of what a human being is.

Start looking at whether a human being is simply the body, and the illusion is revealed... the green curtain gets drawn aside and the ego, sitting on his stool with the controls in his hands, looks up at you with a terrified look in its eyes. Discovered, he starts his fast-talking sales pitch, trying desperately to distract you from the matter at hand... which is, of course, recognition and final acceptance of the absolute FACT that you are not a physical body; you are not a mind.

Colors. Sound. Music. Smells. Tastes. Delightful thoughts... enjoy them in passing. Hold them each for a moment and savor them, knowing all the while that they are illusion. And those pieces and fragments of illusion that seem to cause you suffering, sadness, pain, fear-- savor these all the more, for in remembering that they are nothing more than illusion, they become part of the magnificent feast that is this life stream experience.

Knowing that you are on a roller coaster, that you took your vacation time, paid your money, got your ticket, went through the little gate to confirm that you were tall enough to ride this ride, got strapped in, looked at your beloved sitting beside you and grinned from ear to ear-- knowing that as you climb that first hill, slowing clacking your way up, higher and higher-- knowing that as you look around over the millions of other people standing in various lines, buying their snacks, seeing the sights, hearing the music of the calliope-- knowing that as you go over that first hill and plunge straight down at 90 miles an hour, feeling your stomach in your throat and a lizard-brain panic kicking you in the chest-- knowing that you've chosen all of this, relax and shout and throw your hands in the air.

The apparent danger you perceive is no less and no more than this. Take the ride that you are taking. Enjoy every moment of it, even the tragedy. For soon you will wake up and remember all of the truth that you have been experiencing but not quite recognizing. Soon the body will fall away, the identification with that body and mind will fall away... the credit cards will fall away... the new guitar strings and record collection and receipts for work done on the jeep's transmission will fall away... those loved ones who appear to be separate from you will fall away... and once again you will remember what you have always known: There is only One. And it is You. There is no other.

CHAPTER TEN
Stillness

I was boiling spaghetti when it happened. No 'Thieving Magpie' playing in the background, but the similarities were not lost to me, all the same.

It happened quietly. Without fanfare. No waving banners, no trumpets. No drama. Nothing. Just the sound of the water boiling, and me stirring the noodles to see if they were ready yet.

My mind had wandered back to a couple days prior, the whole 'checkout clerk swiping my driver's license' victim-status bag. And then, before I realized what was happening, my mouth opened and uttered these words:

"Not now, ego. You're not going to take away my peace of mind. I'm driving the bus now."

And that was that. Calm. Relaxed. Happy. And mildly curious at what had just happened. I spread my homemade sauce over the noodles, found my fork and sat down to eat. Glorious calm. This could be nice; I could get used to this. No monkeys flinging feces across the room to keep things interesting. No need to spiral into drama, throwing open the windows and doors so the tornado could blow through, tearing everything off the walls and sending them crashing onto the floor just to have something to clean up afterward.

Just silence. The sound of the fork clinking gently against the plate as I ate. The internal sound of my own spaghetti chewing inside my head. The deep red color of the meat sauce, and the little white chunks of fresh garlic I had crushed and cut up with my own hands. The scrape on the knuckle of my right hand, just above my index finger, where I had knocked it against the doorframe as the door, temporarily sticking due to changes in weather, gave way under my determined shove.

Just quiet. And sunlight. And the ringing of the silence, so loud in my ears. And calm in my stomach. And acceptance in my heart. No need for worry. Stillness in the trees outside. Stillness in the trees inside. Time to walk out in the world and test this new condition for stability.

Eye of the storm

"Rest in the eye of the storm..." That's what kept running through my mind, gently, with each step. With each breath.

While everything else is spinning madly around you, rest quietly at the center, in the eye of the storm. Rest calmly. Quietly. Relax. There in the middle, see that you are part of everything, and it is part of you.

I was walking back from the store, and up ahead I saw a man walking unsteadily. Drunk? Maybe. Not sure. Didn't matter. An older man. As we approached one another, I took off my glasses so he could see my eyes. We got close enough to greet one another, and I looked into his eyes, smiling. "How you doin'?" he asked me. "Hey brother..." I replied. And he grinned and walked past, and from behind me I heard him say, "all right..."

A younger man walking his bicycle ended up beside on the street as we came to a park. We talked easily. It felt good to laugh and share a smile with him. My brother. And the guy with the cigarette who made it across Central and to the bus stop just as I was about to walk by. I smiled and nodded, he did the same.

Where's all the fear? It's in the head, along with all of the other noise. It's stored in the body, in the nervous system. Go back to the heart and feel it all drop away. Feel like taking a nap, relaxed and quiet, yet aware. Feel like watching and listening. Like walking slowly. No need to hurry. Nowhere to be except right here right now. At this moment, there is only this moment, and it is precisely where I sit. When I stand, when I sing, when I take a crap. All of the 10,000 directions intersect at one magical point, and that point is me. The axis mundi.

All directions lead home. And all directions lead back to one point in space: the heart. There is nowhere else because there is no one else. And there is no one else because there is no other. There is only one. And you are it. Nowhere to find it; it's always following you around, or rather, dancing with you as you walk, run, sleep, sit, or do yoga. Wherever you might be, it is right there, inside your chest, waiting for you to stop, take a breath, look down at your own heart, and see it smiling and winking at you, humming your favorite song.

This could go on for days. I hope it does. Slowly, like syrup easing gently from the bottle. Even warm, it takes its time.

This is how you naturally move and breathe and exist when you drop into your heart and out of your head. How to do so? Just by repeating: rest at the eye of the storm. That's all you have to be. That's all you have to do. There's only one place to be. There's only one time in which to be. And whatever you look like to you, that is not it. Your self-image is not what you truly are. For if you saw your true brilliance, you would set aside all worries of right and wrong... you would retire all concerns about money and retirement and bank accounts and tax write-offs. You would let go of all doubts and fears you carry, and you would not take special efforts to shop for new clothing or used clothing and you would not worry about how you look or what you sound like... and if you did, you would not worry about the fact that you were worrying. You would simply see, smile, and accept, dropping it all entirely.

Because it's just the noise of the mind. In reality, there is silence. There is music. And there is joy. That's all there is, in infinite forms, multitudes of shapes and colors to dazzle the mind.

Teacup
A vast calm. Feel it washing over you. That is part of your natural state... We know it may feel unfamiliar to you, as you've spent most of your existence as you know it in a state of perpetual turbulence, trying to find the next emergency to survive; the next storm to weather.

But now you have something new-- you have some tools, including awareness of a deeper truth. Rest there, in the eye of the storm, where all is calm. It is perpetually calm there. All you need to do is recognize whenever things feel like they're flying around the room... that's when you know you've stepped out of the center, away from the eye, and into the surrounding fray. No worries. It's not the world that is going crazy-- it's merely that you've stepped out of your center. Step back into it and watch the business of things from that point.

Don't be worried and don't be surprised by the apparent changes that are going to seem to start taking place. In all actuality, they've been in motion already, but you will only now begin to notice them with your new level of openness, awareness, and spaciousness. There is now more room in you than ever before, as you perceive. More of what has been creating suffering in you has been scooped out, hollowed out... the core removed, leaving space. And you know what the definition of space is, right? "Love."

Love has room for all of the craziness and unpredictability in the world. Love has room for all of the yowling cats... all of the fearful spouses... all of the barking dogs and deadlines in the world... Love has room for all of it. Don't forget: Love is the teacup that everything else swims around in.

Sushi knife

Wow. Today as I sit to write, I find nothing but emptiness. A giant jar, completely filled with emptiness. Perhaps I am that jar. When I am completely filled with emptiness, there is vast space, endless calm. The intellect feels frightened. "What if there are no more words?" "What if I fall short of my goals?" "I will be a failure!"

There is no failure in Reality. There are no successes against which to measure any sort of achievement. There is only love. Everything vibrates at the frequency of love. Space vibrates with love. Emptiness vibrates with love. And love vibrates in emptiness, through emptiness.

There is space and quiet. All sounds added together make the sound of silence. Love flaps in the wind against that chorus, that echo, that choir of silence.

Wherever we can recreate an approximation of space in the world, we create love. Magic happens in space. The space where people come together to sing, dance, and chant is love. The space where dinner is served is love. The space where people can come together to work through their issues, embody their emotions, and do their work is love. Love is space. Space is love.

Your physical body is comprised almost entirely of space. Therefore, your body is created of love. Love is the space between and within the apparently physical reality you call home. Love is the space between two points, where the vibration occurs. And love is the space within each point, where galaxies and universes spin and unfold and collapse endlessly, expressing love always.

Love is the space between phrases. The silence between the question and the answer. The silence between the request and the response. Love is the space of the empty page, unlimited potential, simply waiting to be written upon. Space is a frozen lake on a clear winter morning, just waiting to be skated upon.

Love is the open sky, endlessly waiting to be flown through. Love is the space within the drum, where air waves get generated. Love is the unknown as you awaken to a new morning to find what the day has in store. Love is the honoring of this unknown, and the acknowledgment that Reality may very well unfold with its own agenda at the forefront, simply smiling as your ideas, plans, and timelines are apparently crushed underfoot.

Love is the great inhale, and the great exhale. It is the pause just before climax. The silent repose afterward. And when things appear to be happening quickly and without space, it can be found by subdividing again and again, revealing infinite space between each apparent movement, incident, or event. The space between drum strokes can be measured in universes. The space within the blink of an eye can be measured in galaxies. All of these things reside within the vast field of the heart.

I took a step toward the fire to guard myself against the evening's chill.

So each of those stars up there are actually within my heart?

"Yes, of course they are," he replied. "Your mistake is to assume that what you perceive through your eyes is the way things are actually arranged. Close your eyes for a moment and envision your heart being about 4 feet tall."

It was a weird thing to envision, but I listened and followed.

"Now, imagine yourself standing behind it, looking through it at the world and everything in it. This is one way to express, within the limitations of language, one method for moving toward true perception."

The next time I was walking along the sidewalk, I tried it. A young woman was walking toward me on this crowded downtown afternoon. I was always afraid someone was going to look at me and think of me as threatening or scary, which was about as far from the truth as things could get. I had tried to be scary and tough in the past, and it had never served me well. Now I felt afraid of being wrongly accused of such things, because, well... that was just the kind of luck I had.

On this day, I kept walking. I didn't cross the street or look away or pretend to check my phone for messages or step into one of the local shops until the beautiful woman passed by. Instead, I kept walking. I was honestly just walking along. I truly had no ulterior motives-- so why should I fear that someone would think I did?

I kept walking, and as we approached each other, I brought the vision of my own heart up before me, and I looked at her and everyone else through the "curtain" of my heart. Silently I offered up thanks for her beauty, letting my heart say, 'thank you, sister, for your beauty' and releasing any sexual desire and grasping that habitually arose. As we passed and I smiled with a relaxed face and gentleness in my eyes, I saw my own love and acceptance and space reflected back to me in her eyes.

She passed.

And immediately my ego kicked in. "It worked! Hey, I think she likes us! Let's go back and ask for her phone number! No, wait-- maybe it's too soon. What time is it? We've got to come back to this exact spot tomorrow at this same time and see if we bump into her again. That would be perfect! Then we can get her phone number and see if she likes sushi!"

So I ended up getting sushi, I explained.

He was laughing.

"Well, yeah," he said as his laughter died down. "Sushi is good. Nothing wrong with sushi. Especially good sushi. Gotta have a sharp knife for that.

"But you know, this brings up a good point. Love is the space within sushi. And love is also the space between you and the beautiful woman as she approaches, and as she continues past you. Love is the space between you when your eyes meet for just a split second.

"And what you might not realize is that love is the space between the ego's words. I know it's tempting to paint the ego as the villain, always the bad guy in the movie. Always out to quench its selfish thirst... to satisfy its own petty little hungers and desires and demands. But love is actually the space between each of those apparent demands... Love is within each of those judgments made by the ego. If we keep cutting things down into finer and finer pieces, we find that as we split hairs we find love.

"Even in those moments of apparent rejection, there is only love. Love resides between the words, within the breath that is about to issue the command for execution or dissolution or revolution. Love is inherent in every syllable, every breath. There is no part of this experience that does not issue from love, even in their claims to hate.

"Certainly on this plane, there is apparent suffering, doubt, fear, sadness, grief, and pain. That is what this plane appears to be made of when perceived through the five senses. But now is the time to set aside all reliance on the five senses in the search for true identity and to rely solely on the heart. Only the heart will reveal reality as it truly stands, where waves of love and joyful surrender crash against the rocks of freedom endlessly.

"All is space. All is love. All is freedom. Every movement is a celebratory dance in the name of this freedom. Every painful trial that you've ever endured... every death you've caused and suffered. Every selfish and selfless moment you've ever imagined and undergone... they are all the dance of love spinning wildly and gracefully and clumsily and effortlessly, with ribbons and scarves tied on, whistling through the air like so many kites arching against the wind.

Receptivity as an active state

You need to know that when I drag my ass in here with my cup of coffee, I almost never know what's going to come out. Seriously. I mean, sometimes I have a bit of an idea, but then other times, I'll be crouching by the fire, poking it with a stick to get it going better, and wondering what the hell I'm going to write today. Sometimes I worry that I've used up all the ideas... emptied my word bag, and there will be nothing left. Nothing of value, anyway. That's the ego and the small mind throwing me a little, splintered, poisoned bone to chew on... a bone of doubt. And of course I say, fuck you, doubt. Just like Roy Huntley yelled, "Fuck you, Sister Nancy!" when we were in the 3rd or 4th grade. How do you yell a thing like that to Sister Nancy and live to tell about it? Apparently only fear keeps me from turning away from doubt.

Osiris, Ra, and Thoth... Speak through me now. What guidance and counsel do you have for the world? I am ready to open myself to your wisdom.

Your beauty shines forth brighter each day, beloved one. And yes, you are not mistaken-- you do in fact sense that something is shifting in your perception. Old habitual patterns continue to drive certain behavior patterns, but it's okay-- they are fading as your vibration continues to increase on your plane of existence.

Some of the things you can expect to experience-- a sense of growing distance between you and the drama of the world. A sense of deepened well-being, no matter what is going on. A sense of certainty that what you are seeing is not what you get. A calm, relaxed, joyful presence, knowing full well that there is no death-- only a shift in perspective... from the 'you' you believe yourself to be to the 'You' that you truly are and always have been. A growing sense of acceptance as you embrace the fact that everything truly is sacred, no matter how the manifestations appear to unfold. A deeper sense of remembering that there truly is no 'other'; you are it. You are all of it. Everything that seems to be happening is no more than different manifestations of Yourself. How on earth could anyone harm You if You is all there is?

Increased patience for your brothers and sisters who are at different points along the path. Because remember, they are You, as well. So when we recommend that you 'cut yourself some slack', that's a taller order than you might initially imagine. Yet when you remember and embrace (not in that order) your true identity, then it becomes easier. Suddenly the struggle is over. Victory is achieved; victory over the fear of separation, which was never any more than a mirage anyway. And there's no harm in the mirage... no harm in believing in it. It's simply that taking the mirage to be true generates anxiety and fear in your own self and in those around you. Why not enjoy the truth instead of hiding from it?

Also, your wildest dreams are truly within reach. Where would you like to go, brother? Think about what your dreams are-- what is it that you desire? What do you wish to do? Where do you wish to go? Because all of that, down to the very finest detail, is yours for the asking. Simply begin to get clear and explicit about what you want, and you'll manifest it. Because the world you perceive that you live in, the plane of existence you are experiencing, is truly nothing more than a mirror... offering you the opportunity to experience yourself in endless shapes and forms so that you can remember who you are.

Where would you like to live? Begin drawing it out. What would you like to be doing with your time? How would you like to give in the world? To whom do you wish to be of service? (Yes, do not think we miss the humor in the reply: "I wish to be of service to myself." That's actually the only answer possible.) The more you relax into non-resistance and focus on the energy you intentionally extend, the more you will notice 'miracles' happening around you. These 'miracles' are completely natural, and the natural outcome of releasing attachment to the mirage. As many sages before you have said, the mirage would have you believe that you exist in the world. In truth, the entire world exists in you. This is not poetry... inspect this carefully; investigate as deeply as you can and you will discover that there is no plainer way for us to guide you toward the truth on this plane of existence where language fails so completely to capture the beauty and magnificence of the heart. Your very heart. The one beating in your chest right now. That is the doorway. Go there. Over and over. Again and again.

Take refuge there when things seem to be collapsing all around you. When loved ones die. When innocent people are killed or hurt. When apparent evil seems to reign unfettered while good seems to fall by the wayside. All of these things are a necessary part of the mirage. Take refuge in the heart. Because you know absolutely that you are not the physical body, you are free to live fearlessly, loving courageously with reckless abandon all who stumble into your path. Let the reach of your savage, breathtaking love for life extend far and wide, that the hearts and minds of lands far away may be lifted and strengthened... renewed and reminded by your words, thoughts, and actions. Since there is no enemy to fight, walk calmly and with love through every dark alley you find, for those are nothing more than the dark alleys of your mind. Illuminate them with your brilliance and light, which are nothing short of the light of the Divine.

Would the Divine wear parachute pants? Would the Divine hide copies of Playboy in the heat register? Would the Divine ditch school in order to run home to get his favorite comb so he could fix his hair? Would the Divine drink so much champagne that he pukes in the bushes at 2am, then does it again the next day? Would the Divine accidentally overdose on nutmeg in search for the perfect sleep aid? Yes! Again and again we say, YES! The Divine knows no bounds... no limitations... no boxes, no rooms, no limits, no concepts... On the football field of the Divine, there are no sidelines.

Right and wrong... Listen to your brother Hafiz who was quite correct in saying that now is the time for you to deeply compute the impossibility that there is anything but Grace. He was an active receiver-- feminine energy is very active, though it would appear to be passive. Not simply a radio antenna passively receiving signals, it actively scans for signals to receive. That is your task now. To demonstrate what it looks like to balance masculine and feminine energies, knowing that your ability to scan and listen and follow are what will serve those around you at this time.

CHAPTER ELEVEN
Gratitude

Cuba, New Mexico, that is.

I had visited this particular gas station restroom so many times in the past year I'd even become familiar with the graffiti. This was the one with no paper towels... only the hand dryer that blew air with a noise that made me cringe every time. I wondered how the others did it... apparently I was the only human who found the frequency range reverberating off the walls so physically painful that I had to cover my ears. I'd seen other patrons looking at me out of the corner of their eye. I could only imagine what they must be thinking.

I wondered how they could do it. Just like the barber, back before I started shaving my own head every few days. After every haircut, at the very end, after using the clippers on my neck and brushing my shoulders off with the little whisk brush, inevitably the barber would reach over and grab the blower nozzle and start hitting me with bursts of air. And without fail, no matter how much I tried to crane my neck and turn my ears away, he would always, always manage to blow the deadly stream of air directly into at least one of my ears, causing it to ring for the next ten minutes.

I'd seen photos of myself as a child, with headphones placed on my head when I was only two or three years old, and I had a pained look on my face, tears in my eyes, clearly unhappy. If only they had understood how sensitive my ears were back then, and the kind of pain they were unwittingly inflicting on their little boy, they would have been able to spare him from so much.

But then again, it was exactly the exposure to the elements that made me who I am today. It was precisely those challenges, those times in life when I simply wasn't sure I was going to survive, or how, that were such a precious gift today. The risks were quite real; I know at least one time period when I was considering suicide. Yet the gifts and rewards I reap today make all of that so worth it. No way I could even think of changing one single aspect of life.

Even the past fourteen months of cancer, chemo, and now possibly anti-depressants. Especially these things.

When I shift my focus back to gratitude, I find myself in love once again. And when I take the time to shift my focus away from worry and back to self-care, something I've been neglecting for the past fourteen months, suddenly there is so much more space in my life. And space is love; love is space. There is so much more room to move around... to play... to dance, to sing, to sit, to listen, to share... to enjoy precisely whatever it is that life is manifesting at this very moment.

Since it is not me, I am free to watch with curious fascination. And I am free to interrupt the storylines that the ego spins in order to keep me distracted. Distracted from looking within and remembering my brilliance and magic; the gifts that I have to share with the world. How much more satisfying for the ego to watch me rolling around in the mud, crying, torturing myself, measuring my worth in dollars or belongings or status or whatever. Anything but acknowledging the light that shines forth when I ignore it, the ego.

I'm in love today. In love with my life. With my job. With my wife. With my car. With my friends and family. Even those who perceive me as a threat, or would disown me. For in moments like these, I see clearly that it isn't truly THEM who perceive me as a threat-- it's ego. And it isn't ME who judges himself to be disowned- - it's ego. Basically, ego sees ego in the world and responds with ego, shouting angrily at ego or running away, afraid of what ego will do or say to threaten ego. True Identity is simply love and light. True identity is never challenged or threatened or even bumped or bruised. True Identity simply watches, loving as all unfolds.

True Identity is not restricted by the bounds of time and space. True Identity appears to the intellect to be able to time travel; to stand in seemingly multiple time zones or planes of existence simultaneously. This is all just a house of mirrors. The apparent separation is no more than reflections of the limits of ego-based perception; that is, the intellect.

When you go within, you can go anywhere. You can communicate with masters who can provide guidance and love and direction and understanding. And those masters that you bump into are you. All the funhouse mirrors make your own image appear to be stretched in so many incomprehensible ways. Yet they are all you. They always were. And they always will be. Wherever you go, you bump into you. This gives the concept of 'self care' an entirely new spin.

Suddenly, self care means that every single creature you encounter deserves the care and love you would want for yourself. This is where caring for the immediate self, through healthy exercise, diet, and sleep, can lead to recognizing all other creatures and beings, physical and non-physical alike, as you. Kindness to them is simply kindness to yourself, as they are you, quite literally.

The teacup holds all. There is nothing outside of the teacup. And the teacup is yours. In fact, the teacup and all of its contents, are you. The hand that holds the teacup is actually also contained within the teacup. The intellect or rational mind would have you believe that if it doesn't fall within the rules and strictures posted up on the ego's wall, then it simply cannot be true, and is to be rejected. This is how the ego carries out its work: to measure, categorize, judge, and label.

"The teacup is mine!" it screams, "not yours!" What a hilarious statement to make! It's utterly meaningless. So many presuppositions are made and assumed to be true: 1) that there is anyone else in the room; 2) that there is anything separate that can be 'owned'; 3) that it's possible to distinguish a drop of water from the wave... the wave from the ocean.

You are the drop of water. You are the wave. You are the ocean. When you accept this as true, which requires removing the intellect from the role of leader and returning it to its appropriate role of servant to the heart, suddenly things become much easier. Life is gentler. Suddenly it becomes possible to see 'behind the curtain'... deep beyond the surface of things. While it may appear that you are continuously wrongly accused by others, once you accept that you are all it becomes clear that those who appear to reject you cannot possibly do so, because they ARE you. You ARE them.

And we have the freedom to accept the solidity of what we see in varying extents-- if a particular person appears to reject you, suddenly you can see behind the curtain; beyond the surface, and realize how much that person must truly love you... what kind of love and compassion and sacrifice must it take in order to sign up to play a role that would create this illusion, where you would find yourself believing that they do not love you? What kind of sacrifice must be involved in being willing to be misunderstood for so long, knowing at their spiritual core that these trials and illusions are precisely what you would need to bring forth the love and compassion inherent within you?

Knowing how sensitive your ears are, how deeply someone must love you to push the button on the hand dryer, knowing that their apparent lack of sensitivity, concern, or compassion would help you grow in understanding and compassion yourself.

Knowing all of this in your heart, how could you look around you at all of the apparent noise, panic, chaos, and suffering in the world and do anything other than smile in loving joy?

Sing your song

Dear One! Welcome!

Please close your eyes and think back to a time where you felt completely happy... completely at ease, and completely powerful. Think of a time, a day, a moment, an afternoon, when you felt like things could not possibly go wrong; everything you touched worked out beautifully and effortlessly. Think back on how your heart felt that day or evening. Remember the lightness, the joy. Remember how easy it felt to smile. Remember where you were, who you were with. Remember how connected you felt to the people around you, to your surroundings, and to yourself. Bring this feeling up and up and up... bring it to the forefront of your attention. Put it right here on the front burner. Let it rise up from your heart and spread over you like morning sunshine.

This is the space from which we will be working today. This is where we'll be creating from; this space of love, acceptance, joy, freedom, power, and understanding. This place where we are free to have fun, to goof around, to be silly and playful. This is a space of true power; freedom from the limitations of our everyday world.

From this place of joy, sitting squarely in the center of this calm, relaxed, happy space, know that everything you need for engaging in your creative pursuit is here in this room right now. At all times, wherever you are, you always have everything you need in order to create love, understanding, compassion, and gentleness in your life. You always, at any given moment, have the power to create playfulness, lightness, and freedom for yourself and all those around you. There is no need for more equipment, the right location, the proper time frame, the right wind direction... There is no need to wait for anything anymore.

It is the ego that would have you believe you need to get things right; that somehow there is a set of standards you must follow in order to create an environment of freedom, lightness, and joy. It is the ego that would have you believe you need a certificate or a license in order to move forward with singing, chanting, dancing, playing, writing, drawing, painting... or any other expression of the Heart. The ego would truly have you wait just a little longer, until you have enough practice to do this publicly, otherwise you risk what? You risk being laughed at? Being criticized? Being ostracized? Being seen for who and what you truly are? Being vulnerable?

This vulnerability is the crack in the wall of the ego. It's where light shines in, and light shines out. It's where love passes between you and the world, in both directions. This vulnerability is precisely what you need to step into in order to share your light and love and gifts with the world. And the world is hungry for your gifts. It is hungry for your gold, your brilliance, your expressions of Divine Wisdom. Those around you see you, and they are looking to you for examples of how to be in the world. Whether you know it or not, whether you have asked for it or not, it stands that you are an example in the world; a leader. Your friends, your acquaintances, strangers on the street, enemies... all of these people see you and watch how you engage in the world. They see when you share your art and your brilliance, and they see when you choose to look the other way.

They hear the excuses not to create; I'm too busy. I'm too tired. I don't have the right instruments yet. I'm not sure I'm ready. All of these are not you; they are the ego speaking. The ego, which wants to keep you playing small in order to avoid your delving deep into the heart and swimming in your own light, love, gold and passionate brilliance. The ego, which wants to prevent you from diving headlong into your Heart's Swimming Pool, where you can immerse yourself with reckless abandon, knowing with full certainty that you are safe, you are celebrated, and that you are life and love.

Why would the ego want to keep you from this joy, your natural birthright, the place you envisioned as we sat down? The place you know in your heart is your true home? Simple; the more you recognize your true brilliance, the less you have to rely upon the ego to give you ideas about your identity. And when you finally realize that you are all of the love and brilliance in the universe personified, you will finally draw the correct conclusion that the ego was never your friend, never your ally, and never should have been given the keys to your Mercedes.

So think back again to that time and place when you felt completely at home in your own heart. Think about the activities that take you back to this place, this feeling of being at one with yourself and the world. If chanting, singing, humming, and playing with words and phrases and melodies takes you to this place, then let's focus on that.

You, in all your magical brilliance, have everything you need to write your own chant. You have a heartbeat. You have a voice. That is enough. That is all you need. I hereby certify you and grant you full license to create chants and sing them publicly, as loud as you like. I grant you complete sovereignty over your chants; how you sing them, when you sing them, and where you sing them. You have complete control over whom you chant to and why. All the power of the universe is yours. Simply call upon your heart to guide you and then listen carefully.

The process is very simple. First, hum a melody. Pick any notes you like. Just play with your voice. Take a deep breath and then let it out, and let a sound come out with the breath. Play with your breath and the sound that comes out. Let something fun tickle you and come out. If it's laughter, great. If it's a long, low moan, great. There are no wrong answers here. All tears are welcome; all shouts of joy are welcome, and all fiery, passionate anger is welcome here, too. Fear is also welcome here.

However, the deeper you go into the Heart, the more you may begin to recognize that gratitude is arising. And you can use this as a two-way street; you can go to the heart to access gratitude, or you can use gratitude to access the heart. Either way is fine. As you allow your emotions to come out freely, you have the choice to either judge and criticize them (ego), or honor and bless all that comes out of your mouth, the movements of your body, and your expression. You are an expression of the Divine; to honor and bless all of your musical expression is to honor and bless the Divine. And that's why we're here today, to bless life itself. For we are part of life. We are the dance of life. Poetry in motion.

Now that you've begun to express yourself vocally, find a melodic phrase that makes your heart sing and repeat it a few times. It can sound like 'la la la' or 'doon doon doon' or 'ba pa daa pa daa...'' it doesn't really matter. All expressions are right and correct here; there is no wrong way here upon the Inner Throne of the Heart. For that is where you are sitting right now. You are kings and queens of the Inner Throne of the Heart. All of this is yours. So open your mouth, relax your throat, and let your melody come out freely.

Now pick an energy to honor. All energies of the universe live within you at all times. If we think about the energies associated with the 10,000 directions, they all come together in one point inside your heart. The energy of new awakenings. The angry, protective mother. The destroyer of obstacles. The magician, who creates solutions to problems. The warrior, who takes swift, clean action to get things done. The lover, who is in touch with emotions and embodies them freely. The sovereign queen or king, who sees the big picture and takes care of the realm. The trickster or jester or joker, who uses humor and trickery and folly to point out deeper truths about life. All of these energies live within each and every one of us. And every single one of these energies is available to us at any moment, simply by calling them forth.

So what energy would I like to call forth in this moment? Choose that energy and think of a word or phrase that captures the deepest truth of that energy for you. Now add the melody, knowing that you cannot possibly do it wrong or incorrectly; it is impossible to do so. The concept of 'wrong' or 'incorrect' expressions of love is simply meaningless in the realm of the Heart, which sees truth and recognizes that the ego's tricks are empty.

Now it's time to repeat your phrase and melody out loud. This is your chant. Sing it loudly for all to hear. Sing it quietly for yourself, to remind you of your connection to the universe. There is no other. You are not separate. You and the universe are one. You are one with the Divine.

You are the Divine, embodied.

Manipulation

Man. I find myself flip-flopping... I can go from being the most generous, thoughtful, kind, supportive friend in the world to being the most critical, defensive person in a matter of minutes. Handing over my power to ego, which would have me believe that someone is trying to pull the wool over my eyes instead of treating them with gentle compassion and meeting them where THEY are. Demanding that they cross the field to meet me where I am, rather than honoring their outreach toward me and working to see them as they show up in the world in this moment.

Why is that? Why do I do that?

What is my payoff for playing critical and cold and stand-offish instead of understanding and accepting and letting folks off the hook? Giving them a break when I know good and well what they are trying to say?

Note: When someone is trying to explain something and does not come out and ask for what they want in very clear terms, I commonly feel like I'm being manipulated. I absolutely hate hate hate working to 'fill in the blanks' when I sense that someone wants something from me. I become defensive, like someone is trying to trick me or fool me into doing something that I don't want to do. And if I'm not sure whether I want to do it, hearing and seeing such behavior pushes me toward not wanting to do whatever it is I think (as I try to figure it out) they are asking of me.

Are you asking me for time? Energy? Resources? Are you asking me for connection? Love? Support? Understanding? Why do I have to try to figure it out?

In the case of people who are younger than me, I understand that they are young. They are still learning how to ask for what they want or need. They do not necessarily have the skills to do so yet, and may need assistance. In that sense, I'm usually very happy to help them identify what it is they are trying to ask for, and in a supportive way, so that in the future they can better identify and ask for what they need. So that in the future, they can self-advocate effectively. So they can learn the system and how to navigate within it.

However. When my assumption is that someone already knows (or 'should' know) how to ask for what they need and I perceive them dancing around the question, hesitating, hemming and hawing (all my judgments, I know) instead of just coming right out and asking clearly for what they want, I get angry. I get resentful. I get resistant. Because I feel like they are trying, somehow, to take advantage of me. To lie to me. To cheat me. To steal from me. To manipulate me, which is the most infuriating thing of all, as it takes me back to early childhood.

And I dig in my heels. I become very, very meticulous in my questioning. I become very intellectual and heady. I become the king of logic and the fool of the heart. This is what happens when I think someone is trying to manipulate me.

In the realm of the Heart, it is impossible to manipulate anyone. There is never a desire to manipulate anyone. There is no 'other' to manipulate, for all are "myself". All are simply trying their best to be understood, loved, and accepted in the present moment. In the realm of the heart, all are longing for connection, striving for increased intimacy and shared joy. Looking always for new ways to connect and to experience love and connection and joyful union with each other, for to do so is to connect with oneself, again and again.

It is a trick of the ego that makes you believe that there could ever be some 'other' who would want to take advantage of you. When people do walk away with your money in their hands, laughing to themselves and muttering, "sucker!" under their breath, it is again nothing other than the ego driving their behaviors. To respond from the level of the ego is to give their behavior credence; to bestow some credibility upon their ego. Since the ego is illusion and mirage, responding to it from one's own ego is akin to responding to a shadow with fear.

Acting as if someone is trying to take advantage of you is simply playing small; the ego's way of making sure that you are sufficiently distracted and not looking toward the heart. For, as we've said numerous times already, looking toward the heart means recognition of the Truth: that the ego does not actually exist. Simply a list of preferences; preferences "for" and preferences "against". Looking toward the heart feels risky because close identification with the ego demands constant attention to the ego; constant attempts to satisfy its wildly erratic demands. Looking toward the heart means the ego risks dissolution into its natural state as a mirage. And the ego does not like that one bit.

Sinking into generosity for awhile can feel good, can even feel effortless for awhile. At some point, if the ego sneaks in through the back door, the ego can even whisper things in your ear that seem to support such generosity. Things like, "Wow... I'm a really generous and loving guy. Look how selfless I am! Look how supportive I am! I'll bet I'm this person's best friend... I'm kind of like a savior. Look how amazing I am!"

The ego sneaks in and begins to take credit for the egoless behavior taking place. That's how it hijacks the loving and caring behavior of good people. Good people who are not necessarily on their guard for the ego's tricks and antics. For the ego's sabotage. And then, moments later, when someone else has difficulty expressing their thoughts or desires, has troubles asking for what they want simply because they are not quite able to identify and articulate it clearly, that's when the ego steps forth in a new way, claiming victimhood status. (One of the ego's very favorite claims of all time.) "Why should I have to try to understand what this person is saying? They are obviously trying to pull one over on me. And besides, I just spent the past hour being loving and giving and selfless! What about me? Don't I deserve some attention and care? Why does it always have to be me who is giving all the time? Giving love. Giving attention. Giving support. What about supporting me? What about loving and caring for me? When is that going to happen? If I'm always supporting others, who is going to support me?"

Herein lies the ego's fatal flaw, for it overlooks one of the most basic truths about Love: When one loves and feeds others, he himself is fed through the act of loving them. The ego's demands are based on a zero-sum approach to love: "if I give love away, I have lost love. I have less love." When actually the opposite is true: "the more love, support, and generosity I give away, the more I have... the more I enjoy... the more fully I live my life."

The ego wants you to forget this and will do anything in its power to fool you.

Gratitude

One secret to successfully letting go of what you perceive in the world is to let it pass through. It can feel distracting, we know... all of the sounds, the sights... the pleasant and unpleasant. Keep in mind that it is nothing other than the ego which determines what shall be called 'pleasant' or 'unpleasant'. In fact, the very thing that may be considered 'pleasant' one day may be 'unpleasant' the next day... or the very next moment. This is the fallacy of the ego revealed.

This is where the importance of gratitude comes into the picture. By extending gratitude to everything and everyone, you bypass the ego's circuitry and take your attention directly back to the heart. The more you are able to bless and honor every single sensory perception, the better able you will be to remain in the heart space, which is the center of peace and calm in the stormy world of the senses.

There is no need to be unhappy. Things appear to be a certain way... you know full well that things are not what they appear. And yet you continue to get frustrated and angry... impatient and sad when things don't appear to be going your way. Keep in mind always that everything is going your way... everything is conspiring for your continued growth and evolution. For your final realization that you are all there is. As your brother Hafiz says, sometimes the Divine is in a playful drunken mood and wants to hold you upside down and shake all of the nonsense out. All of eternity is ready for you to wake up and remember that you are Love itself; that you are the one you have been waiting for. And every time you feel frustrated with something in your life, it is because you have, once again, listened to the ego's rantings and have taken them on as your own beliefs.

Again, this is unnecessary. And yet it's perfectly fine to go on for as long as you like, grabbing on to the ego's rantings. But in a world where true happiness is your very birthright, why would you ever even consider listening to the ego? Best simply to set it aside today... this very moment, and to begin pointing your attention in the direction of gratitude and grace.

A simple 'thank you' for everything you see and hear is a great way to start. "Thank you" to the birds, the garbage truck, the nosey neighbor, the police car siren, the cat's meows, your wife's bad mood... 'thank you' for all of it. For as we've said before, all of it resides within the teacup of the Divine, as do you. Choosing to try to reject any part of it is futile, since it is essentially meaningless. How can the ocean reject any single drop of itself?

Simplify. Here is another piece of advice for you. If you are ready to move to the perceived 'next level', simplify your life everywhere you can. It's perfectly fine to start small. How many objects are in your current possession that you do not use, enjoy, or need? Let them go. Find another home for them. Simplify your finances. Your belongings. Your habits. Simplify what you do for fun. Simplify how you look at your own life. For the more you simplify your behaviors, the more you simplify your thoughts. And the thoughts are the playground of the ego. It's like paring down a wildly growing tree... removing all the unnecessary branches that have been running rampant all these years. Simplify your thoughts and you bring yourself one step closer to remembering that you are the Heart.

Service. Place yourself in the service of those around you... community members, brothers and sisters. Every moment that you dedicate to being of service in the world is a moment that you take back from the ego, which would have you believe that the hours you perceive yourself to be experiencing somehow 'belong' to you... are somehow 'yours' to do with as you please. The only result of trying to hang on to these moments is frustration, boredom, and a lack of serenity. For it is impossible, by your perception, to stop the apparent 'flow' of time... even more impossible still to save it up for later. One downfall to claiming any sort of time as 'yours' is to end up wondering how to spend it; having walled yourself off from everything and everyone, you end up in the service of the ego, doing things that are meaningless and help no one, including yourself.

From a broader perspective, of course, all roads do lead back to the Home of the Heart. Indulging in the folly of the ego will simply result in dissatisfaction, over and over, until you begin to realize it in advance and make new choices. This is part of the beauty of following the ego... even the ego's demands lead to the apparent 'destruction' of the ego. So worry not... (for worry is yet another tool of the ego), you cannot possibly go wrong on this perceived journey.

Likewise, no one else can possibly go wrong, either. Remember this when you feel the urge to judge those around you, especially those you love, and who love you. Remember this when you feel the temptation to start proclaiming ultimatums. For all is flexible; all is ever changing and fluid. Your ultimatum is like a seagull's cry for the ocean to stop churning, just for a moment, so it can catch its breath; completely meaningless and actually humorous from the ocean's point of view. Your beloved, who is on his or her own path, is doing precisely what he or she should be doing. And your experiences in relation to that are also perfect. Even your judgments of imperfection are themselves perfect. There is no need to get too riled up about things.

Remember: the practice of non-resistance is the best path for you at this time. Listen. Watch. Understand as best you can. And go back into gratitude, over and over. Go back into the heart, again and again, and listen carefully for your guidance.

You will always find guidance through the heart if you listen; if you just give yourself half a chance to hear something, anything at all, with an open mind and open heart. You will always receive the guidance you need, even if you refuse to accept it or follow it. It will always be there for you. For it IS you.

Another thing; steadfast determination in the face of boredom, tiredness, and general feelings of distractedness will always take you closer to your goal. Steadfast determination to look toward the heart; to create an environment of vast calm around yourself wherever you go, this is the hallmark of a master on the path. Wherever you go, create a sense of easygoing peacefulness. Create an aura of compassionate understanding. This is all within your power. There is no external being or entity who bestows an aura upon you. It is already yours. All you need do is to generate it and extend it, simply by letting your understanding shine through. Understanding for the apparent shortcomings of others. Understanding for your own perceived shortcomings, judgments, and all of those aspects of your personality that you might wish you did not exhibit.

The personality is simply the face of the ego. Whatever personality you judge yourself to 'have', it is not you. It was never you. So all of the selfishness, all of the selflessness... all of the judgments, positive and negative, that you hold for yourself, now is the time to release them into the ether, where they belong. Release them all, turning back toward the heart, creating a sense of calm joy within and around yourself. And when others get stirred up, go more deeply into your calm.

And when they come to you for calm, remain calm. Give them all the calm you have to offer, and then give them more. For they are not actually taking anything from you; they are simply drinking from the well that is flowing through you. And this well is not yours to withhold.

Even if such a laughable concept were somehow possible.

Unfolding

Create space for others to unfold in their own time, to blossom at their own rate. There is no need for, nor benefit from trying to force things to be any particular way. People will choose whom they want to connect with. They will respond to stimuli as they will, whether these responses seem rational to you or not. And perhaps the less rational, the better, for the ego, intellect, small mind would love to have everything mapped out. Would love to have a logical explanation for everything it perceives. A spreadsheet with check boxes all over it. That is the desire for a black and white world, where things are concrete and clearly defined.

As you know by now, this is not reality, in any sense of the word. The rules you set are simply ties that bind yourself. The limits you set only limit your perception and your imagination. The creative force of the heart is limitless, and sets no boundaries on what is possible. Infinite possibility is the true nature of the universe, and this is why you perceive what seems to be chaos in your world. Every outcome is possible, and they are limitless, endless, and without number.

And at the same time, they all lead back to the heart. There is no need to fear.

Stepping forth into gratitude is always the right thing to do when you're unsure. When you feel confused, or doubtful, or tired, or angry or sad... Gratitude is the answer that will always guide you back toward joy. Peaceful serenity is to be gained by giving thanks for all things, precisely as they are, without exception. Keep in mind: it is only your limited perception that would allow you to believe that anything is out of place. All relationships, no matter how they appear, are perfectly unfolding. Do not be confused by what you see. Remember that it is not real. It is finite, and therefore temporary. It is not lasting.

Step toward what is real by turning inward with gratitude. Share your brilliance and gold. Share your joy, for it is the energy of the universe that flows through you. When you share joy and acceptance, you open yourself to the flow of the universe through you. The more you do this, the easier it becomes to surrender the ego and lay it aside. The easier it becomes to serve as a clear mirror for everyone around you. The brighter you shine, the more you light up the room, dispelling the darkness and reminding every other being of their own true light.

Treat yourself as you would treat a king or a queen; a dearly beloved child. Treat yourself with the love and compassion you would offer to someone you respect and admire completely. Offer gifts of silence to yourself. Write love notes and leave them around the house for you to find. Laugh often and enjoy simplicity in life. Simplify. This is important. Step back from those obligations that your ego holds dear. Do your work, then let it go. Give completely of yourself in your work, in your play, and in your silence. Solitude is a key element of your path. Be sure to honor yourself by setting aside time for solitude every day. Only in the quiet of the present moment can you recognize how much noise your ego generates... to keep you distracted, off balance, and moving. Searching. Looking. Seeking.

There is nothing to seek. There is nothing to find. All of what you need is right there in your heart. No need for a fancy house, a new car, an expensive guitar. These things can all seem nice, but they are not necessary. All that is necessary is your heart and all it contains. This is all you need. There is no other.

Sledgehammer or tissue?

Love. Understanding. Compassion. Grace. Wisdom. Care. Gentleness. Generosity. Active receptivity.

These are your lessons. These are your homework. Every time you reach for your hammer and your sword, we say pause. Wait. Breathe. Is that sledgehammer really the right tool for this job? Give it a minute and you may just find that a Q-tip, or a tissue, might actually help you to achieve your goals more effectively than the machine gun you're wielding.

And how much do you really know? What do you know of life and death? Really, truly? What do you know of the universe, dear ego? You believe that you know, and you enjoy moving forward with that shield across your chest. But take it down. Take it off. Step more fully into your true vulnerability, which will always and ever be your true strength. Demonstrate. Show the world what compassion might look like. Give them an example of gentleness. Let them see what understanding sounds like. Looks like. Smells like. Tastes like. Feels like.

Tell me a story. A story about anything. Make these pages black with story. Take off your watch and refill your glass and tell me a story. Tell me a story about love. About passion. Tell me a story about life. Show me what it looks like to hang from the rafters and swing from the chandeliers with your song of life in your heart, breath of the divine flute in your lungs. Dance for me with reckless abandon. And don't worry too much about bumping your head, or pulling a muscle... or forgetting the words or stumbling into someone and causing harm. There is no harm. There is no watch. There is no need for fear.

There is no need to fear shitty marriages; they only exist in the realm of the ego, or small mind, where spiritual sight is limited on your plane of existence. You need not worry, and therefore, need never plant seeds of doubt or fear into the minds and hearts of others. It is needless. Things will always evolve, ever turning and tuning in more sharply and lovingly with kindness, clarity, and insight.

WHY? This was the funniest question you ever heard last night... the idea that one would need a REASON to be grateful for something, otherwise it was bullshit-- otherwise it would somehow not 'count', and would reflect some measure of inauthenticity. It is the ego that would have you believe intellect must justify each feeling of gratitude. And what does it take to 'get' to the place of gratitude? "I'm not there yet..." How far is that stretch? What is the span that must be crossed? How many light years, or miles? How many kilometers or leagues? How many acres? How many yards? How many feet? How many inches? How many centimeters? How many millimeters? How many micrometers? Okay, now we're getting close...

Yeah, actually, the distance can be calculated by the blink of an eye. "I am grateful." There. That's it. For what? "I am grateful for... this shoelace." Brilliant! You've done it! Now just take that one example, that main concept, and apply it to everything you see, hear, taste, smell, feel, and think. And watch what happens. Get ready, though... you'd better put on your space helmet, or at least a welding mask, because what will happen is probably going to blow your skirt back a bit. Might even knock you on your ass. And you'll be thankful, by definition.

Gratitude. Even, no-- especially-- toward those events and situations that felt the most challenging. Those things I once cursed... let me sing songs of gratitude for those very events... Where is my ability to dream up something magically creative? Where is my ability to think outside the box, and to accept nothing on its face, digging always deeper for some hint of truth buried below. That truth... sometimes it's right there on the surface... and sometimes I hide it from my own view. I cover my eyes and pretend that I have somehow been wronged by some outside force. I take on victimhood status. And that is a badge of honor I wear proudly, for all to see... "Oh, did you hear about Tim? Yeah, he really has been suffering lately... he was taken advantage of. Wrongly accused. Cheated. Attacked. Cruelly so. And all he was doing was passively being a saint. Then a garbage truck ran over him. He was praying for the driver of the truck as it rolled over his bones..."

Yeah... the victim. Keeps me from having to take responsibility for every single aspect of my life, from A to Z. Responsibility for who I am, what I am, where I am, when I am, how I am, and why I am. Yet taking responsibility does not suggest omnipotence, or total control, at all. No. It doesn't work like that. In fact, it's kind of the opposite, somehow... By taking full responsibility, I am thereby freed up to release control of that beyond my grasp. Those things I AM able to control, I do my best to handle in a good way. The rest, I acknowledge. I salute. I honor and bless with my sword. That is what gives me access into my true power and strength. As a man. As a leader. As a human.

Tell me a story. Tell me a fun story. I want to have fun. This is too heavy for me right now. I want to play. I want to dance and sing and frolic. I don't want to think about tax preparation or bills or relationships or shadow or the past or any of that stuff. I just want to have fun. Relax for a little while and forget, or refocus, anyway, away from the rigors of reality. I just want to check out for a few minutes... maybe an hour or two... and just float.

Actually, that's exactly what we recommend. Float. But with compassion and acceptance. For when you are truly sitting in a space of gratitude for every single detail in your life, you will suddenly find, to your complete amazement and delight, that there is no need to escape or distance yourself from anything. It will all become a delightful play. And you'll recognize that the guy up on stage playing the lead role is none other than yourself. And those other characters, who come onstage for a moment or two and then exit stage left, are also none other than yourself. You. They're all you. There's no one else in the audience except you. In all your brilliant forms.

Actually, we should say, "You", capitalized. Because You is none other than Us. And Us is none other than the Divine. So really, there's only One here at this show, and it's Him. Her. The Divine. Ain't nobody else around to blame or chide or convince or fix or argue with. Only The Man. The Queen. She's all that, and no less than all that.

If you're looking for anyone other than The Divine to answer the phone, you'll be waiting a long time. She's the Operator. She's the Director of the film. And while you may THINK that you're just you, you're not. Not really. You're simply Her pretending to be you. Just Her, playing another role... manifesting with your face and lifeline and story and baggage and expired passport with only one stamp because Japan is the only actual country you've ever visited and we need to change that because the beaches of Pelacone are so beautiful, especially this time of year.

CHAPTER TWELVE
Ego vs. Heart

Take Heart, and let Heart take you.

Let it take you through fields and over mountains. Let it take you to the edge of comfort, where satisfaction and complacency fall away like mist as you plunge into the night of uncertainty. Let Heart take you down back alleys and dirt roads, cutting paths through knee-high snow in the twilight. Let heart take you beyond what is expected. Let it take you into battle. Into chaos. Let Heart lead you over the edge of the cliff to see if you can fly. You can.

Let Heart take you. Completely.

You will have to surrender. Or what you have mistaken yourself to be will have to surrender itself completely. This will feel like self-destruction, and in the world of misperception, it is. But in the Field of the Heart, it is simply taking off the mask of the ego. Dropping it gently in the sink and looking squarely in the mirror.

You will have to surrender feeling okay about yourself. You will have to let go of the structures you hold so dearly, such as familial ties... friends, enemies, and the like. You will have to release the idea that you're an okay guy who occasionally does good things for others. You will have to sacrifice the image of yourself that you hold, be it underachiever or hero. Neither are true. Both fall flat in the light of Reality.

You will have to summon the courage to be heroic. You will have to summon the courage to be a coward. You will have to set both of those on the table before you. Along with your keys, wallet, watch, and any prescription drugs you may be carrying in your pockets. Please remove your footwear and set it beneath the table. You won't be needing these any longer. Where you are going, they won't serve you any protection.

You'll need to let go of outdated ideas of right and wrong. Good and bad. These are the ego's playground. And when you release them, you'll be flying in the face of the world you believe you live in. Do it anyway.

More than anything, you'll need to sacrifice your need for mediocrity. Your desire to settle for second best. Or third best. Or 51st best. Or third worst. You'll need to set aside your undying urge to identify someone or something to follow. Or join. There is no more joining. There is no more following. The only organization left to you is the brilliant disorganization of Reality. The only leader to follow is your own heart.

Follow your heart into the darkness and find out what life truly is. Hold it up in front of your face and look through its gauzy texture. View everyone around you through this filter and you will see a very different world than you've ever laid eyes on before. The world you've feared drops away, revealing itself to be nothing more than a hall of mirrors. An endless field of creative possibility. What will you create in this world, now that you know it is harmless? Now that you understand you've been frightened of a merry-go-round, are you ready to leap on and take a ride?

Take heart, and let heart take you.

Let it take you all the way. Let it carry you effortlessly. All you have to do is stop protesting. Stop resisting. Just climb on. Relax. Surrender control. You have never had control anyway... no matter what illusions you might have about the world and your place in it. Since all in this world is temporary, all is empty. The shiniest awards lining your mantle will all turn to ashes in your mouth one day. The best reputation will quietly recede into the black swamps of time, bubbling as they slowly submerge themselves back into the darkness of temporality.

Physical beauty passes and fades. Song recedes. The sun sets. Gleaming metal rusts. The newest technology becomes old and antiquated; outdated and useless. The coolest sunglasses become goofy looking. Only the timeless is timeless. And only the heart is timeless.

Timelessness means stepping out of time. It means handing over all of the structures used for identification in the pretend world. It means knowing that you will never get them back. But take comfort: once you surrender them completely and glimpse Reality, you will never want them back. It's like the chewing gum that has lost its flavor long, long ago... the gum that you spit out on the street, even though you know it's impolite, against social norms, and possibly even illegal. And as you continue down the street, you see other little wads of gum in the gutter... how eager will you be to scoop them up and pop them into your mouth?

This is about how tempting your structures will seem to you upon glimpsing Reality through the lens of the heart. Take Heart, and let Heart take You. Let it take you back around to the front door, where You will answer the door. Go ahead. Knock on that door. Knock on it with all your might. Ring the doorbell. No answer? Then smash that door in! Kick as hard as you can. This mansion is not the home of some powerful politician who will call the cops on you. It's not the presidential retreat of some dictator whom you need to fear. This is Your Home! This castle is your birthright! You were born here, and here is where you will live out your eternal life. That's your address on the mailbox. Your guitars inside... Your rocking chair, your perfect sofa... your blender and your delicious food in the refrigerator. Those are your paintings on the wall... your LP's lining the shelves of the record collection.

Peek through the windows. Those are your plants. Your crystal chandeliers. Your golden goblets sitting on the table. All of that fine china and flatware? It's yours. It always has been.

And yet you locked yourself out, long ago. You stumbled down the street, down around the bend, forgetting all this time that you had the key right there in your pocket. You imagined all of these horrific things happening to you... All these adventures and epic sagas you've survived. All of these tales you tell your drinking buddies down at the tavern. You bought crutches and a wheelchair. They were initially props to help you get more in the mood as you fine tuned your tales. Eventually you got so used to them that you relied on them to tell your stories. Then you began to believe the stories. Little by little, they became more and more true for you, until you could recite them in your sleep.

And you did. Sleepwalking through your life came to be how you passed the time... it became your very existence. Someone told you it was all in your head, and they were right. But you simply took it as another arrow aimed at you. It became another trophy on your mantle-- another sacrifice that you believed you'd made to some higher moral ground.

What an exciting night of drinking you had last night! The stories you told! The crowds who listened with excitement in their eyes! The food you ate! The lights! The sounds!

And now, with slightly blurred vision and just a hint of unsteadiness in your gait, you stumble up to the castle wall, climbing over and falling into your back yard. The sprinkler system does not activate and get you all soaking wet, like it might in the movies, but you grin all the same. It's dark, and you left the flashlight inside, so you have to fumble around in the dark to find the doorknob. But the back door is locked. And there's no key anywhere to be found. You've been abandoned again. All hope is lost. It was all true... things are so hopeless... why did you even consider trying to succeed. What you see is what you get. The sobs erupt, the tears cascade down, and the snot flies. Just as you're about to sink down against the back door and really get cooking, you feel something in your pocket.

What the hell is this, you think, as you slide your hand over the protrusion at your side. It's the key. The key to the front door. You go around. You stand at the front door with the key in your hand. And you start banging with your fists. No one is answering, you notice. No one cares! No one is there! You're all alone!

And as you prepare to go back into hysterics and victimhood, as ego makes its one last stand, you feel something jagged in your hand. You look down, surprised to find... yes. The key. You're still gripping it. All you have to do is slide it into the lock and turn it. You do so and the door swings open. Wide open.

Now all you have to do is walk through that doorway, into your castle. Coming back home to a place you've actually never left. Are you ready to return to your rightful place in your Lover's arms?

Conductor vs. Facilitator

Do you know the difference between the conductor and the Facilitator?

The conductor: See me, hear me, love me

The conductor has a preconceived idea of how he wants things to unfold. There is the possibility of failure-- of getting the timing, pitch, or volume wrong. The conductor sees his job as that of getting the group to create something of value; to come together to fulfill the conductor's vision. The conductor exercises control over the pitch and timing of those in the group. Outcome based, this event is a performance, to be measured, critiqued, and labeled. The resulting measurement of the group's performance, as led by the conductor, becomes a measurement of the success of the conductor. The eyes and ears of the group members are trained on the conductor during the event.

During this event, the conductor's stance is: look at me, listen to me. Rhythms and melodies may be complex or obscured, requiring all other members to focus attention upon the conductor. The conscious or unconscious message sent by the conductor to the group is, "Look how amazing I am." The conductor's inherent motive is to get unfulfilled needs met; to receive acknowledgment and appreciation from the group... to demonstrate to the group how unique and special he is; to stand in the spotlight for a moment and to gain the acknowledgment and respect of the members of the group. To demonstrate his talent to the group.

The ego drives the bus when the conductor is leading a song. The ego uses a number of strategies and techniques in order to bring all attention back to itself in order to feed itself, to strengthen the delusion that it exists. To look and feel important and worthwhile. To cover up feelings of doubt, uncertainty, and fear of not being good enough.

Having forgotten that his true identity is Love, the conductor's only desire is to reassure himself that he is okay;

that he is still relevant and worthy of love. The underlying misperception here is that he exists separately from Love, and as such, exists in isolation from love. He mistakenly believes that there is a lack of love; that somehow he needs to get more of it from an external source, and that the external source is other people. He believes that if he can get the admiration and respect of other people, he will receive their love, which he needs since he does not have a sufficient amount of his own love in his life.

The Facilitator: See yourself, hear yourself, love yourself

The Facilitator has no idea what sounds or sights might unfold. There is no possibility of failure... no right or wrong pitches, timing, or volume. All is welcome. The Facilitator acknowledges and encourages freedom, and sees his job as that of inviting each individual member of the group to look within, to express whatever feels right in the moment, any pitch within any timing, including no apparent timing at all, in order to fulfill the universe's vision. Process based, this event is an organic unfolding, to be experienced physically, mentally, and emotionally-- and then released. The resulting acknowledgment of connection of each individual with himself, and with others, is celebrated as a success for each member and for the group as a whole. The eyes and ears of the group members are focused both inward and outward toward all other members of the group, or upon any other individual in the group at any moment, according to what feels right in the moment for the individual.

During this event, the Facilitator's stance is: look at everyone in the group, including yourself. Listen to everyone in the group, including yourself. Rhythms and melodies are simple and clear, increasing the chances of all members following or approximating them, providing a simple and clear framework within which members express their own rhythms; their own melodies; their own truth.

The conscious or unconscious message being sent by the Facilitator is, "Look how amazing you are." The Facilitator's inherent motive is to create space within which each member can freely express... to create an environment of safety and respect where each member has an opportunity to get their own unfulfilled needs met. An environment where each member has the chance to receive acknowledgment and appreciation from herself. To demonstrate to herself how unique and special she is. For each member in the group to simultaneously stand in their own spotlight and gain the acknowledgment and respect of themselves. For each member to demonstrate his talent to himself, all other members, and to the universe.

The Heart drives the bus when the Facilitator is leading a song. The Heart uses a number of strategies and techniques in order to bring the attention of each member of the group inward, back into themselves in order to feed themselves, to remind themselves of their true identity. The Heart has no need to look or feel important and worthwhile-- the Heart has no need to cover up any feelings of doubt, uncertainty, or fear of not being good enough because those thoughts are meaningless to the Heart.

Swimming in Love, the only desire is to help each member of the group remember that they are also Love; that there is only One and each of them is it.

The underlying recognition and understanding here is that nothing exists separately from Love, and as such, there is nothing that could possibly exist in isolation from love. The Facilitator knows that the idea of there ever being a lack of love is meaningless; that the source of all love is within himself. He understands completely that the admiration and respect of other people is temporary, fleeting; impermanent. It has a beginning, middle and an end, and therefore, having a finite lifespan, is inherently empty. He knows that love is immeasurable, since all things are simply love.

Every day, in every moment on your path, you have the opportunity to choose whether you want to be a conductor or a Facilitator. It is one thing to try to get others to act or think in a certain way in order to meet your ideas of what life should be. It's another thing entirely to empty yourself of all expectation and to simply work toward creating space and gentle guidance that points the way for each individual inward, back into his own heart, that he might come to remember the ultimate truth: that he has never lost connection with love because he is love. He merely closed his eyes and told himself a story, imagining it to be true. A story of dragons and demons... lights and colors and sounds and pictures and words... songs of hope and glory; songs of tragedy and despair. Struggles and pain and sacrifice. Confusion and separation and darkness.

All of these reside within Love's teacup.

Revenge?

It's so laughable... revenge upon whom? Yourself? It's meaningless. Withholding love? From whom? Yourself? Here's the deal-- you could never do that. Not the actual You. It's impossible. It's like trying to wash your hands while keeping them in your pockets.

The full moon sighs as she looks down upon you. Sighs with a whisper of delight as you make your way home. For she knows that you will make it back home safely... of that there is no question; no doubt. And along the way, you may very well make up stories to keep yourself amused as you walk along the lane... through the forest... As her light filters down upon you, you keep walking, oblivious to the love that is being directed single-pointedly to your very heart and soul. You walk along in your own little world, completely blind to the magnificence that is pouring down upon you like a waterfall of love in each and every moment. It's not that you are cavalier, or uncaring... it's simply that you don't perceive. And that, too, is completely understood by her love. And she shines it down upon you nonetheless, never ending, and with a smile on her lips.

She carries you on her broad and powerful shoulders, lifting you up above the branches so they won't slap your arms or sting your face. She lifts you up so the salt of the waves won't sting your eyes, won't plug your ears. She shades your face so the sun won't burn your skin. She stands over you in protection, vigilant and ready to crush any enemy. Of course, in the same breath as she does this, she knows there is no enemy; enemy is a concept built upon illusion. There is only you and you and you again, dancing in the light. Dancing in the night. Dancing in sight of the moon, who looks over you every single night, even when you cannot see her. Even when you cannot hear her song. Even when you think you have been abandoned, like a small boy crying and running up and down Aisle Five in the supermarket.

But she is always there. She has never left you. It's impossible for her to leave you for a number of reasons. One: she is you. Two: she hangs there in the sky where she can see you, always. Three: everything upon which her gaze falls IS you. Three good reasons to remember that there is never anything to fear; there never was.

And what of this clumsy physical body? What to do about that? Nothing. Simply nothing. Just relax and let the waves of love wash over you, again and again. Let yourself become quiet and listen carefully for her gaze, buzzing silently in the air. Listen for the feel of her touch, which caresses you in every moment. The dragonfly knows her love, as does the ostrich and the penguin. The dragonfly, with brilliant wings and unconcerned flight path, carries the weight of the world on her shoulders for you, as well. For she, too, is no one other than yourself.

You'd better get used to this... to looking around and seeing nothing other than reflections of your own heart in the faces of every other creature and being on the planet. For this is a large bathroom, great for singing... with high, vaulted ceilings and a wonderful hot tub. A separate shower, like the Japanese have. Yes, this is God's bathroom, and you are invited as the special guest of the hour. This is your bathroom. These are your elegant windows, filled with sunlight and dazzling views. These are your mirrors and tiled walls and heated floors so you never feel cold or afraid at night.

You've seen visions of walking alone in the darkness up a solitary mountain covered in snow. You've looked out through tear-stained eyes at miles and miles of taillights as you've sat in traffic on rush hour highways that seemed to go on forever. In those moments of sadness and despair, it seemed as if your pain would never, ever recede. But look at you now. Here you sit, in this very moment, and those memories are being revealed for what they always and ever were: simple perceptions. Misperceptions, actually. Yet they too held beauty. And only now, as you look back do you begin to recognize the beauty in the pain. The beauty of traveling through that pain... recognizing that it does not last forever.

Now, the next lesson: none of them last forever. And this, too, holds magnificent beauty. For it is truth. And no matter how painful truth may seem in any given moment, through the cracked lens of your limited perception upon this plane of existence, still it is shot through with glory and wonder... The wonder of feeling and living and breathing and crying and falling in love, again and again in each moment, with life. With the moon. With the snow. With your own hands. With your own voice. With the promise of another breath. And when that promise is broken, a larger, more promise steps forward to reveal itself as true: you are not the physical body. When the physical breath ceases, life continues. You continue-- the you that you really are, not the façade that you see in the mirror as you shave. Not the one you imagine retiring one day... not the one who you recall being five years old.

No. For behind each of these masks lies your own true face. This face is revealed every time you look up at the moon. Every time you fall asleep. Every time you die. Every time you are born. Just a celebration of the life that you are, always were, and always will be. What guarantee could be more powerful than this?

Swimming pool

On those hot summer days in Texas, we would ride our bikes to the swimming pool. Do I have enough change to buy a candy bar? A soda? Look at all the pretty girls! Do I have the courage to try to do a gainer off the high dive today? Uh oh, there's a boy who told me he would beat me up... am I in danger today? How hot is it? My feet burn on the dry cement... and such relief when I pay my entrance fee and walk hurriedly in, past the bleach-cleaned dressing rooms and out into the dazzling sunlight.

I throw my towel on a chair and leap in without thinking, seeking relief.

Relief from loneliness. Relief from sadness. Anger. Fear. Self-doubt. Perhaps if I can stay underwater long enough, it will all be gone when I come back up to the surface. But even after a minute and a half, the noise and colors and madness and emotions would still be there, waiting for me as I gasped for breath.

Perhaps the best thing to do is simply to find a comfortable chair on the periphery and have a seat. Just watch the show. Watch the emotions coming up... and invite them over to sit with me. And if I sit with them long enough, they'll eventually excuse themselves and take their leave. They always do, in the end. The only thing that makes me believe they have parked their travel trailer in my front yard is my amnesia. I call them up on the phone again and again, and they agree to come on over and sit with me. And I lean in close, grasping at every word for hidden meanings... clues to why my life is like it is.

They get up to leave and I grab their arm, begging them to stay just awhile longer. "Stay," I implore. "I'll make dinner. Have a drink. Make yourself comfortable. Why hurry off? I love your company. Even though it's uncomfortable, it's what I know. It's what I'm familiar with. If you leave, I'll sit here in the silence."

These are the words of the ego.

"I'll sit here in silence. And if that happens, then I might be exposed for the fraud that I am. Because I am you. You NEED me if you want an identity. Who would you POSSIBLY be without me? You'd better thank your lucky stars that you have me around. I'm the one who keeps you safe. I'm the one who makes sure you look good... sound intelligent... are wearing the right clothing so you'll fit in, stand out, look the part."

Meanwhile, someone does a cannonball off the high dive, splashing me and jostling me with waves. I'm in the deep end.

Heart smiles. He's been sitting right here with us all the time, calm, relaxed, and happy. Just watching and listening. He does not argue or interrupt as the ego is spinning his tales... He does not interject when ego tells a little fib. Or a bald-faced lie. Heart does not point out the ego's endless contradictions. Heart has no need. As it turns out, we're sitting on Heart's couch. And this house? It's sitting on Heart's land. Heart owns this entire block. In fact, Heart owns the whole town. If we were down at City Hall, we could look up the records and find that Heart actually owns every square inch of this county.

And truth be told, if we could get off this rock and stand in the City Hall of some other planet, we could actually find the records that show Heart owns Earth. Zoom out farther still and we discover that Heart owns the whole place. All of it. In fact, Heart IS all of it. The air we breathe. The airless, inky black of outer space. Every square light year: it's all Heart.

Heart sits quietly on the sofa, smiling. She knows a secret. She leans over to me and whispers in my ear, "You know... I happen to own the swimming pool, as well. Lovely day for a swim, isn't it?"

I look outside, and the temperature is climbing... soon it will reach 100 degrees Fahrenheit. I can sit on the edge of the pool and watch. I can sit in the shallow end of the pool and feel the cool waves beating against my chest. I can swim along the bottom in near silence, watching the slow motion action below the surface. I can climb up the 10,000 steps of the ladder to the top of the high dive and throw myself into oblivion, crashing down and making waves of my own. Splashing and jostling the others. Making my mark on the world.

I notice something I'd missed before. That gorgeous woman sitting at the patio table where I've left my towel and my sandals... where my melting candy bar, my bag of chips and my warm soda are waiting for me... She's sitting at my table. She's smiling, unperturbed by the cries of the kid who fell and skinned his knee. (He shouldn't have been running.) Unbothered by the splashing nearby. Not phased in the least when pool water splashes on her hair.

She owns the place. It's all hers. She invites me over to join her. I swim to the side of the pool and get out, dripping. Afraid to drip on her, I stand back a little, grabbing at my towel to dry myself off before shaking her hand. She gently takes me by the hand and pulls me to her, turns me around, and plops me down squarely in her lap. My eyes are wide with horror-- "You idiot! You're going to get her all wet, and she's going to be so angry and disappointed with you... You blew it again!" A wave of sadness and shame comes over me, and I look down at the hot cement.

Still smiling, she gently puts a finger beneath my chin and raises my face up, and looks directly into my eyes. That wasn't you, she says-- that was ego. He's on your back right this moment, whispering into your ear.

I have a hard time believing that, but I say nothing. She smiles wider and reaches into her purse, producing a small hand-held mirror.

Here, take a look, she says. See for yourself. She holds the mirror at an angle, and I look, and sure enough, there's a little guy on my back, looking away, dripping wet, trying not to be seen. He's always there, she tells me. Learning to distinguish the difference between his voice and my voice is the key to knowing whom to follow.

She leans forward and pulls me back into her lap, kissing the top of my head as she holds me close. Mother Heart holds me like that for hours, and I hug her arms as they wrap around me and gently brush my cheek, and run through my hair. Together we watch the boys playing Marco Polo in the corner. We listen to the lifeguard's whistle as she calls 'time out' and sends two angry, fighting children out of the pool for ten minutes to calm down. We watch the retired former olympic champion practicing her seemingly effortless, flawless dives. We listen to the laughter, the screams of delight, the splashing and the sound of the ice cream truck's crazy, tilted music as it stops in front of the gate. We see the teenage boy slowly climb the ladder to the top of the high diving board, waiting his turn... summoning his courage to try to do a gainer without hitting his head on the diving board.

We watch as the sun sets. The moon rises. The pool closes. The people leave. We sit there all night long, counting the stars. Listening to the summer breeze blow through the leaves on the trees. Listening to the cicadas as they sing out in waves.

She tells me things that make me weep with relief. Incredible things that I hesitate to believe... that I am love. That she is always with me. That, in fact, she IS me and I am her. The little guy on my back keeps whispering in my ear, contradicting every single thing she says. "I want PROOF!," he demands. "This is bullshit! She's lying! Think of all the times we've been screwed over the by system! By other people! By those who promised to love us forever! You can't trust this Heart lady! We've got to get out of here!"

She just smiles. She hears him, as well. I look up into her eyes, worried that the little guy on my back might be right... I mean, it really DOES feel like I've been screwed over, so many times. Like I've been lied to... cheated... stolen from... Why? How could all of these experiences be wrong?

She looks into my eyes and reminds me that all of this is hers. Every bit of it. She reminds me that even the little guy riding around whispering in my ear...even he is contained within the experience of Her.

There is nothing to fear, she says. I am here, holding you, always. When you think you need protection, come to me and you will find no protection is needed. When you believe you are being attacked, open your eyes and see that you are still sitting here in my lap. There are no enemies who would do you harm. No matter how terrifying or exciting or romantic things may appear to you, simply open your eyes and see that you are still sitting here with me and you will know grace.

The sun is rising. The pool attendants clean the pool and prepare the cash register. Children and adults alike begin to line up outside the front gate. Promptly at 8:00 am, the gates open and they file in. Splashes and screams of delight resume as if they'd never stopped.

Your own face

If you take this to heart, it will lead to your apparent self-destruction. Nothing will be left but ashes. Of course, in Reality, you will step out of your self-imposed cage. Things may get ugly. But in the end, it's worth it.

No worries if it doesn't seem to happen right away. You're guaranteed freedom from your ego one way or another.

There is no face that your gaze can fall upon that is not a reflection of your own face. The old, wrinkled, pruny face wrenched into a permanent frown... endlessly bickering and biting and grasping at every little straw... inspecting every technicality for a shred of power over her situation, over her world, over others... over her own wellbeing. This is you. The open, young, beautifully fresh and innocent face... the one that looks at you with admiring eyes and a grand, wide, gorgeous, inviting smile... the one who wants to be helpful, who looks to you for reassurance... who trusts you and genuinely believes that you can do no wrong. This is also you.

The bored, poker-faced guy who does not let you see any cracks in his facade... no chinks in his armor... no weakness or signs of humility or uncertainty... The guy who wants to know 'why' before taking a single step, before making any moves... the guy who has an opinion about every matter and refuses to back down from it without documented proof, evidence from a reliable source... This guy is also you. The man child who has not been out in the world, who lives behind the protective walls of his parents, carrying the burden of others without hope of ever getting to spread his wings... delving deeply into a fabricated fantasy world in order to escape the dreary ache of his daily existence. Yes-- also you.

All of these are you, no matter to which extent you adore or abhor them. They all present to you an invitation into your work-- into examining what you prefer, enjoy, disdain, reject, or simply ignore. It is this very examination that is the work of the day. This is the challenge. This is the call to freedom. The examination of these preferences, and the root of each preference, is the work at hand. Set aside the stories that bubble forth endlessly about WHY you hate or love any particular mask. These are simply the ego's way of avoiding the actual examination. Whatever the story, attraction or repulsion, where does this story come from? Who is telling this story? Why does this story feel so important as you carry out your daily existence?

Who or what is it that would have you believe this story? And to what end? What is to be gained for you by telling and retelling this story? What are you losing out on by telling and retelling this story?

More importantly, since the source of the story is not your true self, but rather, the ego, what does it have to gain by whispering this story in your ear, over and over through the years? What does the ego have to lose if you stop and inspect the source of the story carefully? What might happen to the ego if you decide to call a halt to the madness? Yes... it would be revealed to be the empty shell that it truly is... a figment of your imagination... built out of preferences. Preferences 'for' and preferences 'against'. All based on memories... memories of pleasure, memories of pain. All simply attachment. The desire to appear real to itself and to the universe.

Tired of taking a back seat to the ego? Tired of being its servant, day in and day out, with nothing of value to show for it? Want to get a little subversive? Are you ready to stir up a little trouble? Are you ready to make a noise of your own in the world, instead of simply parroting everything the ego whispers in your ear?

Try this: everyone you encounter in the world, bless and honor them exactly, precisely as they are. Including yourself. Everyone you meet, without exception-- show them kindness, acceptance, and love. Show them generosity. Demonstrate to them what non-attachment looks like. Show them what true freedom looks like. Be ready: the ego will kick and scream. The ego will rail against you at every turn. When you are generous and kind to someone it likes, be ready for it to take credit for any signs of gratitude. Notice when those signs of gratitude become expected-- who is it that expects a 'thank you'? Notice when those missing signs of gratitude bring up resentment-- who is it that becomes angry?

Bless and honor them as they are in the present moment. The woman who just found out she has cancer. The boy whose parents just announced they are getting a divorce. The girl who suspects she might be gay. The man whose father refuses to speak to him. The woman whose mother has mental illness and only knows how to respond with rage. The sexually abused child who runs and hides... and grows up to become a woman who runs and hides.

When you know these things about people, it's easier to show them compassion. Your ego pulls out its measuring tape and determines, based upon its rules and regulations (which change from moment to moment, by the way, depending upon the mood and the direction of the wind) who 'deserves' its so-called compassion... it's so-called caring. "This story is a good story; I'd better show compassion or else I'll look like an uncaring asshole." Once again, the ego, looking out only for the ego.

But what about when you don't know their story? The ego does not know what true caring is, for true caring is, by definition, selfless. Every act of the ego is based upon self-preservation; self-creation, in fact. Letting go of attention to the self is meaningless to the ego. There is no point of reference beyond itself from which to view the world.

Seeing the world through the lens of the Heart is where caring comes from... it's what makes caring possible. Caring can only come from the Heart. The reason that practicing true caring can sometimes feel difficult or painful is precisely because it can only extend from the heart; and when this occurs, the ego creates the illusion that something worth holding onto is being lost, surrendered, or given up. The pain comes not from the Heart, but rather the ego, which has just taken a backseat to the Heart as a result of your active decision to turn your attention away from the ego and toward the heart of another.

So you see someone and you do not know his story. The ego takes a few quick measurements and then provides a story for you. Then, if you're not careful, you believe that story as it gets whispered into your ear by the ego. The small mind. The intellect. It draws its conclusions, whispers them into your ear, and if you're not careful, you begin to repeat them to yourself. You accept them as truth. Now you have a story to follow. A story, like all other stories the ego would have you accept as truth, based upon nothing more than conjecture. Thin air. An empty story then judged summarily based upon the ego's rules and regulations. Which, again, may change on a whim.

How many times have you found yourself angry in traffic because someone is not following a certain rule, only to break that same rule moments later, with some special justification in mind? Who is doing that? Who is it that judges the other driver? Who is it that responds with anger? Who is it that later intentionally breaks the same rule? Who is it that creates the justification? And finally, who is it that accepts the justification as valid and goes about his business as if nothing is wrong?

One word: ego.

Resistance, even to another's resistance, is the ego at work. Subvert this crooked politician from your life. All you have to do is recognize when he's telling you his lies and then ignore them. Act counter to what he instructs. When he tells you to go right, go left. When he tells you to get angry, breathe deeply. See the machinations of the ego. Listen to the whirring of its gears. Become familiar with how it responds to certain situations with regularity, predictability. Notice in yourself all of the ego's tricks. And then, when you judge someone else is acting from ego, bless and honor them on their journey. By doing so, you bless and honor yourself as you engage with the ego for yet another day.

This is where Supreme Confidence, Supreme Humility will serve you well. Supreme confidence that what you see is not what you get; therefore, knowing that your true self cannot possibly lose, you smile in the face of whatever experience seems to be unfolding before you. Supreme humility in the fact that, at any given moment, the ego is waiting to trip you up; to whisper in your ear, urging you to apply its judgments to the present situation; and to respond based upon those judgments.

Supreme confidence that viewing the world through the lens of the heart will take you back to the underlying truth of all situations, no matter how seemingly counterintuitive; that all is Love. That nothing rests outside the boundless edges of Love. Supreme humility in the knowledge that something far more powerful than the ego, the intellect, the small mind, could ever invent, ever imagine, or ever even understand is at work, naturally, effortlessly, timelessly.

What does all of this mean? It means you've never been rejected. You've never been hurt. You've never been mistreated, abused, nor ignored.

From the perspective of the ego, yes... countless times, no doubt. From the ego's perspective, you have been fed to the wolves, kicked out of paradise for being not good enough... Attacked when you've shown vulnerability; and have had to fight tooth and nail for what you have today. And whatever it is that you have today, it's not enough. It's not quite as much as you deserve. If everyone knew how deeply you have suffered in this lifetime, they would no doubt erect a statue in your honor. (This is not said mockingly.)

You've played by the rules as much as possible. Or maybe you've played against the rules as much as possible, for the sake of survival. "Only suckers get screwed over. Only the strong survive." Do whatever it takes to get ahead. And maybe you have gotten ahead. Maybe you are the head of a powerful firm. Or maybe you've invented something that others want. Maybe you have thousands of dollars in the bank. Tens of thousands. Hundreds of thousands. Millions. Billions. Trillions. Maybe you own your own car. Maybe you own an island. A jet. Access to resources, which defines power in your realm. You have power. You are powerful. You have the influence to make things happen in your favor. Maybe all of this is true. Maybe you are living the life of your dreams, able to satisfy any desire you may experience... food, vacations, sex, fame, glory. Perhaps you are the most powerful person on the planet.

Thing is, you are not the physical body.

The physical body WILL fail, eventually. It will come to the end of its usefulness, and will fall away. Zoom out far enough, and we see that this so-called power of the ego is very, very finite. And even if we zoom in closer, and look at the lifespan of each individual 'satisfying' experience, we find that it, too, is finite. Sexual satisfaction has a beginning, a middle, and an end. And then it's done. A fancy dinner party, no matter how extravagant, must come to an end, sooner or later. All of the senses that cry out in hunger can only be fed for a limited time before they cry out again. In this sense, the concept of 'satisfaction' in any permanent way is revealed to be meaningless.

The ego is doomed. Doomed to failure. Doomed to death. Doomed to being revealed for what it is: empty. Impermanent. Hollow. Unreal. A figment of the imagination.

But what of the Heart? What does the world look like through the lens of the Heart? Through the lens of the heart we view Reality unadulterated. You, meaning your True Identity, have never been lied to. Lied to by whom? Love is all the only on in the room, and you are It. You have never been hurt. Hurt by whom? You have never been rejected. How could you possibly be rejected when you, being Love eternal, are the very source of all existence? You have never been judged or seen as unfit, unfinished, unbecoming, or insufficient in any way. You have never been regarded as lacking beauty, intelligence, strength, or magnificence. You are, in fact, the very definition of these words, which fall meaningless beneath your feet.

You are the Heart. The Heart is you. The Heart is Love. Love is all. Love contains all. Love defines all. Love transcends all. This means that You, dear one, are that which transcends all.

Do not be in the least bit surprised if your ego is piping up right now, getting defensive, dismissive, protective of its turf in your life. Don't be alarmed if thoughts of blasphemy happen across your radar screen as you read this. Naturally it will argue. Its very job is to argue. And viewing the world, as it does, through such limited scope, the ego, small mind, or intellect is unable, by definition, to wrap its head around the concept of something that transcends it. Therefore, the intellect will never, ever be able to intellectualize its way into knowing your true identity. Don't be surprised if the voice in your ear says something like, "This can't be proven. Therefore, this isn't true. It's all bullshit." The ego would like very much for you to dismiss this fundamental truth of your True Identity. There is nothing it would like more than for you to put this book down and never pick it up again. To never consider the possibility of meaning beyond what can be perceived via the five physical senses. But this book is not written for the ego. It is written for You. You are not the physical body. You are not the small mind, intellect, or ego. You are the cup that contains them all. You are nothing less than Love, creator of all.

Unexpurgated bullshit

Today is a day for great celebration! Joyfulness is your natural state, and so every day is cause for celebration, yet

316

today is especially so, for new awakenings have begun. Your intellect may not understand, and may question. This is all natural and not worth worrying about. Your ego or small mind may say, 'what's all the fuss about? I don't see anything new!', which is precisely what you might expect it to say, given its mission of keeping you knocked off balance and looking away from the prize. The prize is the Heart. And you've been looking toward the Heart. Stop worrying about whether or not this will work for your book and listen! It is only the ego that would have a running dialogue critiquing and determining, based upon its own particular score card, what is worth doing and what is not. Do you see, Dear One?

The Heart is calling and you are answering. Even the way you are responding, feeling slightly aloof from the calls to arms of the ego, is progress in the Heart's point of view. No, you are not doing it perfectly; and yes, you are doing it perfectly! We call upon you to remember the importance of disregarding any 'panic button' moments the ego would have you engage in. For these happen (oh so 'coincidentally') when you are on the verge of a new breakthrough upon your path. You, a powerful spiritual leader, are already and always making strides toward the Heart. For what feels like a long time to you (though not even the blink of an eye to us), you feel as though you have been struggling. Struggling toward what? Toward freedom from the dark cloud of sadness and worry that seemed to hover over you for so long. And today we announce that you have officially (lest you still need some sort of official certification) broken through into the sunshine. This has been happening all along, you understand, but now a new corner has been turned.

Get ready for increased power, increased understanding, increased compassion, and increased responsibility to your fellow man. And fear not; these are all the results of your own requests and demands upon the universe. None other than you, yourself have created this set of situations, where your brilliance and gold may shine to others who may benefit from it. The secret you must now remember, which is actually no secret at all, but through the eyes of the ego, is to continually set aside your intellect's desire to analyze and to determine what is successful and what is failure. Upon the Heart Path, there can BE no failure, no matter how things may appear to unfold. The worse things seem to be, the stronger your attachment to a given outcome that your ego has labeled "success". Deviation from such an outcome, in any way, shape, or form, will naturally appear to the crumpled, crooked ego to be lack of success, or failure.

Do not let your feathers be ruffled. Rest assured that the louder your ego bangs against the bars of its own prison, the closer to the Heart Path you are journeying. Feeling upset? Then you must be on the path, yet mistakenly listening and believing the words of the ego being whispered frantically into your ear. No matter. No bother. Simply relinquish, again and again. When you feel called to get angry, ask yourself who is getting angry. Ask yourself what the source of the anger could possibly be. Getting angry is a very human thing to do, and there is no shame in it at all. At the same time, the Heart is never the source of anger, for the Heart views all existence from a wider perspective. From the Heart's point of view, anger can be a powerful servant, yet there is truly no need to call upon such a servant. For everything is unfolding perfectly.

Where you are not a body, not a mind, what need could there be for anger, sadness, despair, or frustration? There are no losses ever to suffer; no victories to be won except for the victory of realization itself. Once that has occurred, all battles are won. All problems solved. Regardless of appearances from and to the outside world, once realization has occurred, you have arrived at the eye of the storm. The center of calm observation. At this point, it is no longer even 'you' (as identified by your ego) who watches. It is simply the Heart... the Universe observing Herself in action as she dances silently.

Here is the cause for your celebration today. You are witnessing you as you witness yourself unfolding, ever present and ever joyful in your silent dance. The songs that arrive through your Heart are all the song of the Universe, articulated beautifully, perfectly, by the Universe through the manifestation of Herself through your physical, mental, and spiritual being. Through the lens of your limited perception as a human on the planet, this will appear to happen for a short time, a number of years as your ego counts, and then will appear to end. Yet the Universe, in all of Her infinite glory, continues 24/7, 365... effortlessly... without beginning nor end. She has always been dancing and spinning. Which, Dear Child, I will tell you, means that you your very self have been dancing and spinning endlessly since the beginning of eternity. This alone is cause for celebration!

Now comes your next challenge: to begin being even MORE careful about the words you utter. You know precisely what we are talking about. Though you feel no lust toward your sister, you pretend that you do, making suggestive

319

remarks. Though you feel no worry about the daily comings and goings at work or at home, still you create meaningless chatter in order to pretend that you 'fit in' with the world you perceive. And though you know in your Heart that you have been a teacher for eons, still you hold on to antiquated, archaic, outworn concepts of the intellect and the ego that would have you believe that serving as a teacher is something you cannot do well, or properly. That there, somehow, is risk involved.

This, Dear One, is pure, unexpurgated bullshit.

Here's a great barometer for you: if you are experiencing any sensations of fear whatsoever, you are no longer looking through the lens of the Heart. How to fix this? Just remember that it is the ego that would have you experiencing fear, in order to keep you from stepping more fully into your Love Light. For the more deeply and fully you step into your Love Light, the more fully it is revealed how starkly naked the ego truly is... how powerless and empty and devoid of any true substance. What better way to keep you in the dark than to keep you playing small; to continue repeating old messages that seemed to make sense to you when you were a child, a teenager, a young adult. Disparaging messages about your worth, your place in the world, and your true nature. Lies about what and who you are, that connect your being to the physical body... your mind to your life.

It could not be more of a farce, even if you tried to make it so. And sometimes, you do. We see and hear when you choose to bury your face in your pillow, afraid to go out and take actions that you perceive to be risks. But now your perception is more pure than ever before. Simply set aside your habitual need to say and do things that contradict this great brilliance that flows through you. It is not OF you, therefore to recognize and acknowledge it has nothing to DO with you. In turn, there is no need for you to fear that you might be egotistical, or a megalomaniac. These accusations come from, you guessed it, the ego, who would STILL rather have you looking at guilt than at your own brilliance.

It is time to allow the ego to follow the path for which it has always been destined: to release it into the void. This is the ego's rightful place in the world, for the Realm of the Heart contains no rooms for such strangers to stay the night. The Realm of the Heart acknowledges fact and fact only: that the ego does not exist and in all actuality, never has. Only by resting here in the Realm of the Heart may you experience Reality in her full glory and beauty.

So set aside all fear, all judgment, all grudges. There is no need for them here: they are completely meaningless. Only Love, which is the candle that lights all other candles, resides here in the Realm of the Heart. This is your rightful home. Welcome home.

Path of the Heart

How do you know that you are on the Path of the Heart? You are always on the Path, for the Path is all there is. Still, how can you follow the Compass of your Heart? Listen and watch inside yourself for feelings of joy, peace, satisfaction, and comfort. Listen for that feeling inside that bubbles forth into laughter. Be aware of those moments when you feel especially connected to the world around you, to other people, and to yourself.

Feelings of joy and a deep sense of wellbeing are signals that you are viewing the world through the lens of the Heart.

Equally important is to learn to recognize what pulls you away from looking through the Heart Lens. Worry about any subject at all is a sure sign that you are dipping your toes into fear, which is the realm of the ego.

Some things to let go of; some things to stop worrying about-- Anything having to do with your survival; that is, the survival of your physical body. Yes, it is correct and proper to pay enough attention to your physical body to keep it functioning in a healthy way. However, beyond that the ego is sure to take over. Beauty, strength, fashion... these are all aspects of glamour, which are of the ego. They are all temporary, having a beginning, middle, and an end. As such, they are finite, hollow, and empty. Disregard them. Hairstyles, clothing, dining in chic restaurants... it is fine to enjoy these things so long as you realize, in each moment, that they are truly empty. That there is no way to hold on to them. That they will disappear, just as your physical body will, leaving only the infinite behind, smiling calmly.

It is the same with every sensory experience you can imagine. Vacations. Art. Music. Parties. Firewood. Shirts. Records. Going to the movies. All of these things are fine to enjoy. Simply remember, in each moment, that it is not real.

You may find that these experiences, once revealed for their inherent hollowness, will gradually become less and less satisfying, and therefore less and less attractive. The concept of 'living a full life' will take on new meaning as you begin to allow life to flow through you, rather than trying to create a life that defines you. Instead of grabbing on to artifacts and using them as evidence of the identity you imagine that you want, you will gradually let things go, more and more, enjoying them for what they are (illusion) and letting them pass.

Knowing that you truly own nothing, you find that you own everything. Knowing that no one location on the planet can ever truly be your home, you discover that the entire planet is home. Understanding that no single aspect of identity can ever capture who and what you truly are, you find yourself free to embrace all aspects of identity. This is the true gift of life... to recognize that you are infinite, beyond all sights, sounds, smells, tastes, and tactile sensations.

"What can I get?" is transformed into "What can I give?" "How can I gain" becomes "How can I contribute?"

Others may think that you are crazy... that you've "lost your mind." This is not so far from the truth; you have not 'lost' your mind, but simply chosen to stop allowing it to drive the bus, like putting the cart before the horse. The only true Horse is the Horse of the Heart. The cart is always the ego, intellect, or small mind.

Others, feeling unsettled by your behavior, may try to convince you that what you are doing is foolhardy. That in order to 'get ahead' you need to focus your attention and life energy upon such things as building a retirement fund; making political connections; amassing money; and squeezing as much efficiency out of resources as possible. They will do whatever they can to convince you that technology leads to happiness; that increased dependence upon social media is valuable. They will try to get you to agree with them that paying close attention to political and militaristic conflicts is the way to demonstrate your commitment to being a valuable human being; a contributing member of society.

When they see you turn away from such things as concern for money, fame, and resources, they will very likely feel uncomfortable. This discomfort is the hallmark of the ego, which feels threatened by any behavior that turns attention away from it. Others may become angry, frightened, or confrontational. They may take their anger and fear and frustration out on you. This is natural, and not to be feared or avoided.

The cause of their discomfort is your demonstration of shifting perspective from ego to Heart. The appropriate response to someone who is fearful or angry is to continue shifting your perspective from ego to Heart. In fact, this is the answer to every single challenging issue you perceive on your plane of existence. There is no situation in which stepping more fully and deeply into the Heart is ever the wrong answer.

When you step more fully into the Heart, you will begin to realize that there is nothing left undone. Nothing of true importance is ever left undone, for all resides within the infinite container of the Heart. Are you feeling regret for something said, or something left unsaid? Do you carry guilt or fear or anger for wrongs that you perceive you have committed or have suffered at the hands of others? These are simply misperception; nothing more. Rest assured that the compassion your ego would show you is nothing compared to that which your True Self shows you in every moment. And since it is literally meaningless for Love to ever trespass against Love itself, the concept of forgiveness also falls away as meaningless.

Forgiveness, however, does have value in the world. It is a useful tool that serves the function of bringing attention and awareness back to the Heart, where life is fully served in each moment. The practice of forgiving others does assist in releasing attachment to outcomes; releasing desire and fear of someone else's beliefs and behaviors. It also serves to release ourselves from the grip of the ego's attachments to our own beliefs and behaviors. In the end, forgiveness leads our awareness back to the Heart, where it belongs. This is our birthright, not something that 'should' be done because some set of regulations requires it of us, but rather because true joy and deep, unwavering happiness are your birthright. The perception that you do not have this happiness is the very curriculum that brings you back to it.

Since Reality is timeless, you have all the time in the world. There is no urgency; no rush to get it right. The ego thrives on deadlines; "I must learn how to play guitar before this week is over, otherwise I am a failure." This is one technique the ego uses to create a sense of urgency where peace would reign supreme. By creating tension, the ego provides distraction; something to focus on-- something that feels like it demands your attention-- in order to keep you from focusing on the Heart. In the realm of the Heart, which is always and forever your true identity, there is nothing to do and nowhere to go. Even as you strive to perform and to reach the limits of your human potential, which is truly poetry in motion, even the very essence of this, at the very core, is peace, tranquility, and joy.

Releasing attachment to outcome is the way to remember this joy and to 'get back in touch' with it. In reality, it has never left. You have simply turned your head and closed your eyes. Getting back in touch with the Heart is as easy as opening your eyes.

Grieving

Love and compassion. They can look like so many things. One of the most beautiful gifts you can possibly give to another person is to walk with them toward their pain and sadness, as they are ready. Guide them gently but firmly, with complete confidence, toward looking at their role in life. You can do this effectively through serving as a living example of those traits you would have others embrace.

Where in your life are you resisting? Where in your life are you refusing to embrace some aspect of yourself? Where are you avoiding the full embodiment of your sadness, pain, fear, and anger? Where is your heart broken? And where have you yet to grieve? For true grieving is one of the greatest gifts a human can ever receive... the gift of embodying sadness. Letting the sadness flow through one's being, completely. And then releasing it, turning it over to the Divine, which is none other than your own true Self.

Where in your life can you create space for others to experience their lives more fully? Where can you show more love, more light, and more brilliance toward yourself? For the more love you freely offer to yourself, the more love naturally flows to all those around you. Where is there more room for acceptance of yourself, precisely as you are in this moment? Where is there more room to allow resistance to slowly soften, even just a little bit, its protective stance against embodying emotion? Where can you allow yourself to sink more deeply into those tender places in your life, where fear, sadness, and anger currently retain some of their sharp, rough edges?

Where in your life can you give yourself permission to allow just a little bit of your toe to dip into the sadness you so desperately try to hide, repress, and deny? Where does your urge to control the world and others actually reflect a desire to avoid your own discomfort? What gold and brilliance do you recognize in others who have allowed themselves to fully experience and then release their own sadness, pain, anger, and fear? What gold might lie deep within yourself, unacknowledged, just waiting to be unearthed through the process of touching your own grief?

What beliefs do you hold about the grieving process? What kind of person, in your judgment, allows herself or himself to fully experience and embody her own sadness, anger, or fear? How does this belief serve you? Does it lead to expression, release, and freedom? Or does it lead to hiding, repressing, denying, and aching?

The purpose of the journey is to experience the journey. The emotional experience is a key aspect of human existence. It is right and good and natural. When you give yourself permission to fully experience your emotions, you open the doors to release and freedom. By doing so, you give those around you permission to give themselves permission... leading to their freedom. Like a candle lighting another candle, this freedom spreads from person to person, doors being thrown open wide and vistas of opportunity expanding drastically. Trust in self grows, as does trust in others. A deeper, wider sense of freedom arises... freedom to relax and accept with gratitude all that life has to offer. Freedom to accept that this experience of life, temporary as it is, finite as it appears through the limited spiritual perception of the human senses, is perfect in every way, for it represents the endless possibilities of the universe.

When the depths of the broken heart are plumbed, and the stored energies of sadness, anger, and fear are embodied and released, underlying joy is also released. As this stored energy is released, so are misperceptions about your identity. Pieces of the story your ego has been holding on to get released, and no longer fit who you perceive yourself to be transforming into. In the end, it is revealed that the only one with a broken heart was the ego. For the true Heart is never broken; how could it be? It is the very fabric of existence, manifested.

The rivers of sadness, anger, and fear all eventually empty back into the ocean of Love and Freedom. Whether it is during the physical manifestation of the human body or after it has been laid aside, it is guaranteed that the return to the Source is inevitable for all. Your ability to embrace this truth while experiencing life through human manifestation serves as a precious gift to all others whose lives you touch. Turning your attention to the Heart and away from the ego is a worthwhile effort, even as your ego points at all of the things you may lose... The sense of security (false and empty); material wealth (temporary); popularity (transitory and fleeting).

All of the things that you risk losing by turning away from the ego and toward the heart are all things worth losing. Actually, in one sense it is best to lose them sooner, rather than later. And in another sense, you can never possibly lose anything, because nothing on this plane of existence is ever truly 'yours' to begin with. From the perspective of reality, you are only a temporary steward of those material objects in your life that you perceive to be yours. Even what you call 'your life' is simply a story, and will be handed over at the expiration of the physical body.

Your true life never ends. There is only life. And you are it. There is no 'other'.

Unlimited

You are unlimited. You are not what you think. What you think, that is not you.

What you believe can lead you toward your true self: simply point your thoughts, ideas, and beliefs toward the Heart. Whatever they may be, simply send them to the Heart. The Heart receives all, accepts all, knowing that it truly receives and accepts nothing less than its own self in countless manifestations. All things empty, false, and temporary can simply be directed toward the Heart, which is the location of the universe.

Of equal value is to simply turn away from all thoughts, ideas, and beliefs, knowing that they are all conceptually based, and therefore not Real. While appearing to be the opposite of intentionally directing all thoughts to the Heart, this technique is equally effective in returning one to eventual understanding, through the Heart, that there is nothing BUT the Heart in Reality.

Do you find this overwhelming? Keep in mind that the absurdity of what you read is nothing more than yet another judgment from the ego, which would have you believe that it is the dictator of reality. Only the ego is overwhelmed. Recognize this, and withdraw your attention and urge for identification from the grasp of the ego. Simply watch the ego, in all its confusion, feeling overwhelmed. Watch as it scrambles and flops around, trying desperately to convince you that you are a fool for not 'listening to reason'.

"Listening to reason" is what got you into creating your own suffering in the first place. No longer listen to reason. Reject reason. Reject the need to be believed or accepted by anyone at all, especially the ego. Give yourself permission to laugh and dance and spin and sing and just stand silently as the ego shouts and condemns and questions and argues and wrangles with itself, attempting to draw your attention with its antics... with its claims of superiority... with its promises of relief from the suffering it is causing you. It is beating you with a stick, promising to make the pain go away. There is no need for such distraction from the joy and freedom that is your birthright.

Relax. Rest in the absolute certainty that you are unassailable. Surrender to the understanding that you, in all your Divine glory, are beyond reproach. For you are the very definition of the Divine. Lay aside your personality, your uniqueness, your specialness. For what you perceive to be unique and special in yourself does not even hold a candle to your true uniqueness and specialness. In Reality, there is no way for you to understand or grasp just how truly magnificent you are. It is like creativity trying to describe creativity to itself. When you finally realize it, you will understand that there was never anything to understand. You will see Reality, which was right before you the whole time. You will view the world and all its contents through the lens of the Heart, and you will see yourself. You will see Love.

Question of the day
"Who is saying this, ego or Heart?"

That is the question of the day for you, Beloved. When faced with any situation where you are feeling confused, conflicted, concerned... just fall back on this question, again and again. And if you're having trouble teasing it out, don't worry. There are two more questions you can ask, and they are simple ones:

"What would ego have to say about this?" and "What would Heart have to say about this?"

This is so simple, it may seem mystifying. If you find yourself standing speechless, then simply go a little deeper. Close your eyes and take a deep breath, if you need to. Take a moment for yourself to get centered, grounded, and balanced. There is no need to hurry. Take your time. Breathe deeply into your stomach and open up; listen with a relaxed intention, as if simply hearing an airplane go by in the distance or a stream running nearby in the background. No need to put pressure on yourself with this; simply listen for catch phrases or even single words. Listen for thoughts. Listen for feelings. Listen for images. Allow your imagination to serve you in perceiving broadly here.

Ego first. What judgments come rushing forward? What are you tempted to do or say that you might feel somehow you should not? If you were to be completely honest with yourself, what would you say or do in response to the current situation at hand, from the ego's perspective? How might you act that out? What might you say or do? Don't worry about outcomes for now; simply note the possible responses that might come from the ego space.

Now, the heart. Sink deeply into your heart; point your attention there. Take another deep breath way down into your stomach, and let it out. The Heart response is going to very likely sound and look very different from the ego's response. Note the stark contrast in responses. Note any differences in flavor or texture of the responses. What would the Heart have you say or not say? What would the Heart have you do or refrain from doing? What facial expression can you visualize yourself having when carrying out the response of the Heart? What physical stance? Are you sitting? Standing? Lying down? Walking? Running? Skipping? Hopping?

There is no right or wrong way to do this. Only the ego would have you believe that there is anything here for you to "do" or "achieve"; only the ego would suggest that it's possible to fail at this. There is no success nor failure here. If you notice that the response of the ego and Heart seem to be exactly the same, then try again. You have not failed; there is simply room to go more deeply into your own wisdom and perception. Most likely the ego is trying to prevent you from turning back into your Heart; for the Heart will never, can never block you from a wider perspective. In the realm of the Heart, which is Reality, the very idea of preventing Truth from being perceived is meaningless. For Truth is all there is. Trying to hide Truth from Truth in a field of Truth... again, becomes literally meaningless.

Questions are powerful tools. Here you have amazing inquisitive power, and incredible potential to serve more deeply as an Instrument of Peace. The desire to serve as such indicates a readiness to step into the next phase of your journey. If you are here, then you are ready. Often times, there is no need for a question; the Truth is hovering right before your very eyes, and only resistance from the ego would create the desire for hesitation, confirmation, or validation. Yet other times, questions are incredibly helpful. They can ease along the process of identifying and clarifying what perceptions are coming from where.

Of importance is to create space after asking a question of yourself or anyone else. When you ask a question and another person answers it, especially if you note that the question was helpful in bringing the other person's understanding of themselves more into alignment with Truth and Heart, the ego will quickly want to jump in and claim credit. Beware the temptation to follow up the other person's breakthrough with a running commentary of your thoughts, ideas, and recommendations. Often times, what the other person needs more than anything is Love; and Love is space. By sitting in silence, you allow the other person to integrate this new realization about her or himself; to create their own meaning from the new connections they have just made. Adding your own speech may be helpful in some ways, but most likely will simply fill the air with meaningless zeroes, which can obstruct the other person's ability to step more fully into this fresh, new perspective that has opened up before them.

Remember, this is not personal. For you are not truly a person. You are infinitely more. Truly serving as an instrument of peace requires letting go of desires for fame, fortune, and security. Indeed, understanding deeply that these are all empty and devoid of content and reality, it is natural for the desire for such things drops away naturally. Knowing that a cup is empty, who would reach for it for a drink of water?

When those desires for fame, fortune, and security come up for you, you can simply acknowledge them for what they are, and then ask yourself the key questions: Who is saying this? Who is offering this up? The ego, or the Heart? Pay close attention to the response: if story begins to spin wildly out of control, or if resistance to an honest answer comes up, then you are receiving sure signals that the ego is trying to distract and misdirect.

The more you learn to observe and sit calmly in silence as the noise of the world seems to rage on around you, the more others may find themselves either attracted to you or repulsed from you. Pay no mind to this; take nothing personally. For those people who seem to adore you are actually attracted to the Truth of their own Heart that you are reflecting back to them. Likewise, those who seem to dislike you for no apparent reason are responding from the ego, resisting the Truth of their own Hearts that you reflect back to them. There is nothing for you to grab onto here, for none of this is about you. All you need do is rest in the joy of your own heart, and the gears of the Infinite Divine are turning already, effortlessly, and endlessly.

Playing small. On the flip side of things, just as it is important to recognize the ego's temptation to claim credit for the glory of the Truth in the Heart and build itself up bigger, it is equally important to recognize the ego's temptation to play small in order to protect itself from discomfort, harm, or attack. In reality, the Heart can never be attacked. But from the perspective of the ego, the human body can. The human body, like the ego, is time-based, finite, and therefore empty. It is not real, therefore it is limited. The ego's certainty that the human physical body measures Life and reflects the bounds of Life are what drive it to try to avoid calling attention, scrutiny, and possible attack toward itself.

Just as grasping for attention is one side of the coin of attachment, based upon memory of pleasure, repulsion from attention (grasping at safety) is the other side of the same coin, based upon the memory of pain. Both are from the perspective of the ego, and in both cases, returning to an attitude of non-resistance points the way back to the Heart; back to freedom. For non-resistance reminds us that there is no need to grab at anything, or to try to avoid anything. There is no safety to chase, nor danger to avoid, for Life is limitless, boundless... infinite. Serving as an Instrument of Peace means doing the internal 'work' involved to remember this Truth. It means recognizing the web of the ego as you become entangled in it, and then applying the Truth to your thinking in order to return to clearer perception of Reality. The more you do this, the clearer your perception becomes. Fear not. You are the Divine remembering the Divine.

As an Instrument of Peace, step forward with supreme confidence and supreme humility into each moment. Allow others to witness your Divine inner fire; do not try to make it appear smaller or weaker or less than what it truly is. This inner fire is the healer; and you are its servant as bearer of the flame... a channel through which it flows.

A return to wholeness

One guarantee: all beings are seeking a return to wholeness. Whatever you think you see, and whatever judgments you may hold about another person's actions or intentions, know that underneath it all is their desire to return to their true state as the Divine. Addictive patterns are nothing other than this desire to reconnect with the Source of Love. This is based upon their misperception that they are somehow incomplete or less than Divine, which is a natural phase in the progression of the Divine remembering its true identity.

The point here is that if you, as an Instrument of Peace, look deeply enough, you will find that desire to return to wholeness in each and every person you meet, no matter how twisted or distorted their actions may appear to you. The one who spreads lies about your desire for him... the apparent hatred that motivates his supposedly evil behavior is revealed to be nothing other than the ache for a return to wholeness, once you understand that he was adopted. Rejection is a theme in his life, and his desperate attempts to achieve acceptance and completeness feel no less real to him than yours.

Suddenly what once appeared to be an evil person can be seen with compassion. The Instrument of Peace works to set aside the judgments of the ego and to discern the deeper, underlying truth that reflects this desire for the return to wholeness. The Instrument of Peace keeps in mind at all times that everyone is on this same path, and that though the journey may take countless appearances and the judgments by the ego will seem endless, still the duty of the Instrument of Peace is to calmly and with resolve and determination continue to set aside those judgments and look more deeply into the situation, whatever it may be.

What must be sacrificed is the instant gratification of slinging half-baked theories and judgments about other people. What must be sacrificed is the desire for connection with the fellow man through low, base, common means such as gossip and hearsay. Only the ego perceives any benefit through belittling or degrading others. Only the ego would have you believe that you are ever justified in engaging in such habitual thought and speech patterns. The Heart sees, knows, and understands that true reflection and inquiry is very different from gossip, for the desired outcome from genuine inquiry is deeper understanding for all. And deeper understanding for all points the way toward Truth, toward the continued return to wholeness.

The next time you feel compelled to judge another summarily, stop and take a deep breath. Ask yourself, as an Instrument of Peace, whether the judgment arises from the ego or the Heart. If it is any judgment at all, it is of the ego. If it is a vision of the other in his or her quest for the return to wholeness, you are hearing the guidance of the Heart, which is to be followed. Always.

Bridge

The bridge of perception is open and available to you and all who have any interest in gaining access to it. For interest is the only requirement for moving forward. One need only say, "I am ready to be of service to the One through Light" and the wish becomes potential, granted to themselves by none other than themselves.

Each journey is unique, and there are countless winding paths that lead back to the Heart. If you feel at all drawn to doing the work of Light, then the call is emanating forth and outward from within you. There is nothing more for you to do in order to accept your heart's invitation than to begin showing up. Working in the service of the One through Light happens in numerous ways, and involves the release of attachment of the perceived world and all of its ego-based reflections, and turning within, toward the Heart. When you affirm your desire to be of service, you will receive the guidance you need in the form that is right for you in your perceived life story. There are no special requirements, other than to have a heart and to begin to 'take heart'--to examine and explore yourself and your perceived world and life more deeply in order to determine who and what you truly are.

By asking yourself every day, "Who is saying this, Heart or ego?", you open the door to a new world of perception for yourself and within yourself. Keep in mind that turning away from the ego does not require you to take vows of poverty, any oaths of silence, or a promise to follow any particular religion, sect, or tradition. (In fact, doing any of these against your own inner guidance may actually result in feeling like you have prolonged the journey.) There is nothing and no one to block your way in stepping more fully into your own capacity as a servant, healer, and guide on the path of the Heart. There are no particular prayers or practices involved, other than noticing what is happening in your life and reflecting upon the truth that lies behind and beneath the story. When confused, simply ask your heart, "Is this story?"

There is no person who is not adequately suited to look more deeply within her or his own heart and to begin recognizing where they are grasping onto story as their own identity. Take heart and allow a gentle smile to play across your face from time to time, as you recall that joy is woven into the very fabric of life. For life is none other than love, and you are nothing other than an expression of Love itself. Joy is your very nature and birthright.

If you experience what you perceive to be problems and frustrations on your path, remember that this is perfectly natural and a sign of progress. For those who have been strongly misidentifying with the ego, a path on the plane of human existence that everyone travels at some point, it can seem challenging to surrender what feels like your very being. It is common during the process of unfolding and awakening to assume that the resistance of the ego is your own.

Know and understand with conviction and certainty that any areas of your life that you approach without gratitude is an opportunity to take up your work. For any and all work involving service to others in the world starts, by necessity, with healing yourself; that is, with cleansing and purifying your own perception through the release of attachment to what is not real.

In other words, to help make your neighborhood better, get busy cleaning your own yard.

Simply return your attention to your own heart, again and again. If you are able, place a hand on your heart and take a breath, allowing your attention to go to the spot where your hand and your chest make contact. This seemingly simple practice has great power, and can help you along your journey.

Beware attachment to those who would have you believe that listening to your heart and trusting your own inner guidance is somehow wrong, improper, or dangerous. Since all life is grounded in the Heart, it is impossible to do harm to your true self or any other through love, acceptance, patience, kindness, understanding, or by creating space for another. By honoring and blessing all others on their path, and through the practice of gratitude, you will help to create circumstances favorable for all.

And notice any judgments about the 'correctness' of another's path. Pay close attention to any urge you may experience that would have you try to 'save' another from making mistakes upon her or his path. Invariably this will be the ego talking.

A word of caution: Take careful note of any part of you that is attracted to the concept of 'being a healer' or 'entering upon the path of the Light Worker" as a way to gain respect, prestige, admiration, romance, or any other ego-based gain. It is common for the ego to use the very trappings of so-called 'ego-less-ness' as a way to feel somehow superior to others. Know with certainty that any grasping at glamour will always, always result in frustration. But take heart; all frustration eventually leads to the opportunity for deeper learning.

Also, do not concern yourself with timeframes, for there are no deadlines on the path of the Heart other than those imposed by the world of the temporary upon the world of the temporary. Since the physical body and its trappings are not you, their transitory nature does not affect you. At the same time, the more deeply you throw yourself into your "studies", examining where all selfishness, fear, anger, and sadness originate from, the more clearly your growth in understanding can clear the perceived barriers to love on your journey of human existence.

Remember: this is not a race. There is no trophy. No reward save remembering your true identity and the identity of everyone else, which is beyond any other reward you could possibly imagine, fathom, or perceive. And this reward is guaranteed to all beings.

The path is not sexy or glamorous, for it involves recognizing the emptiness that is the true nature of all things "sexy" or "glamorous". Yet you will know if you are called to the path by listening to your Heart. All are on the path always; there has never been a time in your perceived life when you were somehow 'off the path.' All experience is an opportunity to return attention to the Heart.

Where your heart sings, that is the direction to extend and focus your attention. Where your joy and happiness and satisfaction seem limited and short-lived, that is the appropriate direction to extend your focused inquiry. Where there is fear, anger, or sadness, there is an opportunity for release into freedom. For true freedom is your natural state. Love is your home. You are the very field of Love itself.

All perception of 'other' is untrue. Drop your story, drop your fear, drop your clenched posture of self-protection. You are home; home is you. You are safe; safety is you. You are Love; Love is you. There is no Other.

You are a being of rich brilliance and unsurpassable majesty. You are the very gift of the cosmos, perfect in every way. Your success is guaranteed, for there is no such thing as any being or object outside the field of the Divine. As far as you can see, beyond the stars in the sky or the planets in space... beyond the farthest stretches of the imagination, your glory reaches still further. For you are Infinite Love itself.

Do not forget this. Do not accept that you are anything short of your true magic, fire, and brilliance. Do not believe any limitations that others would have you assume about who and what you are. Being inconceivable via the intellect, small mind, ego, there is no way to capture in words your true beauty, grace, and wisdom.

The only way to approach true understanding of your actual identity is through the portal of the Heart. It is not something that can be grasped through words, arguments, theorems, postulates, proofs, or scientific measurement. It is not something that can ever be pointed to or captured in song. There is no way to chase it down in a photograph or to capture it through painting or song.

Your true brilliance can only be experienced directly, through your own inquiry into your Heart and all it contains. There you will find the answer to all of your perceived problems, challenges, struggles, hopes, desires, wishes, and dreams. There you will discover your true identity as light, love, wisdom, compassion, healing, peace, strength, and grace. There you will find the road to freedom; the mirror reflecting your One True Face.

And on that path you will find all others, guiding you and being guided by you, as you dance and spin with joyful abandon to the music of the Heart. The sound of the stars spinning through the sky. The sound of your heartbeat, which pulses the sun and universe into existence in each and every moment. The flare of love that captures infinity in the blink of an eye, and holds it aloft, lighting the way for all who embark upon their own journey into the perceived darkness of the Within.

Embrace all of them and yourself with joyful gentleness and compassion on your journey. For you are all of it. There is no Other.

CHAPTER THIRTEEN
Lens of the Heart

So you see you're not alone. You've never been alone, and we understand that you believe that you 'get it' from an intellectual point of view. But by now you've got to begin to realize how little credibility that holds for us. You've spent your entire life trying to build up the perfect intellect so that you would never have to feel vulnerable; never have to hide and never have to worry about being attacked by someone smarter or faster or better, who could prove you wrong and make you feel worthless.

And we remember watching you that day when, after all those years of study and practice saying what you believed were just the right phrases... replaying arguments in your head twenty years after the fact... "If only I had said 'this' instead of 'that'... then I would have really showed them..." Plotting and scheming and trying to stay one-up on the other guy.

Turns out there IS no other guy. And just to prove it, we're sending people your way to show you how not alone you are. In fact, some of these people you've been interacting with for years, but have never opened the aperture of your heart lens wide enough to see them for who they truly are. It may seem counterintuitive to open up that aperture-- on an f-16 kind of day, your intellect says that you'd better close it down so that only a little bit of light gets through. We say the Heart Lens works the opposite way. Take your intellect and turn it upside down. When the light is shining brightly, open up that heart lens as wide as it will go and let as much of that light and love wash over you. There's no need to protect yourself from it; it is you.

You will begin to discern others who have similar experiences to what you thought were only yours. And similar points of view, and similar heart paths. Now is the appropriate time to step out even farther into the light, to be even more seemingly vulnerable by letting even more of your light, love, and brilliance shine forth for the world to see and experience. Worry not about slings and arrows... politics... getting ahead... being safe and secure in a chaotic, dangerous world. You could not possibly be any more safe and secure than you are as your true being in the universe, for you contain within you the entire universe. There is no getting ahead-- nothing ahead of which to move. No belongings on your plane of existence that will remove your physical body from the path of physical expiration.

All of this is the natural order of things, and perfectly acceptable, agreeable, and even enjoyable to those whose perception is taken through the lens of the heart. When you set aside your ego about being challenged regarding the size of the salad plate on your lunch tray, that is the moment when you begin to see more deeply into the true nature of the present moment. That is when you remember that the woman who appears to be giving you unnecessary hassle is probably scared to death because she has received a cancer diagnosis, and she's afraid. Everything she looks at is a hassle to her, and worse; an actual threat. From where she sits, if she holds the misperception that her true identity is attached to her physical body, then the whole world and everyone in it is a threat. And when you show up with your salad in what she judges to be the incorrect container, suddenly things get messy. We're no longer talking about a salad here, or the one dollar and sixty-two cents you're about to be charged. Although you may feel compelled to dismiss the entire episode as her being unnecessarily picky or targeting you unfairly, it is wise to hold your tongue. Wait. Breathe. Listen. Then follow. You remember her telling you about her cancer diagnosis. You remember her register being staffed by someone else for at least a week, and you remember wondering where she was... and whether she was coming back.

Now she's back. Sitting there, face to face, looking down at your salad. What will you do? How will you respond to her challenges?

And if your ego takes the bait and perceives the interaction to be personal... to be negative... to be threatening or even an inconvenience, it's okay. When you walk away and sit down at the table to eat your salad, you have the choice to shift your perspective downward; down from the center point of your forehead, down through your throat, and down further still into your heart, the seat of the universe, all love, and all compassion. From that lens you can look outward and see the world and everyone in it for what they truly are.

In an instant you can recognize and remember. You can go make things right. You don't even necessarily have to say much; it is the ego, the intellect, the small mind that would have you believe that before offering kind words or emotional support, that there needs to be some formal assessment of the situation at hand... "I felt uncomfortable earlier when you challenged me about the salad, and I want to apologize for my part, but I also feel like you could have handled things differently as well, and for that reason, I think you should apologize to me so I can start being supportive and loving because that is what I have to do to be a 'good person' and I simply MUST make sure that you see me as a 'good person'... you DO see me as a 'good person', don't you? Because I truly am. And if you don't believe me, I've got plenty of proof. Let me tell you about the time when I was seven years old and I was wrongly accused..."

This does no good. You see that, we know. And yet how many times has your ego led you down this path? Attempting to prove that it is right and correct and morally superior before allowing its agenda to be subverted by something so "squishy" and "uncertain" as the heart? Yes... once again it is the trickster ego running its rounds... going through its paces... running its twisted logic... assuming that what it perceives through the five physical senses must be unshakably true. And conversely, that anything not perceived by the five senses must be unshakably false.

The truth, standing on its head. This is the inherent nature of the ego.

It is the lens of the heart that allows you to set all of that aside. To finish your salad, stand up, and walk back over to her, and when she's available, to ask her about the cancer. Ask how she's doing. Ask for an update. Demonstrate that you care. Share with her the connections you share with her; share what you share. This is what it means to be fully human. This is what it means to be fully awake and alive. Not so you can check off any sort of box or punch any sort of ticket that is supposed to get you into 'heaven.' No. In the moment that you establish connection instead of running away from it, you instantly enter the gates of heaven. For heaven lies in the heart. And you can enter at any moment.

Our recommendation is that you drop what you're doing, drag that lumber over, pour yourself a foundation and build yourself a small vacation home here. And stay for longer and longer periods. Soon you'll find yourself setting down roots and building yourself the most magnificent castle ever imagined. You'll live in heaven 24/7. Regardless of what appears to be happening 'out there' in the world of the physical.

This is your purpose. Always. To return home. To your one true home.

In doing so you will find that you actually never left. You only tied a purple bandanna around your head to cover your eyes. You only muffled your ears with your shooting earmuffs. There never was any reason to hide, but it took everything up to now for you to realize it. The journey was the destination. And the destination is home, upon your inner throne, here in the palace of the heart.

Now. Seeing the world through this lens, how will you share your gifts with the world?

Guardian

Have you considered the possibility that you just might be a guardian angel on the planet? An angel of mercy? (Let go of any resistance you may have to the imagery... drop the word 'angel' if it's tripping you up.) Has it occurred to you before that you might be here to do special things? Great things? To lead others by example? Have you ever played around with the idea that you could be as powerful as you perceive great spiritual leaders of your time to be?

Now is the time to embrace these possibilities as truth. As fact. For the same spirit that stirred them to action is the same spirit that stirs in your veins, in your lungs. You may not feel like much. You may think of yourself as a pretty 'normal' person who is just getting by. Doing what you can to make a living, doing your best just to make ends meet.

We are here to remind you that making ends meet is not the limits of your potential. You did not come to this life stream simply to pay bills, buy groceries, and numb your senses with sensory input. The activities of this world are not an end unto themselves. Rather, they are grist for the mill; lessons for the classroom. They are the material, the fabric, out of which you are building opportunities to express your brilliance and your love.

If you ever caught a glimpse of your own magnificence, you might very well fall to your knees, sobbing with amazement and joy. You might possibly have difficulty recognizing the glorious being in the mirror as yourself. Yet we assure you, it is no one else but yourself. You simply fail to recognize yourself. You've put on a halloween costume, looked in the mirror, and tricked yourself into believing that what you see is who you are. And then you've built a life for yourself based upon your beliefs about what you see. You've written stories about how you should act and then worked hard to follow that script. And we remind you that even the script of not following any script at all is still another script.

The ego is the script writer. It's what the ego does.

In order to release yourself from the binds of the script that dictates that you play small in this world, all you need to do is to turn your attention away from the head; away from the senses. Away from the emotional responses that are constantly arising and throwing your boat all over the place like tidal waves. Turn your attention back to your heart. Again and again.

Another step you can take is simply to acknowledge that your brilliance and your power shine far more brightly than you can ever understand, and to start behaving 'as if' you did grasp your true brilliance, genius, and potential. Simply start to practice the act of setting aside judgment when it arises. Simply notice the judgments, notice the anger, notice the responses that want to come out. And then breathe into them. Notice the separation between those thoughts and feelings, and your breath. The more space you can create between them, the easier it becomes to recognize that they are not you. And you are not them.

Offer love to everyone. First and foremost, offer it to yourself. Love and forgiveness need to be at the forefront of the gifts you give to yourself first, and then to others. Love and forgiveness, compassion... these things do not look or sound like punishment, belittling thoughts, or tirades against what you should have done or could have done in the past. These things are all tools of the ego, which would have you believe that you are smaller than you actually are. Love for yourself never begins with the word 'should'. In fact, if you hear the word 'should' in your inner dialogue, you can bet that you are hearing the rants of the ego. And the ego is tricky. Don't be surprised if you hear things like, "I should be done grieving by now..." "I should love myself better than I am..." "I should be able to do this better by now..." These are all the ego's judgments.

The swimming pool of the heart contains none of these statements. Anything less than loving, compassionate, celebratory support is simply meaningless in the sanctuary of the heart. It is impossible to chastise oneself or anyone else while resting in the arms of the heart. For the heart is where reality reigns supreme. All illusion falls away in the heart's gaze.

Your brothers and sisters look to you for guidance and direction. They look to you for strength. Even if you don't recognize it, every display of love, compassion, selflessness, and gentleness... every show of support that you offer to your fellow human is noted. Others are watching. They are listening. They notice. Even strangers on the street notice, and every one of your acts of service and devotion to something beyond your human body has a powerful impact on all those around you. Your perception may tell you that nothing is worth it; that no one notices; that none of it matters. That suffering and sacrificing are the way of this world.

Through the eyes of the ego, this is definitely true. The physical body will perceive suffering, since it itself is temporary. The ego sees only the world of the temporary, and does whatever it can to survive forever in the world of the temporary. This, of course, is quite futile. Like trying to fashion a hammer out of tissue paper.

The suffering and sacrificing, the striving for something beyond the reaches of time and space, the urge to return home to the heart, transform sensory experience and return it to its rightful place in the land of the temporary. Not that it ever truly existed anywhere else; rather, one's perception is corrected when viewing the world through the lens of the heart. The transitory nature of existence is seen for what it is; no more, and no less. And perceived suffering is understood to be temporary as well, which is also its true nature.

Only love itself is timeless. When seeing the world through the lens of the heart, all that is temporary drops away. And all that is left is space, which is love; and love, which is space.

You have the power to step into this awareness at this very moment. You have always had this power, this potential. There is nothing stopping you; nothing blocking your ability to turn your direction away from the outer world and inward toward the heart at any time. Rather than creating self-indulgence, doing so causes love to radiate forth in all directions. Rather than ending up in self-absorption, the small and insignificant 'demands' of the ego are replaced with love, compassion, power, strength, and keen awareness; sharpened perception of the true state of things around you. An increased sense of fulfillment and the realization that, needing nothing, you have all you need.

And seeing those around you who do not yet understand that they, too, need nothing and have all they need, you are there to demonstrate fullness to them. To exemplify what a full heart with no needs can look like. To show them what it can feel like to have your complete attention and your complete care. While some may seem to grab and grab at your fullness with crazed hunger, do not fear depletion. They are drinking from a well that flows through you, rather than taking anything away from you. From the perspective of the human body, you are not the source of this well; you are simply a conduit through which the Divine flows.

However, from the greatest perspective, seeing reality through the lens of the Heart, you are the fullness. You are the crazed hunger. You are the conduit. And you are the Divine, flowing through the conduit. You are all of this and everything around it. You are the very fabric upon which all of this waves in the breeze, dancing and weaving endlessly through time and space.

Something dramatic and sexy

You may ask, "All of this talk of turning attention back to the heart is fine and good, but it is too simple... what is my work? What do I need to do in order to reclaim my birthright of joy and peace?"

We say to you, your work is the very act of turning back to the heart. For being so simple, do not dismiss it as being easy or unimportant. Only the ego would have you believe that it is a) unachievable and impossible; or b) so simple that it must therefore not be worthwhile.

Only the ego would demand something dramatic and sexy before being willing to follow recommendations. Better to move one grain of sand per day toward your goal than to remain stagnant until proof of value through glamour is provided. For that proof will never come.

Cheated

When you feel cheated or like someone has wronged you, or that someone is taking advantage of you, you are simply looking through the lens of the ego, which would have you believe that you have no choice in the matter, whatever it may appear to be. Zoom out. Look through the lens of the heart and remember that in every moment, you have choices. The more deeply you sink into your heart, the greater the number of options and opportunities you have. And the simpler it is to choose, for the ego's endless calculations are not part of the deal in the realm of the Heart. Rather, the heart is more like a huge salad bar with all of your favorite foods offered in endless abundance. What feels right today, Dear One?

Fake I.D.

All identity you pursue is false identity. Anything you can imagine that you can aspire to be or become is not real. Don't be fooled by heroic medals or unheroic deeds or even the one who appears to be completely mentally broken. It's all the ego, and no matter what you see, you are seeing the false when you see with your eyes rather than through your heart.

Like thirteen armies all rushing into battle, all killing each other, it is chaos. There is no order-- no true way to know anything real via the ego. Accept this about everyone and you will move toward truth and clear perception. Those whom you think hate you do not, for they are not who you think they are. They are yourself. There is no other.

Is all this talk of letting go bringing you down? Do not mistake the surrendering of the ego as a sacrifice. It is no more a sacrifice than removing a blindfold and discovering that you are standing in the middle of a surprise birthday party thrown for none other than yourself, finding yourself surrounded by all of your dearest loved ones and closest friends.

It is the ego that would have you believe this is cause for distress. But dropping the attachment to the ego's perspective and seeing life through the lens of the Heart is truly cause for celebration. The more deeply you can go into the heart, the more glorious the beauty of everyday life becomes. The seemingly small details that once appeared to frame your life will sparkle and shine with new beauty. The sunrise, the full moon, the leaves on the trees... you will see them all with new eyes: the eyes of the Heart. When you get one glimpse of Reality as it stands, you'll wonder why you ever chose to cling so tightly to the empty, rusted tin can the ego had to offer.

All identity that is other than the Heart is false. Avoid clinging to any false sense of identity, another's or your own. For you will have to part with it eventually; this is a certainty in the land of the ego.

At that moment, the words in this book will be revealed to you as truth.

Wipe your eyeglasses clean

Turning away from concepts does not mean surrendering all that is beautiful in the world. Quite the contrary-- the more you are able to recognize story and ego for what it is, the more clearly the true beauty of the world will appear to you. For the true glory of Reality has been right in front of you the entire time; you only needed to clean the spots off of your glasses to see it. Feel the warmth of the sunshine on your face. Listen to the song of the wind, the whisper of water. Look deeply enough and you will recognize the beauty underneath the surface of all you see, hear, and experience.

Within the context of Reality, there is no fear, no incompletion, nothing lacking. As you turn inward to the heart through gratitude, you will recognize that reality is unfolding perfectly in your life at this moment, no matter what circumstances you perceive.

Healing is nothing more than cleaning your glasses, purifying your perception by looking through the Heart lens. This allows you to more clearly recognize the misperceptions in your life, for only misperception allows you to create suffering for yourself. Ask yourself, what wants to happen in this moment? Let the heart guide you as you ask this question, allowing thoughts to simply recede into the background. The heart is constantly communicating, radiating its wisdom at all times, 24/7, 365 days a year. There is no instance where the heart is not extending its wisdom and glory through Love.

Only resistance allows you to perceive yourself to be lost without a guide in a dangerous world. Only identification with the ego would allow you to take on misperceptions that are not yours as your truth, marching a parade of fanciful mirages across your field of vision. Mirages of wolves out to get you, of dreams and opportunities lost... of unrequited romantic love.

True love can never be unrequited; it can never be bargained for, exchanged, bartered, weighed, or measured. True love is not something that you have any control over. It is not something that is gained or lost. True love is what you already ARE.

The emotions commonly associated with romantic love have ALL of their roots in the ego, which would have you believe that concepts are love. Surrender all ideas about sex, beauty, power, glamour, and desire. Beyond all concepts lies a field. This is where you will reawaken to the ever-present Love that you have always been.

Fix

There is nothing to correct in the world, save your own perception. When you see other people looking at the world and at you through the lens of the ego, generating a fearful story for themselves, it is not necessary to point this out verbally. Some may hear a few of your words, but even words of truth will be filtered through the lens of the ego in their perception. Of deeper service, then, is to simply honor and bless them where they are, which is how you can lead by example.

Doing good work in the world has value; simply do the work of your heart. Releases all outcomes to the Heart. If you find it helpful to consider things in these terms, then keep in mind that the Heart is taking care of all details at all times. The Heart in truth is not separated from any shred of Reality, and the worries of the world are not Real. Yet within the limited spiritual scope of human perception on your plane of existence, it causes no barrier to clearer perception to think of the Heart in this way.

In any event, there is no need to try to 'save' or 'fix' any other person. Your work lies only in the purification of your own perception-- removing the ego lenses and putting your heart glasses back on so you can see the world as it truly stands.

When you hear advice such as, 'don't worry, be happy,' know deeply and with all certainty that any and all resistance to such advice is of the ego. In all actuality, the wisdom contained in this seemingly simple phrase can be considered true Guidance toward the Heart. For all worry originates from the ego. And all arguments for the validity of worry come from the same place, and are designed to keep you distracted so that the ego can continue to prop up its flimsy stance as real.

The ego will say, "It would be nice to not worry... but I must worry. There are so many threats in the world that if I stop worrying, I won't be prepared and some unexpected threat will end my existence." It will say, "If I had enough money, then I would not need to worry. In order to get enough money, more is needed." Then the ego will say, "Since you ARE me, it is you who needs to worry. And since you and I ARE the physical body, our survival depends upon the survival of the human body. We have no CHOICE but to worry! Only a fool would believe that it's okay to say, 'don't worry, be happy.'"

And so the cycle of distraction continues, viewing worry and fear as valuable activities. Seeking to gain pleasure, comfort, and security... Seeking to avoid discomfort and the transitory nature of human existence. Seeking to avoid fear by actively worrying, which is based UPON fear. Do you see the futility in this?

There is no way to win the games of the ego through engagement with the ego. The only course out of that hole is to turn attention away from the ego and back to Reality by viewing life through the lens of the Heart.

How to do this, you may ask. Our question to you is, Where is your heart? Put your hand on your chest. Feel your heart beating. There. Now pay close attention to how it feels, beating there beneath your hand. Sense the warmth of your hand on your chest. Feel the warmth of your chest with your hand. What do you hear? Close your eyes. Envision your heart physically beating in your chest.

Your heart is not a metaphor for life energy; it is literally the portal to all life. The container of all life, manifested in human form. And it resides in every living human. Surrender the urge to debate philosophical ideas about life and death. That is simply the ego's way of keeping you, even now, from placing your hand upon your heart and turning your attention inward. Freedom lies in surrendering the ties that bind. The ego, intellect, or small mind make valuable servants to the Heart, but when you over-identify with them and mistake them for yourself, they become the very ties that bind.

Thirteen armies

Thirteen armies converge in battle. Chaos ensues, as soldiers try to discern who is who. Treaties were signed. Treaties were repealed. Leadership tries to discern who is who. Confusion reigns as each individual misidentifies another... friend or foe? Enemy or ally?

In every day you face the same chaos, for you view the world through the lens of the ego. As such, it appears to be a hostile battlefield where you must discern to which of the thirteen armies every individual you meet belongs. "Is this friend or enemy? Well, they haven't spoken to me for seven years, but I was rude to them but it wasn't my fault because I was having a bad day..." And on and on.

You walk through life misidentifying everyone. For you look at them and accept what you see with your eyes and hear with your ears as truth. The one who loves you most, you take for enemy. And everyone, including yourself, you label as enemy, for you label them as other. By refusing to recognize the Divine for who it truly is, you close your eyes to Reality, creating an imaginary battlefield and then responding to it as if it is real.

This nightmare can end for you at any given moment, once you choose to let the charade end. It holds no more danger or glamour for you than what you give it, for it is of the ego. And it is guaranteed to end, to fade away into the vapor it truly is at the moment of your realization. Your true identity can never be threatened, for there is no war. There are no thirteen armies. The tragedies and victories, the epic dramas that unfold across your mind's screen... they are all as fictional as the back yard production performed by the neighbor children.

Thirteen armies converge in battle, and they are all you. When seen through the lens of the ego, they are all enemies. When seen through the Heart lens, they are all one. Masks drop away. Fear and anger becomes meaningless. Sitting alone in a room, who else is there to fight? Who else with which to get angry? Against whom will you hold that lifelong grudge? From where can stem a feud? It all goes down the bathtub drain as meaningless.

The one whom you thought abandoned you, withholding love, treating you unfairly for no reason whatsoever... The one who does nothing... The one who believes lies about you and spreads them to protect himself... The one who failed you miserably... The one who will never return your love... The one who takes and takes and never gives back... The one who has hurt so many others, leaving them scarred and broken... These are the thirteen armies. Treaties have been signed and repealed. The ego has assigned and reassigned blame and forgiveness, endlessly. On any given day, it seems impossible to tell if you are standing next to friend, foe, or stranger. Either way, most of the time you feel fear is justified. Justified for your very survival in the world.

The thirteen armies are all masks of you. You are the you perceived to be one sitting on the couch, condemned. You are the one you perceive to have failed you miserably. You are the one you perceive to have taken and never given back... to have hurt so many others, leaving them scarred and broken. These perceived others are all you. End the war that you create in your head. End the chaos you generate in your life. Remove their masks from your perception by viewing them through the lens of the Heart and see their true identity as none other than the Divine.

This will require surrendering all of the perceive romance, glamour, glitter, and gold, as well. It is all false anyway. It is all empty. Being of the world of the finite, it can be no other way. Only the human spirit, the spirit of the Divine, is life. Cars, watches, retirement funds, vacations... these are not life. They cannot capture life. They cannot measure life. Life is not under your control. Life is the Divine. And the Divine simply is. And what or who it is, is You.

Pie in the sky

Concepts come from the intellect, small mind, or ego. Behavior that is agreed upon according to shared opinions about concepts are of the ego. This describes religion perfectly.

Religion is the spear and shield of the thirteen armies. It is the reason for war and the instrument of war, all in the same breath. Its sole purpose is to divide; to create the appearance of division... to support the illusion that there is an 'other' and the 'other' is dangerous. When we get together to sit in the dark and whisper about our fears, the fears we attribute to the 'other' who lives somewhere else, or wears something else, or eats something else, or believes in some other habitual thought pattern, we are doing nothing other than investing in the thirteen armies.

Agreeing to agree upon which of the thirteen armies to which we belong is still agreeing to participate in delusion.

True power is not gained by wielding anything over another person. True power is simply remembered, for it was never lost. And it is remembered by returning to the Heart. By sinking back into the Heart, you will see the One you truly are and always have been. You will realize that there are no thirteen armies. Not in Reality. They never existed. While it may have seemed enjoyable to belong to a group who agreed to agree about the imaginary thirteen armies, the enjoyment you perceived was based upon the misperception that there existed an other. It was based upon the mistaken belief that you were separate; that you, yourself, were an 'other', and as such, that you somehow were not whole. You sought wholeness, completeness, by joining groups, by entering into agreements with other people, by making promises about who you would 'be' and who you would 'become'.

All of it was the ego whispering into your ear. The ego would have you believe that you are separate, in need of more love, more support, more anger, more weapons, more acquisitions, more safety, more security... all in order to create the illusion of being real.

The truth is, you never needed to become complete or whole. You are already whole. You are already complete. You are already far more than you have ever, or could ever imagine. You cannot possibly be rejected by any group or individual... in reality, the concept of rejection is meaningless. You cannot possibly ever get fired from any position, for in reality, you are all positions. And you cannot possibly ever win a competition against any other, for there IS no other. You are the only one sitting in this room. Not 'you' the physical body, as seen through the ego, but rather You, the Divine, the one free from all identifiers. Free of all labels. Beyond all tags or description.

That is what makes this so-called 'work', the work of returning to your rightful place upon the Inner Throne of the Heart, appear to be so difficult. The intellect, ego, or small mind simply shakes its head, claiming that to speak of anything beyond its perception is simply 'crazy talk.' It would have you believe that if you cannot see it, feel it, touch it, taste it, smell it, have sex with it, or eat it, that it cannot possibly be true. This view of the world is precisely upside-down.

If you are ready to view Reality as it stands, look through the lens of the Heart. You will find that whatever you can see, feel, touch, taste, smell, have sex with, or consume is finite, temporary in nature, and therefore empty. These things are guaranteed to fall away, leaving the taste of ashes in your mouth. Only that which is left, that which is beyond all perception, is real.

In these words lies no promise of some 'pie in the sky'... No guarantee of a 'better life' if you simply make certain sacrifices for the benefit of some person or organization or religion. There is no sacrifice to be made that will line the pockets of some powerful individual.

Quite the contrary. You are the one who will gain everything true by releasing attachment to everything that is false, imaginary, and empty. And when you do, you will realize that who you have believed yourself to be is not the one You truly are.

Through the lens of the ego, these are dangerous words. Through the lens of the Heart, they are simply the truth. Nothing more, nothing less.

Weary traveler

Dear Traveler,

Fear not. You are entering the season of the Magician, and it is well. The time is right for you to go inward. Curse not your cave, for it is the womb in which your transformation is underway. You are becoming that which you have always been, but have forgotten. Little by little, you are remembering your True Face. The skies appear to be gray now, and energy appears to be lacking. I assure you that alchemy is taking place, even as you experience habitual thought patterns of frustration, anger, sadness, loneliness, and any sort of sense of worthlessness. The mirage that you are unlovable is hilarious to us, though we recognize that it feels incredibly real to you on your plane of existence, where spiritual perception is limited.

Yes. You are a Traveler. Yet you are not alone. There are many among you who have chosen this path... the path of the seeming transient, where roots seem to be pulled up, or never even established at all. You sometimes worry about not having a 'place' in the world, or a specific location to call your 'home'. You use this to fuel feelings of being homeless, worthless, and fearful. I step forward this brilliant morning to remind you that this story is nothing more than a child's fairy tale; a make-believe performance on a rainy Sunday afternoon, supported by forts made of blankets, couch cushions, and the rocking chair. Your imagination is brilliant and powerful, so much so that you have created a world and have taken it to be real.

If you need an anchor, a grounding point to remind yourself of this, remember this: the entire planet is your home.

Wherever you happen to be standing, you are Home. In Iceland. In Texas. In the Himalayas. At the bottom of the ocean. At Subway eating a sandwich. You are Home. Welcome Home, Dear Traveler!

Rest assured that whatever world you imagine for yourself, no matter how scary or threatening or challenging, it has no impact whatsoever on Reality. Your One True Face shines forth, down upon yourself, in all your waking moments, sleeping moments, and deep dreaming moments. Whether you are sitting, standing, or lying down, You shine down, and up, and outward from within. And there is nothing but brilliance and fire and passion and love and light to sing forth into the skies that you paint gray with your imagination.

The key to your believing the dream you create is imagining yourself to be limited to the shape and size of your physical body. We have said it so many times that we know you may simply disregard its importance. However, this one detail is the key that unlocks the door to your expanded perception of Reality. Where does 'me' end and 'not-me' begin? What is 'me' made of? Where is 'me'? If I am this body, then why do I refer to its parts as 'mine', signifying that they are not me, but rather, possessions belonging to some 'me' that exists separate from these parts? "My" arm? "My" leg? "My" torso? "My" heart? "My" brain? Clearly without the brain or heart, the body does not survive. Yet you refer to these key components as "mine"... what does that imply?

I'll tell you a secret: the best part of all of this is that you are victorious already. You are already a hero, regardless of the story you happen to tell yourself about who or what you are. You are already the Absolute Divine, expressing life in endless, countless forms. You are the light dancing off the leaves of the trees. You are the vapor of the clouds that seem to block the sun forever. You are the spoon that stirs the coffee. You are the sound waves being generated by the 80's new wave record in your cd player.

You are all those things you wish you could be, and all those things you fear being.

In this Reality, where you are already everything there is, without end, forever and ever amen, there is truly nothing to lose and nothing to gain. So we say embrace this time of turning and transformation. Lean back against the wall of your cave and let yourself go. Into the gray clouds. Into the chill of the night. Into the warmth of the fire. Into the candle's glow. Into each breath as you do yoga. Into each delicious swallow of coffee. See the cold, stark outline of the raven as it lands on the fencepost. Hear its cries and know that they are your own.

Taste the water you splash on your face, and truly feel the guitar strings under your fingers. Do you think for one moment that it is an accident that you love music so dearly? That it means so much to you? You ARE music, at your very essence. It's no wonder at all that you would feel drawn to creating and hearing music, narrowly-defined though it may be on your plane. Now is the time to acknowledge that all of it is music. The sound of defecation. Waterfalls. Lawn mowers. Vomiting. The rustle of your boots on the leaves and twigs as you walk across your yard. The sound of the automobile's emergency indicator telling you that all four wheels have lost traction and your car is sliding out of control toward the ditch. Your wife's cries of fear. Her anger. Her sadness. Her arguments. And yours. All of this is music. Release attachment to old judgments that no longer serve the growth of your vision and step more fully into clear vision of Reality.

Now is the season of the Magician. Your magic and brilliance glows like golden fire within, and shines at a frequency too high to be recognized by your human eyes, but easily recognized by your human heart. Open the eye of the heart. Reach out with it, and embrace everything that happens to wander into your path. For every wandering being you meet is driven by love, regardless of the mask you perceive. Regardless of the movies you project onto their screens. Regardless of what you may believe or think you know with your intellect, or small mind. The Great Mind resides everywhere. If you believe you need a doorway to get to it, fine: we provide you with the doorway of the heart. Look to the heart, in the middle of your chest. Use it as your eyes, ears, nose, and tongue. Use it as your hands and feet. Use it as your lungs, breathing in everything you can, and breathing out pure love.

This is the secret to your happiness. You will find it within, where it has always existed, without beginning, without end. Just like you.

We understand that in your physical manifestation your focus and energy can feel limited. Take breaks as you need. Listen. Then Follow. Then listen again. And so forth. In addition, here's a little test for you, to help you gauge whether you are stepping fully into your heart. In your day to day existence, ask yourself this question: am I experiencing fear? That's all there is to it. If the answer is EVER "yes", then you have just identified an area where there is additional room for you to step more fully into your heart, using it as your eyes and ears.

"Am I experiencing the illusion of separation? Am I holding a grudge? Am I feeling a desire to disconnect, or a resistance to deepening connection? Am I feeling compelled to turn this situation into something else in order to make myself feel comfortable?" These questions are great, too. If the answer to any of them is 'yes', then you've just done great work: you've identified somewhere in your life where Love can remove the blinders you are wearing. Blinders of your own design that you are wearing with full freedom of choice, by the way, regardless of how circumstances on your plane of existence may appear.

Relax. Feel your way into your heart. Walk the path of No Resistance. And when I say 'no resistance', I mean NO resistance. To anything. For all of it is your creation; all of it is you. Don't cut off any part of your experience of Yourself. Embrace ALL of Yourself. What does that look like? Embrace all parts of everyone around you. They are You. Language fails, but is still better than no communication; no learning. Trust. Give yourself permission to give your intellect a rest and just move from the heart. That is all that is needed at this time.

Worries of the world

Something to keep in mind: Let the worries of the world pass over you unheeded. You've heard us say this before. All is unfolding perfectly.

Each has her own path to walk; his own lessons to learn in his own time. Just as you do. Don't be alarmed by what you see or hear in the world. Don't mistake it for reality. It's simply the Divine unfolding and manifesting and expressing with infinite love and grace, no matter what judgments you may want to put on things. For example, you are judging negatively that you were woken up by the cat. Yet here is your opportunity for gratitude. You were not woken up by a burglar. Or a rapist. Or a murderer. And you slept in a bed. Not on a floor. Not in a cardboard box outside. There is much to be grateful for.

And we understand your need for sleep. We understand you don't simply want it for comfort; you serve best when you are well-rested. We understand. Take your present experience into your day with you; take your gratitude and your compassion for those around you who also struggle today, for whatever reasons they have experienced during their morning hours. For everyone is facing challenges of some sort.

Finally, can you laugh? Can you see the humor in it? The cat woke you up because she's hungry... she's hungry because your beloved cuts back on food... which happens because she's stressed about money and change and transition... And what is your role in financial stability? You've been buying a lot of records lately... and your beloved just threw you a wonderful birthday party with delicious food and expensive N/A beer...that had to cost some money. Could it be that you have a hand in the financial stability of things, and are impacting it by spending for emotional comfort? Something to think about as you ride around on that high horse of yours.

You asked for our input and guidance. We give it. We give it with love and compassion, and we give it firmly when needed. You are not one who needs to be coddled or shielded from true wisdom or truth. You can handle truth. And that is why when we come across in a clear, blunt way, we do so without hesitation. And without apology. You are a strong, powerful man who sometimes acts in ways that do not align with heart vision. And that's okay. You're learning. Just be aware that your actions do have an impact on those around you. You have more of an impact than you might imagine.

Our suggestion: walk softly. Smile often. Laugh. Joy and tranquility are still your catchwords for the day. Use them often. These two practices will carry you far. Now go create a beautiful day!

CHAPTER FOURTEEN
Invocation

May the wisdom of Divine Perfection flow through me now. May I see through the lens of the Heart. May I hear with divine ears and taste with divine tongue. May I recognize the divine in each person I encounter, and acknowledge it in every word I speak, every thought I think, and every breath that the Divine breathes through me.

May I have compassion and understanding for the shortcomings I perceive myself to have. May I offer love, acceptance, and forgiveness to myself when I am impatient with others, and may I offer love, acceptance and forgiveness to others as well, when I perceive they have become impatient, angry, or distracted.

May I make it my life's work to turn more fully to the heart for guidance and instruction, allowing the noise of the sensory world to roll by unheeded, like a garbage truck in the street. No need to throw myself in its path. I'll only get crushed. Over and over.

May I recognize that in this very moment, I am already enough. As a slice of the Divine, the perfection of all of the energies comes together and meets at one single point, and that point is my heart. As I recall this, may I realize more deeply each day that I have access to infinitely many energies, and can call upon any of them in any moment during my waking hours. In any situation, one of my options is always to choose love, to choose compassion for self and others, and to choose to take a deep breath before drawing any conclusions. I always have the option to pause and simply observe the intellect, ego, or small mind as it goes through its machinations, leaping to whatever conclusions will allow it to play victim, conqueror, or any other role that generates and relies on inner conflict and turmoil.

May I remember in each moment that inner peace is true power, and as fear rises, may I see it for what it is; a passing emotion generated by the ego to distract me from my work of stepping fully into my power, fulfilling my potential and playing my role as servant, as part of the ever changing fountain of Love.

May I acknowledge and thank every being who has ever played a part in my life, and may I recognize that every single one of them has made great contributions and sacrifices in order to support me on this journey. May I expand my perspective widely enough to recognize that those behaviors I once judged negatively were actually in service to the Divine. May I see that any so-called trespasses against me have actually been in support of my growth in understanding and wisdom. May I recall these moments of my own past perceived pain that I may recognize suffering in others and treat them with compassion.

May I recognize the ways that I hold myself hostage to the ego, with manifestations of selfishness, attitudes of helplessness and victimhood, and habitual thought patterns that would have me believe I am other than my true identity of the Divine. May I perceive my ego at work in the moment and catch myself before submitting to those habitual behavior patterns. May I find space between the thoughts, and may I create opportunities for myself and others to step into that space with laughter, joy, and freedom. May I remember that at any given moment, I have the ability, power, and choice to step deeply into that space between thoughts and judgments, where infinite potential lies waiting to be tapped.

May I walk the fine line between supreme confidence and supreme humility, embodying both simultaneously. May I shine light and love forth in ways that bring others back home to the realization of their own confidence and humility. May I accept all feelings, perceptions, and passions as part of the process of the Divine manifesting in human form. May I recognize the difference between my true identity as the Divine, and the human form it takes through me. May I release any and all attachments to outcomes, knowing fully that the ultimate outcome is simply a return to Love, which is timeless. Knowing that, may I demonstrate unshakable confidence to others, that they may relax in the knowledge that their true identity is bullet proof, and cannot possibly be threatened.

May I surrender the rags and scraps of paper and trash that I grip tightly in my fist, letting them fall aside to reveal the brilliance of my true clothing. May I share with the world the diamonds, emeralds, rubies, and other precious gems of my true identity, letting them shine and ring forth with no hint of trying to dampen their music or hide their brilliance. May I remember that anyone's jealousy is simply resistance and fear in them; hesitation toward casting off their own delusions and revealing their own gold, brilliance, light, love, and wisdom. May I use every trick in the book that I know in order to help them remember their own true Self. And may I simultaneously surrender my need to use any tricks from any books at all to try to force or generate any specific outcomes, knowing full well that the ultimate outcome is always safety and freedom.

May I recognize fear and uncertainty in others and shower that fear with blessings. May I honor and bless every being in ways that release them and myself from the imaginary bonds of fear and uncertainty. May I keep in thought, word, and action understanding of the truth that the physical body is not me; the mind is not me. May I relinquish the luxury of indulging in fearful and meaningless talk of not having enough money, food, clothing, shelter, or safety. Simultaneously, may I help others to achieve the recognition of their own abundance. Where worldly abundance lacks for any one, may I help them achieve it, that they may relax enough to remember that what they thought they lacked, they have always already had within them.

May I surrender my need for competition, and my urge to one-up the next person. May I surrender my desire for gratification of all worldly desires, knowing that they are all temporary, finite, and empty in nature. May I dig more deeply into fully embracing and embodying generosity, knowing that in my true identity lies all of the abundance, all the comfort, all the riches I could ever want or need. May I breathe deeply when I feel frustration coming on.

May I cut cleanly, and with a sharp sword, when the time is right to set and maintain healthy boundaries. May I accept and embrace every emotion as part of the human experience in the realm of the Divine. After embodying it fully, may I express it in healthy ways and then release it back to the Divine, the source of everything. May I remember that all is within the bounds of the teacup of the Divine, including those things I would judge as being less-than-divine. In those moments when I perceive anything as being less-than, may I reawaken to the truth of the perfection of everything in every moment.

May I remember always that there is no 'other' to vilify. There is only One, and everyone I see is that.

Honor and bless

The infinite wonder of the Divine is everywhere. In a pizza parlor. On a school bus. In a concert hall. A park bench. A subway car. Within every molecule of a pile of dog crap. There is nothing and nowhere that is not a reflection of the infinite wonder of the Divine. Only the clarity of your perception through the Heart limits your ability to see and recognize it for what it truly is.

The more you work to empty yourself by turning away from the ego's demands, again and again, the better able you will be to recognize the Divine everywhere, in the present moment. You may notice as this happens that the impact of what you used to consider the 'normal' world is decreased... almost as if someone is turning down the volume of the noise in the world the deeper you drop into your Heart.

Only the ego would have you believe this is cause for alarm. For the noise that it considers 'normal' and 'home' is actually nothing more than the surface level of perception; the level of story. The deeper you engage the world at the level of the heart, the more peace and tranquility are revealed behind and underneath the activity you perceive with your human physical senses. Simultaneously, you may begin to notice that magical details, like a family enjoying a slice of pizza together, talking and laughing and connecting at the heart level, will seem to shine and glimmer with a new sense of crystal clarity. Do not fear these apparent changes in the way you perceive the world, as unfamiliar as it may seem to the ego.

It was only your misidentification with the ego, your mistaking it for your true being, that ever allowed you to see the world through its eyes; to hear with its ears... to adopt its demands, fears, and struggles as your own. And now that you are emerging from your sleep, waking up from the slumber that was your life as you experienced it through the lens of the ego, now you begin to hear the beat of every heart as the One. Now you begin to recognize yourself in every face you encounter... in every experience, unfolding endlessly in the present moment.

The more you recognize the truth of the matter, that you are all One, the more you will realize that there is no one from whom you can truly withhold love, for to resist extending love and acceptance to any other person or being is to resist extending it to yourself. The block that you believe will protect you from rejection or disappointment from the other person is simply a block that prevents you from carrying that love as a clear channel. The love is always there; your awareness of it is hampered and dampened by your own resistance; through your own perception of some 'other' that has the ability to threaten, harm, or destroy your wellbeing. This is the calling card of the ego.

Whenever you feel the temptation to give in to resistance against any other person, know that the ego is speaking in your ear. It is the ego that would have you cut off your own arms and legs... cut off your own nose to spite your face. There is no 'other' whom you can possibly punish without punishing yourself. There is no 'other' whom you can love unconditionally without loving yourself in like manner. There is only The One, and you are It.

Love freely. Love unreservedly. Love unconditionally. Love openly. And notice the tidal waves of love that come back to you, crashing over you and soaking you to your core with acceptance, joy, and support. Surrender the ego in each moment. Bow to the Heart; the inner wisdom that lies deep within your own self. Trust your own wisdom, your Heart's wisdom, before all others. For within lies the answer to every problem you have ever perceived; the solution to all riddles that the ego would have you believe are real.

Notice how long you have been putting off the process of allowing yourself to channel this wisdom. For years, literally years, you have been asking people, 'when are you going to write a book?' and 'are you working on your book yet?' People have looked at you with wonder, and you felt as though you were doing a good deed. But now the truth comes out: Every time that question left your lips, it was your own heart asking YOU if you were ready to begin what you have known is one of your callings. You have projected your gold, brilliance, and insight onto others around you, refusing to accept that the Divine might possibly live within you, or even express Itself through you.

Know, through this process of 'taking dictation' as you like to call it, you come to realize that not only does the Divine speak and flow through you; it speaks and flows through all others, as well. And now you understand just a little more clearly that since the human physical body is not you, but rather a channel, the Divine that flows through what you refer to as 'your' physical body is none other than yourself. You ARE the Divine flowing through that physical body. The wisdom that flows through is none other than your own wisdom, for it bypasses the ego and flows from the Heart.

Now that you have opened the door just a crack, you are free. Free to continue sharing your insights with the world. Free to remind all those around you of their own inner fire and brilliance. Of their own potential for remembering their own limitless self. You are the candle that lights the next candle. You never 'own' the flame, per se; yet it is carried by you. Now that you see the different levels of perception, the vanity of story, and the unshakable strength of the Heart, you are free to drop the ego's rants and ravings at any given moment.

You are free to treat yourself with kindness, consideration, thoughtfulness, dignity, and respect in all given moments. You are free to do so openly, for all to see. For in doing so, you give permission to every person around you to treat themselves with the same loving kindness. When they do this, they are moving in the direction of Life; in sync with the vibrations of Love that surround and penetrate every subatomic particle of our beings. Walk freely. Smile openly. Show your inner warmth and gratitude. There is nothing at risk by doing so. There is no danger of the sky falling.

Celebrate the successes of those around you. Release any attachment to envy; it only serves to strengthen the misperception that anyone could possibly have anything that you do not; that anyone could be something that you are not. The differences exist on the level of story only, driven by the ego. Allow all story to pass by you, and bless and honor all beings wherever they may be within the context of their story.

Honor and bless yourself for the journey you are taking. Honor and bless yourself for all of the perceived shortcomings you might believe you have. Honor and bless yourself for all of the struggles you have endured and survived to this moment. Honor and bless yourself for the pain, sadness, and loss you perceive yourself to have experienced in your past... the tragedies, the disappointments, the losses, the regrets. Honor and bless each regret you may hold in your consciousness, thanking it for the lessons it offers you.

Honor and bless every single one of your perceived loved ones. See that they are not the separate entities they appear to be. Honor and bless the many perceived acquaintances in your life, all of those who are living with their own struggles and battles; victories and defeats. Honor and bless the perceived billions of strangers with whom you share the planet, the ecosystem, and dreams of a return to wholeness. Honor and bless all of the ones you would call your enemies, those whom you perceive to have victimized yourself or your loved ones. Send them more love than you can ever imagine yourself freely offering to them, for they, no less than all of the rest, are the Divine manifested, and only the ego's demand that story be accepted as reality causes you to perceive them as anything less.

Wherever you can, offer yourself gratitude for all you have experienced. Offer yourself a daily blessing for the way you bring brilliance into the world. Let yourself be blessed and honored by those around you; fear not any accusations of being egotistical. Only the ego would have you protect yourself against such claims. With an open heart and as much vulnerability as you can demonstrate to the world, let the waves of love that flow in all directions at all times flood your very field of vision. May you drown yourself in happiness, without fear of the ego's eventual disappearance.

Honor and bless yourself for the time and effort you offer up in service to something larger than yourself. For all the energy you spend searching and digging and doing your own internal work. For all the energy you expend working to see how you can take more responsibility for your actions. For all the effort you put forth exploring how you can release the habitual thought patterns that keep you in the role of victim in your own life story. Honor and bless yourself simply for your human experience, knowing with all certainty that there is no other ending accept a triumphant one.

Honor and bless yourself in the face of every other human on the planet, in every manifestation possible. And wherever apparent differences bring up resistance for you, dive even more fully into that honoring and blessing, sending love into the very resistance that would have you close down and play small. There is no 'other' to avoid, or protect. There is no 'other' who knows more than you do about Truth, Reality, or Love. You are The One, the source of all love and creation. This is the Truth. Know it. Embrace it. Remember it. And live it. Deepest blessings and honoring to you in this very moment.

Want more?

www.timbirchard.com

To share your review of this book and to sign up for Tim's
email list, contact us at: timbirchard@gmail.com.

CPSIA information can be obtained at www.ICGtesting.com
Printed in the USA
LVOW10s1336280615

444176LV00001B/211/P